C. S. Lewis on Higher Education

Also available from Bloomsbury:

A Philosophical Walking Tour with C. S. Lewis, by Stewart Goetz
C. S. Lewis and the Church, edited by Judith Wolfe and Brendan N. Wolfe
Contemporary Perspectives on C. S. Lewis' "The Abolition of Man," edited by Timothy M. Mosteller and Gayne John Anacker
God and Meaning, edited by Joshua W. Seachris and Stewart Goetz (Anthology Editor)
Freedom, Teleology, and Evil, by Stewart Goetz
The Purpose of Life, by Stewart Goetz
The Soul Hypothesis, edited by Mark C. Baker and Stewart Goetz

C. S. Lewis on Higher Education

The Pedagogy of Pleasure

Stewart Goetz

BLOOMSBURY ACADEMIC
LONDON • NEW YORK • OXFORD • NEW DELHI • SYDNEY

BLOOMSBURY ACADEMIC
Bloomsbury Publishing Plc
50 Bedford Square, London, WC1B 3DP, UK
1385 Broadway, New York, NY 10018, USA
29 Earlsfort Terrace, Dublin 2, Ireland

BLOOMSBURY, BLOOMSBURY ACADEMIC and the Diana logo
are trademarks of Bloomsbury Publishing Plc

First published in Great Britain 2023

Copyright © Stewart Goetz, 2023

Stewart Goetz has asserted his right under the Copyright, Designs and Patents Act, 1988, to be identified as Author of this work.

For legal purposes the Acknowledgments on p. x constitute
an extension of this copyright page.

Cover design by Louise Dugdale
Cover image: Magdalen College, Oxford © Neil Ginger / Alamy Stock Photo

All rights reserved. No part of this publication may be reproduced or transmitted in any form or by any means, electronic or mechanical, including photocopying, recording, or any information storage or retrieval system, without prior permission in writing from the publishers.

Bloomsbury Publishing Plc does not have any control over, or responsibility for, any third-party websites referred to or in this book. All internet addresses given in this book were correct at the time of going to press. The author and publisher regret any inconvenience caused if addresses have changed or sites have ceased to exist, but can accept no responsibility for any such changes.

A catalogue record for this book is available from the British Library.

A catalog record for this book is available from the Library of Congress.

ISBN:	HB:	978-1-3503-5512-5
	PB:	978-1-3503-5511-8
	ePDF:	978-1-3503-5513-2
	eBook:	978-1-3503-5514-9

Typeset by Integra Software Services Pvt. Ltd.
Printed and bound in Great Britain

To find out more about our authors and books visit www.bloomsbury.com
and sign up for our newsletters.

To William,
for whom learning a new word is a source of pleasure

Contents

Preface · viii
Acknowledgments · x

Introduction: Why Higher Education? · 1

1 The Intrinsic Goodness of Pleasure · 29
2 The Pleasure of Higher Education · 55
3 Higher Education and Being a Christian · 85
4 Higher Education and Naturalism · 101
5 Lewis and Higher Education Today · 119
6 What Do I Think? · 145

Notes · 180
Bibliography · 207
Index · 217

Preface

C. S. Lewis wrote that "[a] pleasure is full grown only when it is remembered" (Lewis 2003a [1938]: 74). I remember well the pleasure I experienced when I first seriously read a book by C. S. Lewis. My wife and I had been looking for something to read to take with us to an ocean beach. I picked up several Lewis paperbacks at a local used bookstore and shortly thereafter settled into a chair by the sea to pass the day. It did not take long to realize that there was much pleasure to be had from what I had purchased.

I have written this book with two major audiences in mind. The first is people who have a serious interest in the philosophical thought of C. S. Lewis. If you are such a person, then I believe you will be intrigued by what he thought about the justification for the intellectual activity that occurs in higher education.

The second audience for this book is people who are interested in the contemporary discussion about the purpose of higher education. Though Lewis lived the majority of his life in the first half of the twentieth century, he offered thoughts about the goal of higher education which merit hearing now, if only because no one else is voicing them.

My method of citing from the works of Lewis makes explicit the time at which he wrote what I quote. When I write (Lewis 1988 [1960]: 43), I am quoting from page 43 of a 1988 edition of a book that originally appeared in 1960. When I write (Lewis [1958] in 1987: 85), I am quoting from page 85 of a 1987 edition of a paper that originally appeared in 1958. I have followed these methods of citation because a reviewer of this manuscript claimed that "Lewis's thought was not static but developed and changed over the course of his life. So, quoting what Lewis thought at one time does not necessarily entail that Lewis held that view for the remainder of his life." I believe Lewis's thought on the topics discussed in this book (and, indeed, on most topics of philosophical interest) did not change substantively from when he was roughly in his mid-twenties in age until the end of his life, which occurred just short of his sixty-fifth birthday. But for those who might disagree, I have made clear, as best as I can, the years in which Lewis wrote what he did (in a couple of cases, the year of writing is not known, which I indicate with "?" or "n.d." for "no date").

Acknowledgments

Many individuals have helped me with the writing of this book. Several read or talked about the manuscript at different stages in its development, including Patrick Casey, John Cottingham, Carolyn Goetz, Derek Keefe, Jenny Frisby Lander, Jonathan Marks, Martin Dunkley Smith, Nicholas Waghorn, and Michael Ward. Patrick Casey and Nicholas Waghorn provided particularly valuable comments as we dialogued back and forth about C. S. Lewis and the purpose of higher education.

Colleen Coalter oversaw the publication of the book, and I am deeply grateful to her. I also thank Suzie Nash for her administrative assistance with the cover design and general correspondence. And it was a pleasure to work with Hemavathy Ramamoorthy in the typesetting of the manuscript.

Introduction: Why Higher Education?

It's All about Questions

I am a professor of philosophy at a small liberal arts college. Several years ago, an admissions officer of my college asked me to be a member of a panel composed of an equal number of faculty members and current students to answer questions from invited prospective students and their parents. The hour-long session was thankfully not as nerve-racking as I had feared, until the final minutes. The session moderator announced that he would take one more question from the audience. A gentleman raised his hand and asked if any panel member would like to explain to him why he should spend tens of thousands of dollars to send his daughter to our, as opposed to some other, college. I thought: "Great question, and I'm going to let someone else answer it." The panel member at the opposite end of our table took a stab at answering the question, and then, to my dismay, every other panel member in order took his or her best shot until it came to me, seated last.

What could I add to the responses already given? I took a deep breath and told the father that if his daughter were to come to our college and take a course from me, I would try to teach her how to think, where thinking is essentially learning how to ask the right questions. I then said that learning how to ask the right questions is not easy, and that I believed I failed in my educative task with about 75 percent of my students, most of whom received no pleasure from and consequently were not interested in fulfilling my purpose for them in my classes.

That was it. I had managed to give an answer and breathed a sigh of relief (though I wondered silently what my administrative superiors might think about my statement that I failed in my educative task 75 percent of the time). The audience members were thanked for their attendance; the session was over. As I sat watching the audience disperse, I noticed the gentleman who had asked the last question making his way down an aisle toward the panelist table. "Where is *he* going?" I muttered to myself. I suddenly realized that he was heading toward me. Not knowing what to do, I got up from my chair as he approached, whereupon he began jabbing my chest with his index finger and pronounced: "YOU gave the right answer!" "I did?" I responded sheepishly. "Yes, you did. I'm a *judge*." And with that declaration, he abruptly left. I stood there wondering why he had told me he was a judge, and I concluded he must have sat in courtrooms listening to countless lawyers asking questions of witnesses and pronounced quietly to himself "Great question" or "Lousy question." As a judge, he understood the importance of asking the right question.

This is a book about the question "What is the (correct) purpose of higher education for the individual person involved in it?," where "higher education" (or synonyms like "university," "college," or "the academy") is understood in its strict sense as the thinking, reasoning, and knowing that typically occur in college. I will term such intellectual engagement "higher-level" or "advanced" intellectual activity.[1] In theory at least, higher-level intellectual activity builds on the intellectual activity that takes place in secondary or high school education, where the intellectual activity in secondary or high school education is in turn higher than, because it builds upon, that which is found in primary school education. Lower and higher levels of intellectual activity are a function of conceptual difficulty. At the lowest level of conceptual difficulty are simple concepts, from which arise complex conceptual relationships that involve those simple concepts.

The intellectual activity that occurs at any educational level beyond the lowest can change in terms of its conceptual complexity and difficulty. For example, I have friends in higher education who complain that the level of conceptual complexity and difficulty of the intellectual activity that occurs in contemporary secondary schools is lower than it used to be years ago. As a result, these friends complain that they are unable to engage with their students in intellectual activity at a level of conceptual sophistication that goes beyond that which used to be reached in secondary schools. I am not criticizing the education that is provided in contemporary secondary schools. Rather, I am pointing out that the degree of conceptual complexity that is found in lower and higher education can vary with time and place.

The justification of higher education is a matter that weighs heavily on the minds of many people. With the cost of a college or university education[2] beyond the reach of many individuals and families, and growing concern about the suppression of speech inside the institutional structures within which higher intellectual activity is supposed to take place, more than a few individuals are wondering about higher education's role in society. Having worked all my life inside the university, I have found myself asking what purpose it serves. This book attempts to answer this question in terms of the views of a well-known academic, C. S. Lewis.

C. S. Lewis is widely thought of and discussed today as a writer of children's stories (the Narnia books) and as a Christian apologist. His Narnia tales have sold millions of copies, as have his books about Christianity such as *Mere Christianity, The Screwtape Letters and Screwtape Proposes a Toast*, and *The Problem of Pain*. What many people do not know is that Lewis was academically trained as a philosopher, classicist, and specialist in medieval and renaissance literature. As an academician and student of the study of human nature and affairs, he held interesting views about the purpose of education generally, and higher education in particular. Though I briefly touch upon what he thought about lower-level education, which occurs in primary and secondary schools, in the following chapters my focus is on his views about higher education. Lewis himself spent his entire adult life in two universities, and while he is not well-known for his thoughts about the purpose of the university, what he did say can be woven together into a largely neglected answer to the question about the academy's purpose.

As we would expect, different understandings of the purpose of higher education have been put forth by very thoughtful people, some of whom Lewis read. By considering those perspectives, we will be better able to understand Lewis's view which calls into question what today are commonly assumed to be the only viable explanations for attending, teaching, or researching at an institution of higher learning. Some of the explanations that have been developed make for difficult reading, and I will try my best to clarify them. In comparison with these justifications of higher education, Lewis's own explanation for it will likely appear quite simple, perhaps even laughable. I suspect its simplicity is one reason why he found it so persuasive, even though it raises difficult questions to which there are few easy answers. But first things first. What have people other than Lewis proposed as the explanation for the existence of higher education?

Possible Instrumentalist Justifications for the Existence of the Academy

People who go to college because they believe, in philosophical terms, that it is useful as a means to a further end have a utilitarian or instrumentalist justification for trying to earn a university diploma.[3] Most of the students whom I have taught over the course of more than three decades have thought of themselves as potential employees and attended my liberal arts college for the purpose of earning a degree (becoming credentialed) to get the proverbial good job (sometimes just "job," with "good" understood). And my students seem not to have been the exception to the rule. According to Rickard K. Vedder,

> data from the Freshman Survey of the Higher Education Research Institute at UCLA and other polling data suggest that most college students indicate their primary goal in college is to get a good job. For

example, in the 2015 Freshman Survey, over 60 percent of respondents, referring to the college they chose to enter, said it was "very important" that "this college's graduates get good jobs."

(Vedder 2019: 17)

It seems reasonable to affirm that in the minds of the majority of university students, the purpose of getting a good job likely explains either seeking a degree in a subject matter that they believe would enable a way of life which they had settled upon before matriculating or using college as a tool for choosing a course of life and earning a degree that they believe will enable them to live that life (see Storey and Storey 2021: 181).

And why would the majority of college students have believed anything other than that securing a good job is the most plausible explanation for entering higher education? After all, the culture in which they have grown into adulthood has for the most part focused on the quality of future employment as the most plausible justification for attending college, where in the case of those financially less well-off a good job is seen as a means to economic and social mobility. For example, in a letter to the editor of *The Wall Street Journal*, Catherine B. Hill, President Emerita of Vassar College, supposes that we want "higher education to act as an engine of economic and social mobility ..." (Hill 2021). This purpose is affirmed in a comment of Father Joseph M. McShane, President Emeritus of Fordham University, that Fordham was founded in 1841 "'to break the cycle of poverty for people living on the margins of society,' which remains salient today" (Bobrow 2022). Both Hill and McShane seemingly assume that no reasonable person could fail to share this instrumentalist justification for attending university.

The purposes of making more money and becoming socially mobile which justify higher education from a potential employee's point of view are not the only utilitarian reasons for the existence of the academy. An employer can share the instrumentalist point of view for justifying higher education. For example, Will C. Wood, in a recent letter to the editor in *The Wall Street Journal*, writes the following:

> Historically, the reason for an employer's emphasis on a degree was simply its bottom line. Requiring a particular degree provided a

low-cost employment application-filtration system that eliminated the need to hire extra human resources staff to process and interview a higher number of applicants ... Companies accepted that this policy might result in their missing a good employee or two, but it was an acceptable trade-off.

(Wood 2020)

While agreeing that we all need incomes for food and shelter, some people find the idea that higher education is useful for earning a higher wage, enjoying a better quality of life, and saving an employer an added expense too materialistic and/or capitalistic in nature. In their minds, the justification for higher education, while it should not neglect the good of the individual, ought primarily to aim at the common good of the polis. To achieve this purpose, the university should aim to produce competent citizens. For example, in the seventeenth century, John Milton, though obviously not discussing today's higher education, believed that the good of the nation, indeed its very survival, is one of the aims of a virtuous and noble education: "I call therefore a complete and generous education that which fits a man to perform justly, skillfully, and magnanimously all the offices, both private and public, of peace and war" (Milton 1957: 632).

C. S. Lewis is an example of a person who spent some of his pre-university years in the English public school system,[4] which his brother, Warren Lewis, despite the needs of the state, believed was no place for his brother Jack ("Jack" being the name C. S. Lewis chose for himself at a very young age) because its purpose was to supply parts for the governmental and commercial machinery:

The fact is that Jack should never have been sent to a Public School at all. It would have been a miracle if the boy who in his first term wrote Carpe Diem[5] could have found a congenial companion amongst those of his own age, or for that matter at any age level ... [H]e would have found himself much more at home amongst first year undergraduates ... For the main function of the Public School in those days was to produce a standardized article. With two or three notable exceptions they were factories turning out the spare parts and replacements needed to keep Imperial and commercial machinery functioning efficiently, and obviously it was essential that the new part should be identical with the worn-out one. But no polishing, filing, or grinding could have made Jack a cog in any machine.

(W. H. Lewis n.d.: 35–6)

And not a few people believe that what Warren described as the purpose of the existence of the English public school is still what justifies the existence of the university today.

However, that the parts of the governmental and commercial machinery function well is not the only public good that might justify the existence of the academy. For example, the American liberal arts college Hope College justifies its plan to have students pay for their tuition out of gratitude after they graduate through the lens of "social justice, since college equalizes earning potential for students from diverse economic backgrounds" (Olgers 2021: 9). Also thinking in terms of social justice, the American pragmatist philosopher Richard Rorty believed higher education exists for the purpose of inculcating the ideas that lead to a more just society in which the vocational skills taught and learned in the academy are put to good use both within and without its walls. Rorty maintained that the university's purpose is social protest, and he wrote that "[a]ll universities worthy of the name have always been centers of social protest. If American universities ever cease to be such centers, they will lose both their self-respect and the respect of the learned world ... For intellectuals are supposed to be aware of, and speak to, issues of social justice" (Rorty 1998: 82). Intellectuals are supposed to speak to social justice because as John Dewey, for whom Rorty's "admiration ... [was] almost unlimited" (Rorty 1998: 104), understood, "the point of society is to construct subjects capable of ever more novel, ever richer, forms of human happiness" (Rorty 1998: 31). And if we think of social justice as a genus of which racial justice is a species, then Ibram X. Kendi is an example of a contemporary academician who makes clear that he is in higher education to bring about social justice: "I became a college professor to educate away racist ideas, seeing ... mental change as the principle solution, seeing myself, as educator, as the primary solver ... [But] I had to forsake the suasionist bred into me, of researching and educating for the sake of changing minds. I had to start researching and educating to change policy" (Kendi 2019: 230–1).

Employment, social mobility and status, governmental functioning, social justice. While these are proposed justifications for the existence of higher education, Michael Sandel, in his recent book *The Tyranny of Merit: What's Become of the Common Good?*, reminds us that the academy derives much of its prestige from "its avowedly higher purpose ... [which is] to prepare [students] to be morally reflective human beings and effective democratic citizens, capable of deliberating about the common good" (Sandel 2020: 191). Anthony Kronman affirms a higher reflective purpose of the academy for the individual, where fulfillment of this purpose promotes the good of the polis. In his book *The Assault on American Excellence*, he maintains that "some ways of living are better than others" (Kronman 2019: 214), and just as there is a best at playing a flute, reading a CT scan, and diagnosing a creaky carburetor, so also there is a best at being a human being. The best way of being a human being includes the development of human capacities for intelligence, imagination, wit, etc. The more a person develops these capacities, the more fulfilled (perfected) he is as a human being. Kronman maintains that the purpose of the university is to provide the liberating knowledge which enables the cultivation of human excellence, which he defines in terms of the development of the just-mentioned distinctly human capacities. Stated slightly differently, Kronman thinks the study and learning provided by higher education help a person progress toward the goal of becoming a better member of the human species (Kronman 2019: 154). According to Kronman, it is because of higher education that some persons realize more fully their human potential than others (Kronman 2019: 158).

Kronman acknowledges that he is defending a thoroughly aristocratic conception of higher education. Indeed, higher education has the duty "to protect the aristocratic ideal that some human beings [those in higher education] get further than others in mastering the art of living" (Kronman 2019: 215). The result is that those who experience the benefits of higher education define a natural aristocracy, and because our statesmen should be aristocrats, our universities are necessary for providing the polis's leadership (Kronman 2019: 188–9). However, seemingly as a concession to those of a more plebeian persuasion, Kronman maintains that higher education's aristocratic purpose does not preclude it also having the purpose of preparing students for rewarding careers (Kronman 2019: 161).

With his claim that there are better and worse members of the human species, and that higher education has the purpose of enabling those in it of achieving human excellence, Kronman is advocating for an elitist conception of living life: just as there are elite basketball players among those who play basketball and elite mathematicians among those who do mathematics, so also there are elite human beings. However, like actions generally, higher-level intellectual activity that is pursued for a purpose can have side effects, some of which might be good and others of which might be bad, and Sandel is concerned about the bad side effects of an elitist view such as Kronman's. Like many words, "elitist" has different meanings, and Sandel recognizes that those who affirm an elitist view of living life according to which excellence requires higher-intellectual activity all too often develop an elitist attitude of a morally repugnant kind toward others who do not get a college education:

> Elitists have so valorized a college degree … that they have difficulty understanding the hubris a meritocracy can generate, and the harsh judgment it imposes on those who have not gone to college … [T]he reign of technocratic merit [whose work force is almost totally supplied by those who have passed through higher education] has reconfigured the terms of social recognition in ways that elevate the prestige of the credentialed, professional classes and depreciate the contributions of most workers [to the common good], eroding their social standing and esteem.
>
> (Sandel 2020: 26, 29)

[I]nsisting that a college degree is the primary route to a respectable job and a decent life creates a credentialist prejudice that undermines the dignity of work and demeans those who have not been to college; and ... insisting that social and political problems are best solved by highly educated, value-neutral experts is a technocratic conceit that corrupts democracy and disempowers ordinary citizens.

(Sandel 2020: 73)

Sandel believes that even if the highly educated technocratic elite were good at deliberating about the common good and pursuing it effectively, which they are not ("recent historical experience suggests little correlation between the capacity for political judgment, which involves moral character as well as insight, and the ability to score well on standardized tests and win admission to elite universities" (Sandel 2020: 99)), it would still be wrong to suggest to the general populace that everyone should go to university to obtain social esteem and good employment. Why "[s]hould colleges and universities take on the role of sorting people based on talent to determine who gets ahead in life?" (Sandel 2020: 172). And why not just recognize as a fact that many people are not suited for higher education so that "[c]onstantly admonishing them to better their condition by getting [a college degree] ... can be more insulting than inspiring?" (Sandel 2020: 169).[6]

If not everyone should go to university, what is the alternative for those who do not? Sandel believes we should make clear to everyone that entering technical and vocational programs while in or immediately subsequent to secondary education is just as honorable and prestigious as attending a name-brand institution of higher learning: "Learning to become a plumber or electrician or dental hygienist should be respected as a valuable contribution to the common good, not regarded as a consolation prize for those who lack the SAT scores or financial means to make it to the Ivy League" (Sandel 2020: 191). Others agree with Sandel. For example, Josh Mitchell, a reporter for *The Wall Street Journal*, has recently pointed out that because more than a few university graduates do not get an adequate financial payoff from a four-year degree and an employer frequently needs to provide the college-educated employee with on-the-job training, the age-old idea of an apprenticeship is now receiving more serious consideration (Mitchell 2020). While apprenticeships have long provided a way into skilled trades such as plumbing, carpentry, and masonry, more and more people are looking at apprenticeships for work not only in these professions but also in others like automobile manufacturing. According to James McCaslin, provost of Southcentral Kentucky Community and Technical College in Bowling Green, Kentucky, "[b]ecause the machines have become so sophisticated and because the margins are so thin, companies are looking for people who can [through apprenticeships] do all the things we deliver" (quoted in Mitchell 2020).

Higher Education as a Source of Pleasure

Is there any other plausible justification for the existence of higher education than those mentioned in the previous section? Sandel himself seems to think there is, but he has little to say about what it is, beyond that colleges and universities have an "educational mission" (Sandel 2020: 172) or "educational function" (Sandel 2020: 182). John Rose cites what he regards as the conservative goal of "passing down wisdom" (Rose 2021), and Mary Harrington notes the goal of "transmitting the best that's been thought and said in our culture to a new generation" (Harrington 2022). Jonathan Marks adds the academy's obligation to "conquer unhealthy individualism" to the list of proposed purposes (Marks 2021b).

With so many instrumentalist justifications for higher education's existence on the table for consideration, someone might respond:

> Why all the fuss? At least some of the utilitarian aims of higher learning are reasonable, whether they are primarily concerned with the good of the person as such or that of society at large. Who in their right mind would question their adequacy, considered either individually or jointly? Is there really another instrumentalist justification for higher

education other than getting a good job, the company's bottom line, the functioning of the government, the achievement of social justice, or becoming a better human being?

Perhaps surprisingly, there is one other purpose for the existence of higher education as a means to an end that has received little, if any, serious attention by those who currently think and write about the justification for the existence of the academy.

When our son was ten years old and already seriously interested in mathematics, my wife and I, along with our son, watched a British Broadcasting Corporation (BBC) television show about the Princeton University mathematician Andrew Wiles and his discovery of a proof of Fermat's Last Theorem, which states that $x^n + y^n = z^n$ has no non-zero integer solutions for x, y, and z when n > 2. Wiles's dream since childhood had been to find a proof of Fermat's Last Theorem. Two of Wiles's mathematical colleagues were interviewed for the BBC production. One, John Conway, stated that "not all mathematical problems are useless. Fermat's one really is useless ... It's got no practical value whatsoever." Another, Peter Sarnak, added that "if it's true, it doesn't imply anything profound, that any of us know. It doesn't lead to anything that's useful, that any of us know" ("Fermat's Last Theorem," 1996). But if Fermat's Last Theorem is really as useless as these mathematicians claimed, what might explain Wiles's interest in providing a proof of it, something at which he succeeded while he was in higher education? Is there an instrumentalist explanation that is nevertheless useless in the way described by Conway and Sarnak?

C. S. Lewis believed there is. And he would have affirmed that it is the explanation for the existence of intellectual activity generally and higher-level intellectual activity more specifically. Lewis maintained that the simple utilitarian justification for the existence of higher education is the purpose of experiencing the pleasure (happiness) that is enjoyed by those thinking about and wrestling with ideas, understanding the conceptual connections between them, and recognizing those which are true and their practical applications (when there are such).[7] "The experience of pleasure?" many individuals will respond. "People in higher education can derive happiness from being a professor or a student in the academy?" Lewis could and did, and believed others, like Wiles, could and would. If there are pleasures that come from such diverse things as agreement with another person, imagination, talking business, associating with and being approved by others, and a good scratch (Lewis 1939a: 27; [1948a] in 1969: 235, 245–7; [1942] in 1969: 300), then, thought Lewis, why can there not be pleasures which come from higher-level intellectual activity? When he explained how he had become interested in Christianity, Lewis wrote that

> Christendom ... reached me at first almost entirely through books I took up not because they were Christian, but because they were famous literature. Hence Dante, Spenser, Milton, the poems of George Herbert and of Coventry Patmore ... Later, when I had become interested in Christianity—been *caught* by truth in places where I sought only pleasure—came St. Augustine, Hooker ...
>
> (Lewis 2007: 978)

And he advised a new tutee, "[t]he great thing is to be always reading but not to get bored—treat it not like work, more as a vice! Your book bill ought to be your biggest extravagance" (Lewis 2007: 1541).

As was the case for Ransom, the main character in Lewis's science-fiction story *Out of the Silent Planet*, so also for Lewis "[t]he love of knowledge [was] a kind of madness" (Lewis 2003a [1938]: 56). A tutee of Lewis's, John Wain, in his review of his mentor's magisterial work *English Literature in the Sixteenth Century*, wrote that "[m]ost dons have moved a long way from any recognition that literature is something that people read for *fun*. Mr Lewis, now as always, writes as if inviting us to a feast" (Wain 1954). A recent obituary of Kathy Wiltsey, a former vice president of Amgen Inc. and a philanthropist, notes that she devoted much time to "persuading young people that math and science could be fun" (Wiltsey 2021: A11). Similarly, Will Frazer's Buchholz High School math team in Florida has won thirteen of the last fourteen American national mathematics championships, and "one of Mr. Frazer's methods for pulling off a feat that many consider impossible [is] making math fun" (Cohen 2022). Hailey Lin, a Buchholz junior "knows how it sounds when people hear about math practice. 'But it's not, like, "Oh, my God, I have to do math."' … She loves the collaborative elements of team competitions and challenging herself against the best of the best" (Cohen 2022).

Like Wain, Wiltsey, and Frazer, Lewis did not hesitate to invoke the idea that learning could be enjoyable, even in higher education. In a response letter to Mary van Deusen who was considering attending classes (the nature of their subject matter is unclear from Lewis's response), Lewis wrote the following:

> Unless it attracts you as an amusement I wouldn't advise you to start attending "classes." My idea is that unless one has to qualify oneself for a job (which you haven't) the only sensible reason for studying anything is that one has a strong curiosity about it. And if one has, one can't help studying it. I don't see any point in attending lectures etc with some general notion of "self-improvement"—unless, as I say, one finds it fun.
>
> I never see why we should do anything unless it is either a duty or a pleasure!
>
> (Lewis 2007: 96)

Lewis's approach to attending classes extended to writing. In an interview, he was told "You write as though you enjoyed it." He responded, "If I didn't enjoy writing I wouldn't continue to do it. Of all my books, there was only one [*The Screwtape Letters*] I did not take pleasure in writing" (Lewis [1963a] in 1970: 263). Lewis's belief that you should attend lectures and write for pleasure, and, at least in the case of the former, not for self-improvement, extended to his view of the reason for reading books. He wrote the following thoughts about reading books to his lifelong friend Arthur Greeves:

> And you ought to rely more on yourself than on anyone else in matters of books—that is if you're out for enjoyment and not for improvement or any nonsense of that sort.
>
> (Lewis 2004a: 190)

The book you refer to is "How to Form a Literary Taste" by Arnold Ben[n]ett: the edition is pretty but the book is not of any value. The very title—as if you set out to "learn" literature the way you learn golf—shews that the author is not a real book-lover but only a priggish hack.

(Lewis 2004a: 240)

As to Bennet[t]'s book, if a person was really a book-lover, however ignorant, he wouldn't go and look up a text book to see what to buy, as if literature was a subject to be learned like algebra: one thing would lead him to another [and] he would go through the usual mistakes [and] gain experience. I hate this idea of "forming a taste."

(Lewis 2004a: 246)

My own pupils still seem to me in many ways older than I. Indeed (nice men as many of them are) I am a little worried by the fact that so few of them seem ever to have had youth as we had it. They have all read all the correct, "important" books: they seem to have no private [and] erratic imaginative adventures of their own … [T]he modern world is so desperately serious. They have a taste for "books of information" [with no goal of forming a taste to enjoy other books for experiences of pleasure].

(Lewis 2004b: 756)

This past summer, I was with a friend who was showing me a part of England I had never before visited. As we emerged from a bookstore, he stopped and said to me, "I think in my entire life I have never read but two or three books more than once." I rolled my friend's comment over and over in my mind and remembered that he had never attended university. Lewis believed the reading habits of people mirror the purpose of higher education. He made this point by contrasting two types of readers, the minority and the majority. People who are members of the minority of readers, the literary readers, read the same book ten, twenty, or thirty times during the course of their life because they get pleasure from what they are reading.[8] They also are always looking for leisure and silence in which to read with their undivided attention. Furthermore, those in the minority sometimes, upon the first reading of a book, undergo a momentous life-changing experience that is comparable to experiences of love or religion. And finally, readers in the minority constantly have before their minds what they have read. They talk to one another about what they have read, often at length, and think about their own lives in terms of the scenes and characters in what they have read (Lewis 1961a: 1–3).[9]

By contrast, those in the majority of readers, the unliterary readers, read a book once and consider "I've read it already" a conclusive retort against reading a work again. They also turn to reading as a last resort and pursue another activity as soon as it comes along. Furthermore, those in the majority of readers are largely unchanged by what they have read, and they seldom think or talk with others about what they have read because it is rarely before their mind (Lewis 1961a: 1–3).

In Lewis's view, higher education is for individuals who, like those in the minority of readers, derive pleasure from intellectual activity. In higher education, the pleasure comes from higher-level intellectual activity. The academy is not for individuals who belong to the majority of readers. Nevertheless, the classes I and my colleagues teach are regularly filled with young adults who read a book only because it is required, and they rarely, if ever, read a book more than once. These "students" do not derive pleasure from reading and learning, and they think of higher education as a required pit stop in the competitive race for a good job. Hence, they view their time there as something to be endured, not enjoyed. Lewis wrote about

> the plain man [who] has been captured and made into a pathetically willing and bewildered university student [who] will sometimes praise the great works which he has dutifully read and not enjoyed, for the excellence of their style. He has missed the jokes in the comedy, remained unmoved by the tragedy, failed to respond to the suggestions of the lyric, and found the episodes of the romance uninteresting; utterly at a loss to explain the value traditionally set on what has proved to him so tedious ...
>
> (Lewis 1939a: 104)

Similarly, Sheldon Vanauken described in his book *A Severe Mercy* his return to teaching students at a college in Virginia in the 1950s, after having enjoyed living and studying at Oxford University and becoming friends with Lewis: "The students at the college were not ... students ..." (Vanauken 1987: 126). At the end of an academic year, I sometimes ask my students what they hope to read over the summer. More often than not, I receive a puzzled stare and silence. Many of America's colleges today are populated with individuals who do not enjoy books and advanced thought, and Lewis would have had us at least ask ourselves whether they should be filled with such persons.[10]

But surely, someone might respond, even if learning (and reading) is fun for some people, that fact cannot itself justify its pursuit. There is a large list of activities that people regard as fun but which we nevertheless believe they should not pursue. Lewis agreed, but maintained that "giving up fun for no reason except that you think it's 'good' to give it up, is all nonsense" (Lewis 2007: 871). One needs a good reason not to pursue what is fun. Lewis acknowledged that there are such reasons. Most obviously, he thought, there are the ordinary rules of morality which typically set down guidelines for what you should not do to have fun. But Lewis believed that if one has no good reason to refrain from an enjoyable activity, then one will, given one is able, go ahead and engage in it. And this is the situation some people find themselves in with respect to intellectual activity. It is fun and they are unaware of any good reason not to enjoy it. So they understandably pursue the experiences of pleasure that come with intellectual activity in higher education.

If the purpose of experiencing pleasure is the explanation for the existence of higher education, how is it that so many people seemingly do not see this? Lewis was often looking for universal principles or laws, and he believed that it is a universal principle that what is most obvious is often overlooked or seen through and not noticed:

> When you are looking at a garden from a room upstairs it is obvious (once you think about it) that you are looking through a window. But if it is the garden that interests you, you may look at it for a long time

without thinking of the window. When you are reading a book it is obvious (once you attend to it) that you are using your eyes: but unless your eyes begin to hurt you, or the book is a text book on optics, you may read all evening without once thinking of eyes ...

[T]hese instances show that the fact which is in one respect the most obvious and primary fact, and through which alone you have access to all the other facts, may be precisely the one that is most easily forgotten—forgotten not because it is so remote or abstruse but because it is so near and so obvious.

(Lewis 2001c [1960 rev. ed.]: 63–4)[11]

Lewis believed that those who are so "near" to higher education because they are a part of it and who think about what justifies its existence more often than not see through the obvious explanation for their involvement in it, which is that it provides them with pleasure. Were Lewis to have read Rorty's defense of higher education in terms of social justice and the realization of forms of human happiness, he would have insisted that one of the ways of experiencing that happiness is found in the rooms, halls, and cloisters of higher learning. The university is a place to share with others a source of happiness made possible by a just society. And while thinking about the nature of a just society and how to make it a reality might be a source of pleasure for some who participate in the life of higher learning, Lewis would have maintained that the university's own being is not justified in terms of the purpose of agitating for the existence of a just society. Were Lewis to have lived today, he would surely have sounded an alarm to the effect that higher education has forgotten the purpose for which it exists, which is the happiness of those in the academy. However, because many politically active people believe politics is an end in itself, they have, not surprisingly, slowly but surely taken over the academy for the purpose of realizing their political vision.[12] Lewis believed a society whose universities are political bodies is seriously ill:

> A sick society must think much about politics, as a sick man must think much about his digestion; to ignore the subject may be fatal cowardice for the one as for the other. But if either comes to regard it

as the natural food of the mind—if either forgets that we think of such things only in order to be able to think of something else—then what was undertaken for the sake of health has become itself a new and deadly disease.

(Lewis [1945c] in 2001g: 162)

An Important Reminder

At this juncture, one might be thinking that the different conceptions of the purpose of higher education are really different conceptions of higher education itself (what higher education is). For example, Andrew Delbanco, in his book *College: What It Was, Is, and Should Be*, writes that

> [t]here are roughly four thousand colleges in the United States: rural, urban, and suburban; non-profit, for-profit; secular, religious; some small and independent, others within large research institutions; some highly selective, others that admit almost anyone who applies and has means to pay ...
>
> Even a quick scan of this landscape reveals how radically the meaning of college is changing ... For a relatively few students, college remains the sort of place ... where [a] class [takes] place at the home of a philosophy professor ... For many more students, college means the anxious pursuit of marketable skills in overcrowded, underresourced institutions ... For still others, it means travelling by night to a fluorescent office building or to a "virtual classroom" that exists only in cyberspace.
>
> (Delbanco 2012: 7)

Different people define "college" differently, and it is not the aim of this book to show that one definition is right and the others wrong. Rather, a reader should remember that the meaning of "college," "university," and "the academy" in this book is "higher education," where "higher education" means higher-level intellectual activity. It is true that higher education as I am thinking of it regularly occurs in the physical spaces (e.g., academic buildings, laboratories) of the social institution that we call college or university. However, it is possible and plausible to distinguish between college or university as higher-level intellectual activity and college or university as the physical bricks and mortar of the relevant social institution. When people ask about the purpose of higher education (college, university), they typically are not asking about the purpose of certain physical spaces. They are asking about the purpose of what goes on in those physical spaces, where what goes on is intellectual activity of a certain kind. They are wondering whether the purpose of that intellectual activity justifies the significant time and money the culture is telling them they should devote to it. This book is concerned with making clear what C. S. Lewis thought that purpose is.

Lewis and the Academy

In reading C. S. Lewis for his views of the purpose of higher education, one should always remember that he was an author who wrote in many different genres, including philosophical and theological books and essays, science fiction and children's stories, literary criticism, and autobiography. What one must often do is piece his views together from these different genres on topics which he did not address systematically in a single piece of work. And because he wrote in so many genres, one must not apply standards of rigor appropriate for his philosophical work to, say, his science fiction or children's literature. If one forgets this important critical principle one might end up either ascribing a view to Lewis which he did not hold or maintaining that he consciously held incompatible positions on a certain topic. With an author like Lewis, a charitable reader will read and reread the entire library of his work to get a sense of what he thought about this or that. Above all, one must not pull an isolated sentence from here or there to prove a point that is at odds with what he obviously thought about a topic in light of everything else that he wrote.

My explication of Lewis's view of the purpose of a university education begins in Chapter 1 with an overview of his thoughts about the purpose of life as the experience of pleasure. Not surprisingly, Lewis did not think about higher education in a vacuum, and his belief that God exists and creates us for the purpose that we be perfectly happy, where happiness is composed of nothing but experiences of pleasure, provided him with a framework in which to situate his consideration of the purpose of higher learning. Chapter 1 is the most straightforwardly philosophical in this book. As it unfolds, you might find yourself thinking that I am making what is simple and obvious complicated and obscure. If you do find yourself thinking this, I ask for your patience. Philosophy is often difficult because it in part involves considering what is conceptually complex and trying to discover its compositional conceptual simples. The philosopher Elizabeth Anscombe, a contemporary of Lewis's and critic of his argument from reason (see Chapter 4, endnote 4), once told her friend, Iris Murdoch, that "[n]o *second rate* philosophy is any good ... One must start from scratch—& it takes a very long time to reach scratch" (Cumhaill and Wiseman 2022: 188). In terms of Lewis's philosophy of the purpose of higher education, pleasure is scratch and understanding Lewis's thought about it provides the basis for his view of the goal of higher-level intellectual activity.[13]

In Chapter 2, I examine Lewis's views about pleasure as they apply to higher education. Lewis held an instrumentalist view of higher education in the sense that learning and knowledge are good when they lead to experiences of pleasure. A non-instrumentalist view of higher education understands learning and knowledge as goods in themselves, regardless of whether or not they lead to pleasure or anything else, and it is clear Lewis did not hold this non-instrumentalist view.

Given that Lewis was a Christian from his early thirties until the day he died and the fact that more than a few people within the Christian community are deeply suspicious of higher education, it is worth spending some time considering Lewis's justification for his own involvement in the academy as a Christian. This is the subject of Chapter 3.

Chapter 4 is a treatment of Lewis's response to what is known in the academy as "naturalism." Naturalism was becoming increasingly popular with academicians in Lewis's day, and is the reigning orthodoxy in higher education today. Lewis believed that were it true, it would undercut any reason for the existence of the university and everything else in life. Given its ongoing and controlling presence in the academy today, it is important to understand Lewis's criticism of it.

In Chapter 5, I take brief looks at practical issues concerning the implementation of what Lewis believed is the purpose of higher education. Not surprisingly, easy answers to many legitimate and difficult questions are hard to find.

Chapter 6 is devoted to my own thoughts about higher education in light of my treatment of Lewis's views. Readers of various earlier drafts of this book, while they were keenly interested in Lewis's thoughts about the purpose of higher education, told me that they also wanted to know what I thought about the aim of advanced intellectual activity. Therefore, I conclude the book with some of my own reflections on the purpose of the academy.

As with my previous two books on the thought of C. S. Lewis (Goetz 2015a, 2018a), I frequently and sometimes extensively quote Lewis's own words. There are two reasons for this. First, Lewis was a master of the written word, and one derives much pleasure from reading what he had to say. Second, without quoting Lewis to back up my claims about his views, many will dismiss what I say about his perspectives on the topics of this book because they have an erroneous preconception of what he was like and what he said. With respect to the second issue, Lewis, though theologically orthodox, had views that many who write about him and his thought have either never addressed, misunderstood, or understood and purposely suppressed.[14] If Lewis was anything, he was his own man, and it is time that people recognize him for what he was without trying to make him into something he was not. Lewis repeatedly stressed to his readers that they should let texts speak to them: "The first demand any work of art makes upon us is surrender. Look. Listen. Receive. Get yourself out of the way" (Lewis 1961a: 19). The "true reader ... makes himself as receptive as he can" (Lewis 1961a: 11). Many readers of Lewis need to get themselves out of the way and read, hear, and receive what he wrote, even though it is at odds with their preconceived notions of what he thought. Lewis wrote about critics that "[a] great many people start by thinking they know what you will say, and honestly believe they have read what they expected to read. But for whatever reason, it is certainly the case that ... you will find yourself repeatedly blamed and praised for saying what you never said and for not saying what you have said" (Lewis 1994 [1966]: 47). This point is especially apropos with respect to what Lewis wrote about pleasure. The vast majority of scholars and biographers of Lewis not only never tell their readers that Lewis's written work is overflowing with positive references to experiences of pleasure and their importance for understanding human life, but also state that Lewis held this or that view concerning a particular issue of value, when in fact he never said anything of the kind.

Lewis came to intellectual maturity in a world where education was primarily for males. In the quotations that I provide from his work, it will be obvious that much of his thought about education, both lower- and higher-level, was stated in terms of boys and men. Like all of us, Lewis was a person rooted in time. He reminded his readers with the words of Alan Gunn (an author of a book about the medieval poem *The Romance of the Rose*) that "[e]very artist deserves to be judged first by the standards of his own time" (Lewis [1953] in 2013: 241). While Lewis was highly critical of the belief that human history was always inevitably moving forward in the sense that humans were continually making things better for themselves and the planet as a whole, he nevertheless believed that progress was sometimes achieved in different areas of life. And the opening up of higher education in his day to females was one such area.[15]

Like any other rational person, Lewis understood that both men and women experience pleasure and its positive value. When Lewis discussed what he termed the "Headship doctrine" of the husband in Christian marriage in a letter to Mary Neylen, a former student of his, he wrote that one has to distinguish between woman as woman (her human nature as a woman) and other modes of her being as a citizen, musician, teacher, etc. And one "needn't transfer to all these personalities everything that is said about [her] as wife *quâ* wife ... [Thus] the Headship doctrine [would not] prevent women going in for education" (Lewis 2004b: 395–6). In a letter to I. O. Evans about pre-university education, Lewis wrote "I have no brief against co-education. I am, in principle, inclined (having no school-mastering experience I [would] not go further than an inclination either way) to approve it" (Lewis 2007: 373). Moreover, Oxford University, in Lewis's early years there, was in the initial stages of admitting and awarding degrees to women (in discussing Chaucer, Lewis wrote "as more and more women take up the study of English literature" (Lewis 1936: 182)), and Lewis himself tutored and gave lectures to both male and female students.

That Lewis believed intellectual activity is not restricted to men was reflected in his discussion of friendship. When we think of friendship as a kind of love, Lewis maintained the question "Do you love me?" means "Do you see the same truth?" (Lewis 1988 [1960]: 66). He went on to point out that "[w]here men are educated and women not ... they will usually have nothing to be Friends about." "But," he added, "we can easily see that it is this lack, rather than anything in their natures, which excludes Friendship; for where they can be companions they can also become Friends. Hence in a profession (like my own) where men and women work side by side ... such Friendship is common" (Lewis 1988 [1960]: 72). Thus, it is evident that Lewis clearly believed men and women could share together the pleasure of higher-level intellectual activity. And Lewis's belief that women could be equals with men in intellectual activity was further evidenced by the fact that, as he himself wrote in a letter, "[i]t isn't chiefly *men* I am kept in touch with by my huge mail: it is *women*" (Lewis 2007: 195). Women were most certainly not put off by the fact that Lewis was a man and, when he wrote this letter, a bachelor. Any reader of Lewis's vast personal correspondence cannot help but notice the thoughtfulness of his replies to both men and women, most of whom initiated letter contact with him and whom he never met face to face.

Lewis sometimes served as a literary critic, and in a piece devoted to the topic wrote that there are two senses in which an author might be dated (Lewis [1946d] in 1982: 115). One sense is in terms of the "paraphernalia" which are of a particular age and include the terminology and categories of thought that an author uses to discuss his topic. In this way, Lewis's language and focus on education for males are dated. Another sense in which an author might be dated is in terms of the topic he treats, which while at one time of interest to readers is no longer so. In this sense, Lewis's views on higher education are not the least bit dated because the topic is of enduring interest.

Thus, in answer to the question "Why read C. S. Lewis for his views of higher education, when he is a dead white male from the previous century?", the answer is because he has important things to say about a topic that is a subject of interest in each generation. Furthermore, as one who thought about the purpose of higher education, Lewis believed it is important to read and learn about the views of others through asking questions about why they see things as they do, whether they are our contemporaries or predecessors in time, and whether we agree with them or not. Lewis himself reveled in seeing the world from someone else's point of view:

> We therefore delight to enter [derive pleasure from entering] into other men's beliefs ... even though we think them untrue. And into their passions, though we think them depraved. And also into their imaginations, though they lack all realism of content.
>
> This must not be understood as if I were making the literature of power once more into a department within the literature of knowledge—a department which existed to gratify our rational curiosity about other people's psychology. It is not a question of knowing (in that sense) at all. It is *connaître* not *savoir*; it is *erleben*; we become these other selves. Not only nor chiefly in order to see what they are like but in order to see what they see, to occupy, for a while, their seat in the great theatre, to use their spectacles and be made free of whatever insights, joys, terrors, wonders or merriment those spectacles reveal ... Those of us who have been true readers all our life

seldom fully realise the enormous extension of our being which we owe to authors ... The man who is contented to be only himself, and therefore less a self, is in prison. My own eyes are not enough for me, I will see through those of others ...

Literary experience heals the wound, without undermining the privilege, of individuality ... But in reading great literature I become a thousand men and yet remain myself. Like the night sky in the Greek poem, I see with a myriad eyes, but it is still I who see. Here, as in worship, in love, in moral action, and in knowing, I transcend myself; and am never more myself than when I do.

(Lewis 1961a: 138–41)

So whether you end up agreeing with Lewis's view about the purpose of higher education or not, you will, in reading this book about his view, hopefully transcend yourself by seeing the world of academia through the eyes of someone who thought seriously about its nature and purpose. And in transcending yourself, perhaps you will find yourself developing friendships with others who enjoy reading, thinking, talking, and writing about the purpose of higher education and other topics that interested Lewis. Lewis was a lifelong lover of Norse myths, and in his autobiography *Surprised by Joy* he recounted a visit he made in his early teens to see his friend Arthur Greeves, who was ill at home:

I found Arthur sitting up in bed. On the table beside him lay a copy of *Myths of the Norseman*.

"Do *you* like that?" said I.

"Do *you* like that?" said he.

Next moment the book was in our hands, our heads were bent close together, we were pointing, quoting, talking—soon almost shouting—discovering in a torrent of questions that we liked not only the same thing, but the same parts of it and in the same way; ...

(Lewis 1955: 130)

Toward the end of his life, Lewis wrote about friendship that it

arises out of mere Companionship when two or more of the companions discover that they have in common some insight or interest or even taste which the others do not share and which, till that moment each believed to be his own unique treasure ... The typical expression of opening Friendship would be something like, "What? You too? I thought I was the only one."

(Lewis 1988 [1960]: 65)

While no reader of this book can become a literal friend of C. S. Lewis, perhaps a less-than-literal friendship with him will develop through the consideration of his ideas about the purpose of higher education. Perhaps more than a few readers will have a "What?-You-too-think-that?" experience as they consider his thought concerning the justification of the existence of the academy.

1

The Intrinsic Goodness of Pleasure

The Serious Business of Life

C. S. Lewis was well aware that many people regard preparation for a job as the justification for the existence of higher education. In the minds of such individuals, to claim higher education is for some other purpose, especially that it is for pleasure, is to render what is serious, frivolous. However, Lewis believed pleasure is serious business. Indeed, he thought it the most serious business, because experiences of it constitute happiness and happiness is what life is ultimately all about. The experience of pleasure is a foundation stone for the view of happiness affirmed by hedonists. As the philosopher Nicholas White has written, because hedonism [about happiness] is a view "everyone finds attractive, or even attractive in the extreme ... virtually every philosopher who's not a hedonist [about happiness] has felt obliged to explain why not" (White 2006: 53–4). Lewis, because he believed happiness consists of nothing but experiences of pleasure (in this sense, he was a hedonist about happiness), did not feel the weight of the obligation. Indeed, as a Christian Lewis thought experiences of pleasure are "shafts of the [divine] glory," "the sunbeam [of] the sun," a kind of theophany (Lewis 1992a [1963]: 89, 90), and comprise the life of the blessed, the life of heaven (Lewis 1992a [1963]: 92–3).

Hedonism

Early in 1941, Canon Oliver Chase Quick wrote to Lewis about the latter's recently published book *The Problem of Pain* and raised questions about the relationships between self-surrender, self-awareness, and the experience of pleasure. In his response, Lewis pointed out to the clergyman that "I wasn't writing on the Problem of Pleasure! If I had been you might find my views *too* hedonistic" (Lewis 2004b: 463). Many years later in a letter to Mary van Deusen, Lewis approvingly exclaimed about God's provision of pleasure described in Psalm 36:8, "And what unabashed Hedonism in 8!" (Lewis 2007: 685). And in his book *The Screwtape Letters and Screwtape Proposes a Toast*, Lewis had the chief devil, Screwtape, complain that God is

> a hedonist at heart. All those fasts and vigils and stakes and crosses are only a façade. Or only like foam on the seashore. Out at sea, out in His sea, there is pleasure, and more pleasure. He makes no secret of it; at His right hand are "pleasures for evermore." ... He's vulgar ... He has a bourgeois mind.
>
> (Lewis 1961b: 101)

In light of Lewis's frequent references to his and God's hedonistic views about pleasure and happiness, a reader might understandably ask "What is hedonism?" Strictly defined, hedonism is the philosophical view that there is one and only one intrinsic good, which is the experience of pleasure, and one and only one intrinsic evil, which is the experience of pain. As I will elaborate momentarily, Lewis, though he believed in the hedonistic understanding of happiness, was not, strictly speaking, a hedonist. But before I clarify Lewis's thought about this matter, it is important to understand what it means to say something is intrinsically good or intrinsically evil.

What is intrinsically good is good in itself. What is good in itself or simply good is good independent of its relationship to anything else, which implies that it does not derive its goodness from its relationship to anything else. Lewis wrote "I have no doubt at all that pleasure is in itself a good ..." (Lewis [1940] in 1967: 21),[1] and earlier in the letter to Canon Quick mentioned above Lewis stressed that he thought "*all* pleasure simply good: what we call bad pleasures are pleasures produced by actions, or inactions, [which] break the moral law, and it is those actions or inactions [which] are bad, not the pleasures"

(Lewis 2004b: 462–3). So even though Lewis was a Christian theist, he did not believe that pleasure receives its goodness from God declaring that it is good, because that would imply pleasure receives its goodness from its relationship to a decision made by God. In believing pleasure is intrinsically good, Lewis thought pleasure is good because its nature as pleasure (what pleasure is like as an experience) entails its goodness, and no one, including God, has a say about this being the case.[2]

And what about pain? Lewis believed it is evil in itself; it is evil independent of its relationship to something else. He wrote "I have no doubt at all that ... pain in itself [is] an evil ..." (Lewis [1940] in 1967: 21). "Pain is unmasked, unmistakable evil ..." (Lewis 2001f [1940]: 90). So in affirming pain is evil in itself, Lewis was affirming that pain does not derive its evilness from its relationship to anything else. Pain's nature (what pain is like as an experience) entails its evilness, and no one has any say about the matter, not even God.

Lewis's assertion that evil is an intrinsic property or feature of pain might be a source of some perplexity. David S. Oderberg points out that in ordinary discourse

> "evil" has come to be used solely for that which is egregiously bad or seriously bad enough to warrant a special kind of opprobrium (... as in an evil deed or an evil person ... or ... as in the evil of some terrible disease or disaster). Evil is thought of as the worst kind of badness, a superlative requiring its own special appellation or attitude.
>
> (Oderberg 2020: ix)

However, Lewis, like philosophers more generally, used "evil" to mean the same thing as "bad," with no suggestion of great or more serious wrongdoing, awfulness of suffering, etc. When Lewis wrote that pain is evil in itself, he meant that pain has the property of being evil intrinsically, but he could just as easily and truthfully have written that pain is intrinsically bad, where "bad" is just a synonym for "evil" and picks out the very same property had by pain.

An extrinsic good is a good whose goodness is dependent on its relationship to something else that is good and from which it derives its goodness. And an extrinsic evil is an evil whose evilness is dependent on its relationship to something else that is evil and from which it derives its evilness. If, like Lewis, we maintain that pleasure is intrinsically good, then an action that produces pleasure is extrinsically good because its goodness is derived from the pleasure to which it leads. For example, eating chocolate ice cream is extrinsically good when it leads to pleasure. And if one derives pleasure from reading a book, then the act of reading the book is extrinsically good because it leads to the experience of pleasure. If, like Lewis, we maintain that pain is intrinsically evil, then an action that produces pain is extrinsically evil because its evilness is derived from the pain to which it leads. For example, drilling a tooth is extrinsically evil when it leads to pain, though it is extrinsically good insofar as it leads to future experiences of pleasure that accompany eating. And if you derive pain from reading a book, then the act of reading the book is extrinsically evil because it leads to the experience of pain. Actions are typically termed *instrumental* goods and evils insofar as they are means to the experiences of pleasure and pain respectively.

Some expositors of Lewis's thought fail to understand his belief that pain is intrinsically and thus, always evil. For example, Harry Lee Poe writes that "nerve endings, or 'pain fibres' as Lewis called them, tell how close to a fire we may come before we pass from safety to danger. Thus, pain serves a helpful purpose and is not necessarily evil" (Poe 2021: 237–8). However, Lewis believed that what is intrinsically evil can also be instrumentally good. Pain, which Lewis claimed is intrinsically evil, can be instrumentally good as a preventative warning about the presence of fire which can cause bodily damage and additional pain.[3]

Because Lewis believed an experience of pleasure is intrinsically good, he believed you desire it for its own sake. And because he believed you desire an experience of pleasure for its own sake he believed you will pursue a pleasurable experience, unless you have what you believe is a good reason not to do so. No one gives up pleasure just to give it up. As I quoted Lewis in the Introduction, "giving up fun for no reason except that you think it's 'good' to give it up, is all nonsense" (Lewis 2007: 871).

Similarly, because Lewis believed an experience of pain is intrinsically evil, he believed you desire not to experience it for its own sake. And because he believed you desire not to experience pain for its own sake, he believed you will avoid it, unless you have a reason not to do so. In the midst of his grief over the death of his wife Joy Davidman, Lewis wrote "[b]ut we are not at all—if we understand ourselves—seeking the aches for their own sake" (Lewis 2001a [1961]: 54). And elsewhere Lewis said,

> [W]e have no experience of anyone liking badness just because it is bad. The nearest we can get to it is in cruelty ... [But] no one ever did a cruel action simply because cruelty is wrong—only because cruelty was pleasant or useful to him ... In order to be bad he must have good things to want and then to pursue in the wrong way.
> (Lewis 2001b [1952]: 43–4)

Lewis insisted that in this case what is true of human persons is also true of God who is not a being "who loves tragedy and tears and fasting *for their own sake* ..." (Lewis 2001c [1960 rev. ed.]: 221).

To say that an experience of pleasure is intrinsically good does not entail that the absence of an experience of pleasure implies the existence of that which is intrinsically evil. The nonexistence of an experience of pleasure does not imply the existence of pain, a positive reality in its own right, because it is possible not to experience pleasure without experiencing pain. In other words, pain is not the logical opposite (negation) of pleasure; not-pleasure (the negation of pleasure) is not the same as pain. As Lewis wrote, "[p]ain ... puts mere loss of pleasure quite out of account" (Lewis 2007: 883–4). When he addressed the purpose of stories for children, he wrote "[w]e must of course try to do them [children] no harm: we may ... sometimes dare to hope that we may do them good" (Lewis [1952] in 1982: 42). A state of being in which you experience no pleasure and no pain, where the goodness of pleasure and evilness of pain are the respective positive and negative *values* of these experiences, is a state of being that is without value; it is a value-neutral state.[4]

Hedonists believe that experiences of pleasure are intrinsically good. They also believe that experiences of pleasure constitute happiness. So if you are experiencing nothing but pleasure, then you are happier than when you are experiencing both pleasure and pain, or only pain, or neither pleasure nor pain. Lewis's hedonism about happiness is reflected in his frequent substitution of the word "happiness" for "pleasure"; he regarded the words as interchangeable. In his discussion of Eros (being in love) in his book *The Four Loves*, his belief in the identity of pleasure and happiness is evident in the following statement: "As Venus [the animally sexual element] within Eros does not really aim at pleasure, so Eros does not aim at happiness" (Lewis 1988 [1960]: 106). When Lewis wrote about readers of literature in his book *An Experiment in Criticism*, he said that "they like stories which enable them—vicariously, through the characters—to participate in pleasure or happiness" (Lewis 1961a: 37). In a paper about the literary work of William Morris, Lewis pointed out that "[a]s [the poet Lord] Byron had said, there is no sterner moralist than pleasure; and so for Morris it is not unhappiness but happiness which is the real fountain of misgiving, making us 'more mindful that the sweet days die'" (Lewis 1939a: 46). About Jane Austen, Lewis wrote that "[s]he has, or at least all her favourite characters have, a hearty relish for what would now be regarded as very modest pleasures. A ball, a dinner party, books, conversation, a drive to see a great house ten miles away, a holiday as far as Derbyshire—these ... are happiness" (Lewis [1954] in 1969: 185–6).

Lewis also affirmed the conceptual identity between pleasure and happiness in the life of Paradisal man in the Garden of Eden:

> Now Paradisal man always chose to follow God's will. In following it he also gratified his own desire, both because all the actions demanded of him were, in fact, agreeable to his blameless inclination, and also because the service of God was itself his keenest pleasure, without which as their razor edge all joys would have been insipid to him. The question "Am I doing this for God's sake or only because I happen to like it?" did not then arise, since doing things for God's sake was what he chiefly "happened to like." His God-ward will rode his happiness

like a well-managed horse ... Pleasure was then an acceptable offering to God because offering was a pleasure.

(Lewis 2001f [1940]: 97)

In Lewis's mind, happiness occupied an important place not only in the Edenic myth concerning mankind's origin but also in the divine purpose concerning mankind's ultimate end. God, according to Lewis, created us for the purpose that we be perfectly happy, where to be perfectly happy is to experience blessedness or beatitude. In his book *The Great Divorce*, which is about a fantastical bus trip to heaven, Lewis has one of the ghostly visitors say "I wish I'd never been born ... What *are* we born for?" To which a heavenly Spirit answers, "For infinite happiness ..." (Lewis 2001e [1946]: 61). In a letter from 1933 to Arthur Greeves, Lewis wrote that "God not only understands but *shares* the desire ... for complete and ecstatic happiness. He made me for no other purpose than to enjoy it" (2004b: 123). To be perfectly blessed is to be perfectly happy, and Lewis said we must suppose "the life of the blessed to be an end in itself, indeed The End ..." (Lewis 1992a [1963]: 92). In a letter written at the outset of the Second World War, Lewis stated that God not only made him for the purpose that he experience perfect happiness, but also made others for the same purpose, even a member of the German Gestapo:

> I provisionally define Agapë as "steadily remembering that inside the Gestapo-man there is a thing [which] says I and me just as you do, which has just the same grounds (neither more nor less) as your 'Me' for being distinguished from all its sins however numerous, which, like you, was made by God for eternal happiness."
>
> (Lewis 2004b: 409)

As I mentioned a moment ago, while Lewis (and God too, according to Lewis's understanding of "God") affirmed a hedonistic understanding of happiness (in this sense, again, he was a hedonist about happiness), he was *not* strictly speaking a hedonist.[5] Strictly speaking, a hedonist believes that pleasure is *the one and only* intrinsic good and pain is *the one and only* intrinsic evil. A hedonist also believes that happiness consists of nothing but experiences of pleasure. A person like Lewis who is a hedonist about happiness agrees with the strict hedonist that pleasure is intrinsically good (and pain is intrinsically evil) and that experiences of pleasure constitute happiness. However, a hedonist about happiness might believe there is at least one other intrinsic good (and one other intrinsic evil), where the additional intrinsic good is not a constituent of happiness. For example, in addition to believing that pleasure is intrinsically good, Lewis believed justice is intrinsically good (and injustice is intrinsically evil),[6] where roughly he thought of *ultimate* justice on the one hand as the morally justified experience of nothing but perfect happiness and on the other hand as the morally justified denial of the experience of that happiness.[7]

Another Understanding of Happiness: Eudaimonism

A hedonist about happiness maintains that happiness consists of nothing but experiences of pleasure, and a life that is maximally happy is one that at every moment consists of nothing but experiences of pleasure (it contains no experiences of pain, so that a maximally happy person is one who is never unhappy). According to the neuroscientist Emiliana Simon-Thomas, who teaches an online course entitled "The Science of Happiness" at the University of California, Berkeley, "[o]ne of the myths about happiness is that it means always feeling good, always [being] in a state of enjoyment ... It's a misnomer and a regrettable one if you try to aspire to that" (quoted in Ansberry 2021). Simon-Thomas seemingly reasons that given that perfect happiness as conceived by the hedonist is not obtainable in this life, the hedonist's idea that happiness consists of nothing but experiences of pleasure must be mistaken. Lewis would have regarded this as an instance of bad reasoning. Why not conclude there is something wrong with our world, not with the hedonist's idea of happiness?

Is there a different conception of happiness than that espoused by the hedonist? It might come as a surprise to a reader that the hedonistic view that happiness consists of experiences of pleasure, though commonsensical, is very much a minority view in higher education. At present, the most popular understanding of happiness is what is known as *eudaimonism*. According to the philosopher Nicholas Wolterstorff,

> [t]he eudaimonist holds that ... the well-lived life [is], by definition, the happy life, the *eudaimōn* life ... It is important to understand what sort of goal happiness is [according to the eudaimonist]. "Happiness" is not the name of experience of a certain sort. "Pleasure" names experiences of a certain sort; "happiness" does not. The eudaimonist is not saying that one's sole end in itself is or should be bringing about experiences of a certain sort, everything else being a means ... [T]he ancient eudaimonists insisted that *eudaimonia* is activity. Happiness does not consist in what happens to one but in what one makes of what happens to one.
>
> (Wolterstorff 2008: 150, 151, 152)

I will have more to say later in this chapter about the distinction between an action, which is something you do, as opposed to a passion, which is something that happens to you. At this point, it is important to make clear that eudaimonists identify happiness with the actions a person performs, not with the pleasures he or she experiences from those actions. Eudaimonists concede that the identification of happiness with actions is not the conception of happiness held by ordinary people. One of the most well-known eudaimonists, the ancient Greek philosopher Aristotle, said that the highest good attainable by action is happiness, and when he asked "What is happiness?" he recognized that the first thing that comes to mind for the common people is the experience of pleasure: "But when it comes to defining what happiness is ... the account given by the common run [of people] differs from that of the philosophers. The former say it is some clear and obvious good, such as pleasure ..." (Aristotle 1962: 1095a17–23). The contemporary eudaimonist philosopher Julia Annas has this to say about ancient eudaimonist theories vis-à-vis common sense:

> [A]ncient [eudaemonistic] theories are all more or less revisionary, and some of them are highly counterintuitive. They give an account of happiness which, if baldly presented to a non-philosopher without any of the supporting arguments, sounds wrong, even absurd ... [A]ncient theories greatly expand and modify the ordinary non-philosophical understanding of happiness, opening themselves up to criticism from non-philosophers on this score.
>
> It is in fact common ground to the ancient theories that, on the one hand, we are all right to assume that our final end is happiness of some kind, and to try to achieve happiness in reflecting systematically on our final end; but that, on the other hand, we are very far astray in our initial assumptions about what happiness is ... So we should not be surprised that ancient theories have counter-intuitive consequences about happiness.
>
> (Annas 1993: 331)

As will become clear in Chapter 2, it is in part because Lewis affirmed the common person's belief about the nature of happiness as pleasure and rejected that of the eudaimonists that he also rejected eudaimonistic views of higher education. Eudaimonists think of human beings having a purpose (either bestowed by a creator, e.g., God, or inherent in human beings as entities in the natural world) which is defined in terms of *activities* that are required to make them good members of their species or kind (i.e., a good human being, for which we have the terms "happy," "flourishing," or "fulfilled"), just as they think of plants having a purpose which is defined in terms of requisite root structures, fruit, foliage, height above ground, etc., to make them good members of their kind (i.e., a good plant), of knives having a purpose which is defined in terms of requisite sharpness, proper weight, length, grip, etc., to make them good members of their kind (i.e., a good knife), and of stories having a purpose which is defined in terms of requisite plot, character development, moral, etc., to make them good members of their kind (i.e., a good story) (see Goetz 2012b: 89–91). Eudaimonists about higher education (see Hitz 2020) believe that higher-level learning or knowing is one kind of activity in which human beings *must* be engaged in order to be good members of their kind (to be fully human or a perfected human being and, thereby, happy).

Lewis understood all too well that some persons believe politics, in the form of the activity of the polis or state, is essentially about promoting the happiness of its citizens. He wrote that the political "Left ... [maintains] that it is an absolute duty to labour for human happiness in this world" (Lewis 1939a: 53). It is not too hard to see how a belief in this duty conjoined with a eudaimonistic conception of human happiness leads to a conviction that everyone should go to college. If human happiness consists, at least in part, of higher-level intellectual activity, and it is a duty of the polis actively to promote the happiness of its citizens and human beings more generally, then the demand made by some people that everyone should attend college (and, further, that government-subsidized college should be made available to everyone) makes sense.[8] While hedonists about happiness like Lewis believe someone in higher education can be very happy, they also think that someone who never passes through the gates and halls of the academy can be just as happy, and the reason hedonists about happiness espouse this view is because they have a different conception of happiness from that held by eudaimonists.

Pleasure and Its Relationship to Morality

Pleasure is a *non*moral good, and pain is a *non*moral evil. That is to say, pleasure and pain are instances of value that are *not* moral in nature. However, one should not conclude from this statement that pain and pleasure are *immoral*. Lewis, like many others, believed there is an important distinction between *nonmoral* (or *amoral*) and *moral* value. In *Poetry and Prose in the Sixteenth Century*, he wrote that "Machiavelli had no more notion of the amoral as distinct from the immoral than of the steam engine" (Lewis 1954: 51). And in his book *The Allegory of Love*,

Lewis recapitulated Hugo of St. Victor's view, with which he disagreed, that pleasure is "evil, but not morally evil …" (Lewis 1936: 15). Again, in a letter to Brother George Every, Lewis stressed that the distinction he made "between moral and non-moral good" is not a Christian notion (neither is it unchristian) but "comes rather from secular ethics" (Lewis 2004b: 447). For example, Lewis was convinced that Christians and non-Christians alike recognize the intrinsic nonmoral goodness of pleasure (e.g., that which comes from eating your favorite ice cream) and the intrinsic nonmoral evilness of pain (e.g., that which comes from stubbing your toe), and the intrinsic moral goodness of acting justly and the intrinsic moral evilness of acting unjustly. As a hedonist about happiness, Lewis thought that if there were no nonmoral values in the forms of the intrinsic goodness and intrinsic evilness of experiences of pleasure and pain respectively, then there would be no moral value in the forms of acting justly and unjustly. David Oderberg, though not a hedonist about happiness, makes this point about the relationship between the moral and nonmoral in what he admits is a deliberately provocative way by stating that "if you want to understand morality, the very *last* place you should look is morality" (Oderberg 2020: xi). Lewis would have agreed. He believed that if you want to understand morality, you must first look to the intrinsic goodness of pleasure and the intrinsic evilness of pain. Without the existence of these nonmoral values, there would be no moral values.

In his book *Letters to Malcolm*, Lewis expressed the distinction between nonmoral and moral value in terms of the theft of an apple and the accompanying pleasure of eating the apple, where the pleasure of eating in such a case is thought of as a bad pleasure: "'bad pleasures' [is a common way of expressing the idea of] 'pleasures snatched by unlawful [unjust] acts.' It is the stealing of the apple that is bad, not the sweetness" (Lewis 1992a [1963]: 89). The sweetness of the apple is the pleasure that comes with eating it, and it is the intrinsic goodness of the pleasure that "makes [the stealing] worse. There is sacrilege in the theft" (Lewis 1992a [1963]: 89). Lewis believed that, were the stealing of the apple in principle never to lead to experiences of pleasure (or the mitigation of experiences of pain) for anyone, whether the thief, the owner of the orchard, or anyone else, stealing the apple would not be morally evil. There would simply be the action of taking the apple or, more likely, the existence of apple trees whose apples are never purposefully picked by human beings.

When people think about the idea of value, their minds often immediately focus on the idea of moral, as opposed to nonmoral, value, because they assume the ultimate purpose or end of life is that they act morally. It is likely that contemporary culture's focus on social justice leads many persons to believe that what life is ultimately all about is being moral. Lewis was convinced that this belief is seriously mistaken, because moral or just action is not only different from the experience of perfect happiness, but also will not be needed in the heavenly life of perfect happiness:

> You may ask, do I then think that moral value will have no place in the state of perfection? Well it sounds a dreadful thing to say, but I'm almost inclined to answer No [it will have no place]. It [the state of perfection] is never presented in Scripture in terms of service is it?—always in terms suggesting fruition—a supper, a marriage, a drink. "I will give him the morning star." May not that be one of the divine jokes—to see people like Marcus Aurelius and [Matthew] Arnold & [John Stuart] Mill at last submitting to the fact that they can give up being *good* and start *receiving* good instead.
>
> (Lewis 2004b: 463–4)[9]

Lewis believed that the good that is received is perfect happiness. He thought reason plays a role analogous to that of a schoolteacher, and what it teaches is that while happiness and acting morally are different from each other, we will never experience the perfect happiness for which we were created unless we take the moral life seriously:

> [The moral realm] exists to be transcended ... [It is a] schoolmaster, as St. Paul says, to bring us to Christ. We must expect no more of it than of a schoolmaster; we must allow it no less. I must say my prayers

to-day whether I feel devout or not; but that is only as I must learn my grammar if I am ever to read the poets.

But the school-days, please God, are numbered. There is no morality in Heaven. The angels never knew (from within) the meaning of the word *ought*, and the blessed dead have long since gladly forgotten it.

(Lewis 1992a [1963]: 115)

Successful students reach an endpoint after which they no longer need to go to classes, do their homework, and take exams. And Lewis maintained that when we experience perfect happiness, we will no longer need moral value. Lewis also believed that Christianity affirms what is reasonable about the respective everlasting and transitory natures of perfect happiness and mere morality:

All right, Christianity will do you good—a great deal more good than you ever wanted or expected. And the first bit of good it will do you is to hammer into your head ... the fact that what you have hitherto called "good"—all that about "leading a decent life" and "being kind"—isn't quite the magnificent and all-important affair you supposed. It will teach you that in fact you can't be "good" (not for twenty-four hours) on your own moral efforts. And then it will teach you that even if you were, you still wouldn't have achieved the purpose for which you were created. Mere *morality* is not the end of life. You were made for something quite different from that ... The people who keep on asking if they can't lead a decent life without Christ, don't know what life is about; if they did they would know that "a decent life" is mere machinery compared with the thing we men are really made for. Morality is indispensible: but the Divine Life, which gives itself to us and which calls us to be gods, intends for us something in which morality will be swallowed up.

(Lewis [1946?] in 1970: 112)

While the need to act morally is transitory, we are nevertheless subject to it in this life. Why? What is the purpose of being moral? Lewis answered that with our everyday idea of morality,

[w]e take as our starting point our ordinary self with its various desires and interests. We then admit that something else—call it "morality" or

"decent behaviour," or "the good of society"—has claims on this self: claims which interfere with its own desires. What we mean by "being good" is giving in to those claims. Some of the things the ordinary self wanted to do turn out to be what we call "wrong": well, we must give them up.

(Lewis 2001b [1952]: 195)

"[t]o *act* unselfishly ... [is to act] justly ..."

(Lewis 2007: 1027)

Lewis insisted that when morality requires that you, a self, sacrifice fulfilling your desire for your own pleasure, what is ultimately at issue is the *happiness* of other selves:

If you asked twenty good men today what they thought the highest of the virtues, nineteen ... would reply, Unselfishness. But if you had asked almost any of the great Christians of old, he would have replied, Love. You see what has happened? A negative term has been substituted for a positive, and this is of more than philological importance. The negative idea of Unselfishness carries with it the suggestion not primarily of securing good things for others, but of going without them ourselves, as if our abstinence and not their happiness was the important point. I do not think this is the Christian virtue of Love. The New Testament has lots to say about self-denial, but not about self-denial as an end in itself.

(Lewis [1941] in 2001g: 25)

Lewis was so convinced that unselfishness and/or sacrifice for its own sake is not the correct reason for being moral that he had Screwtape instruct his nephew Wormwood in *The Screwtape Letters and Screwtape Proposes a Toast* to "teach a man to surrender benefits not that others may be *happy* ... but that he may be *unselfish* in forgoing them" (Lewis 1961b: 121; my emphases). When a person is interested in rightly restraining himself, he is concerned that others have an opportunity to experience justly the happiness for which they are created. Hence, Lewis wrote in *Mere Christianity* that "fair play ... between individuals" is the first concern "when we start thinking about morality ..." (Lewis 2001b [1952]: 72).

Mental versus Bodily Pleasures

When people think of pleasure, they not infrequently think of bodily actions with which experiences of pleasure are associated. Sexual pleasures are those which accompany sexual activity, and there are pleasures which come from eating and drinking, and athletic games. But not all pleasures have bodily sources. Many accompany mental activities like thinking, believing, hoping, and desiring. For example, you might *think* that your friend who has been ill is getting better, *believe* that your friend who has been ill is getting better, *hope* that your friend who has been ill is getting better, *desire* that your friend who has been ill is getting better, etc. In each case, there is what philosophers term the mental *attitude*—thinking, believing, hoping, or desiring—and its *content*, which is "that your friend has been ill and is getting better." When a person reads and/or writes papers, articles, books, poems, etc., he or she is concerned with content, where content consists of ideas or concepts. The content might compose a fictional story, report a historical event, urge us to take an action of some kind, fuel one's imagination, etc.

Most importantly for present purposes, content read or written can be, and for most people at least occasionally is, accompanied by experiences of pleasure. When you read a report that your favorite team has won the championship, you typically experience pleasure. If you read a fictional story in which the villain is captured, you also normally experience pleasure. On many occasions, Lewis expressed how intellectual activity in the forms of reading and writing was a source of pleasure for him. About reading, he wrote in a letter to Arthur Greeves that "I think re-reading old favourites is one of the things we differ on, isn't it, and you do it very rarely. I probably do it too much. It is one of my greatest pleasures: indeed I can't imagine a man really enjoying a book and reading it only once" (Lewis 2004b: 54). Not only did Lewis believe that a reader not uncommonly reads for pleasure, but he also thought that when there is more than one plausible reading of a text, the correct reading is likely the one that brings the reader (the most) pleasure. Thus, when commenting on a particular reading of Chaucer's *Canterbury Tales*, Lewis wrote that "the pleasure which not a few generations have now had in Chaucer thus read is strong, though not conclusive, evidence that they have read him correctly" (Lewis [1939b] in 1969: 54). Lewis believed that pleasure could serve as a criterion of a correct reading only because an author like Chaucer wrote with the purpose of giving his readers experiences of pleasure. And pleasure was not only for the reader. As Lewis pointed out, he sometimes wrote for the sake of his own pleasure: "The truth is that I have a constant temptation to over asperity as soon as I get a pen in my hand, even when there is no subjective anger to prompt me: it comes, I think, simply from the pleasure of using the English language forcibly ..." (Lewis 2004b: 187).

Lewis's hedonistic understanding of happiness also surfaced when he addressed the question of Christian literary theory and criticism as opposed to that of the cultured pagan. According to Lewis, the Christian literary theorist/critic "will feel less uneasy with a purely hedonistic standard for at least many kinds of work" (Lewis 1939a: 195). The cultured pagan, by contrast, "wishes to maintain his superiority to the great mass of mankind who turn to books for mere recreation" (Lewis 1939a: 196). The cultured pagan regards the Christian's view of literature written for pleasure as "shallow and flippant" (Lewis 1939a: 196). But Lewis maintained the cultured pagan's response reflects a misunderstanding. When literature is aimed at something other than recreation, then it should be judged as to whether it fulfills its purpose. What bad literary criticism often fails to acknowledge is that a good bit of literature is written for fun:

> For a great deal (not all) of our literature was made to be read lightly, for entertainment. If we do not read it, in a sense, "for fun" ... we are not using it as it was meant to be used, and all our criticism of it will be pure illusion. For you cannot judge any artefact except by using it as it was intended. It is no good judging a butter-knife by seeing whether

it will saw logs. Much bad criticism, indeed, results from the efforts of
critics to get a work-time result out of something that never aimed at
producing more than pleasure.

(Lewis [1940] in 1967: 34)[10]

Lewis was deeply at odds with what he regarded as the ridiculous
claim that literature is valuable simply (in itself) as literature: "The real
frivolity, the solemn vacuity, is all with those who make literature a self-
existent thing to be valued for its own sake" (Lewis 1939: 196). Lewis
believed literature is not intrinsically good because it has no intrinsic
value whatsoever. Any value it has, insisted Lewis, is no more than
extrinsic in nature. And its extrinsic value ultimately consists in its
being an instrument for experiences of pleasure.

The Right to Happiness, Pleasure, and Passivity

Lewis believed we commonsensically think happiness is composed of
nonmoral, intrinsically good experiences of pleasure. He also was well
aware of the pronouncement by some people in certain quarters that
there is a natural right to happiness which is validated by the American
Declaration of Independence's claim that all men have been endowed
by their Creator with the additional inalienable right to pursue
happiness "by legitimate means" (Lewis 2007: 1465). Lewis added that
this declaration "demands that whatever means of pursuing happiness
are lawful for any should be lawful for all; that 'man', not men of some
particular caste, class, status or religion, should be free to use them"
(Lewis [1963c] in 1970: 319).

Though embraced politically by many individuals, Lewis found
the idea of a natural right to happiness and its pursuit philosophically
odd. He believed it is odd because "we depend for a very great deal of
our happiness ... on circumstances outside all human control" (Lewis
[1963c] in 1970: 318), and it is strange to think we have a right *per se*
to something that is outside our control. Thus, "[a] right to happiness
doesn't, for me, make much more sense than a right to be six feet tall, or

to have a millionaire for your father, or to get good weather whenever you want to have a picnic" (Lewis [1963c] in 1970: 318). But why was Lewis convinced that happiness is something outside our control? To answer this question, we must remember that Lewis was a hedonist about happiness and believed that happiness consists of nothing but experiences of pleasure. But with respect to an experience of pleasure, we are directly patients, not agents. That is, an experience of pleasure is something with respect to which we are directly passive, not active.

According to Aristotle, happiness is an activity of the soul in accordance with virtue (Aristotle 1962: 1098a16–17; 1099b26), and pleasure accompanies this activity and perfects or completes it: "Pleasure is intimately connected with the activity which it completes" (Aristotle 1962: 1175a29–30). Aristotle recognized that because pleasure is so intimately connected with the activity it completes, it is tempting to think that the two are identical: "[P]leasure is so closely linked to activity and so little distinguished from it that one may dispute whether <or not> activity is identical with pleasure" (Aristotle 1962: 1175b33–4). And "because [pleasure and activity] are never found apart, some people get the impression that they are identical" (Aristotle 1962: 1175b35). However, Lewis would have said it is a mistake to think that they are identical.

Lewis disagreed with Aristotle's claim that happiness is an activity. Nevertheless, he agreed that the pleasure that constitutes happiness typically accompanies activity. For example, as Lewis put it, "[t]he act [which] engenders a child ought to be, and usually is, attended by pleasure. But it is not the pleasure that produces the child. Where there is pleasure there may be sterility: where there is no pleasure the act may be fertile" (Lewis 2007: 567). An Aristotelian about happiness believes that pleasure, though it does not constitute happiness, accompanies activities and is a sign that all is working as it should. Lewis would have had us ask why pleasure, and not pain, indicates that things are functioning well, and he believed the answer is that God, who is just and fits things together in the right way, conjoins pleasure with its intrinsic goodness with the activities of entities that are functioning as they should. Moreover, he was convinced that we ultimately have no control over whether our activity will be accompanied by an experience of pleasure. If an experience of pleasure is not an activity but an event that accompanies an activity and with respect to which we are immediately passive, then whether we experience pleasure is something that is ultimately beyond our control. The Aristotelian scholar Gerd van Riel puts this point as follows:

> [W]e never know for sure what to do in order to attain pleasure: it is never guaranteed. As an additional element, pleasure can occur, but it is just as likely to fail to appear. [Consider] Beethoven's fourth piano concerto. It is not certain that I will experience pleasure in attending a performance of this work. Even if all the circumstances are in an optimal state, I cannot be sure that I will enjoy the concert .... If this is true, it should be possible that an activity is perfectly performed even without yielding pleasure. But this dismisses the immediate link between pleasure and a perfect activity, and moreover, it implies that the perfection of an activity is not enough to secure our pleasure. Even if all circumstances are perfectly arranged, and the activity perfectly performed, pleasure is not guaranteed. This "escape from our control" is not an accidental quality of pleasure, dependent on circumstances, but a characteristic of the very essence of pleasure.
>
> (van Riel 1999: 219–20)

Because happiness, on a hedonistic understanding of it, consists of experiences of pleasure, one would expect to find van Riel affirming that happiness is also something over which we have no absolute control. And this is exactly what he claims. Pleasure is like happiness insofar as "it is something which we may hope to attain, without ever being sure how to behave in order to guarantee its appearance" (van Riel 1999: 219).

What Lewis believed is our passivity with respect to experiences of pleasure is evidenced by the phenomenon known among athletes as burn out. Someone can spend years training to compete at the highest level in a sport and wake up one day with no desire to go on the field or court again. Such an individual loses his or her love for the game because participation in it no longer provides pleasure. No matter how hard the person tries to rekindle the desire to play, it often just cannot be done.

The Paradox of Hedonism

Lewis thought that the truth about our passivity with respect to the experience of pleasure and our lack of a right to happiness goes hand in hand with what is known as the paradox of hedonism, which essentially is the idea that the more you make your future happiness the purpose of your actions, the more difficult it is for you to be happy. Hence, in order to find future happiness, you must not make it the object of your pursuit, the reason for your actions. For example, the philosopher Immanuel Kant believed that if the purpose of an individual's existence is that he be happy, then it is a very bad arrangement if reason is provided as the tool for fulfilling this purpose (Kant 1956: 63). Why so? Because it is impossible for even the most intelligent person to have any certainty about what will bring him happiness:

> Is it riches he wants? How much anxiety, envy, and pestering might he not bring in this way on his own head! Is it knowledge and insight? This might perhaps merely give him an eye so sharp that it would make evils at present hidden from him and yet unavoidable seem all the more frightful, or would add a load of still further needs to the desires which already give him trouble enough. Is it long life? Who will guarantee that it would not be a long misery? Is it at least health? How often has infirmity of body kept a man from excesses into which perfect health would have let him fall!—and so on. In short, he has no principle by which he is able to decide with complete certainty what will make him truly happy, since for this he would require omniscience.
>
> (Kant 1956: 85–6)

According to Lewis, among the ten most influential books that shaped his philosophy of life was James Boswell's *The Life of Samuel Johnson* (Lewis 1962). Johnson, an eminent eighteenth-century English literary figure who prayed that he might be "received to everlasting happiness" (Johnson 1807; quoted in Jacobs 2013: 105), wrote words much like Kant's:

> Life is not long, and too much of it must not pass in idle deliberation how it shall be spent; deliberation, which those who begin it by prudence, and continue it with subtilty, must, after long expence of thought, conclude by chance. To prefer one future mode of life to another, upon just reasons, requires faculties which it has not pleased our Creator to give us.
>
> (Boswell 2008: 273)

The hedonist John Stuart Mill penned in his autobiography that "I now thought that this end [happiness] was only to be attained by not making it the direct end. Those only are happy (I thought) who have their minds fixed on some object other than their own happiness ... Aiming thus at something else, they find happiness by the way" (Mill 1964: 112). And the philosopher Henry Sidgwick, following Mill, acknowledged as the "fundamental paradox of Hedonism, that the impulse towards pleasure, if too predominant, defeats its own aim," and he added that "the principle of Egoistic Hedonism ... is practically self-limiting; *i.e.* that a rational method of attaining the end at which it aims requires that we should to some extent put it out of sight and not directly aim at it" (Sidgwick 1966: 48, 136). In line with the thoughts of Kant, Johnson, Mill, and Sidgwick, Lewis wrote in a letter, "[h]ow right you are: the great thing is to stop thinking about happiness. Indeed the best thing about happiness itself is that it liberates you from thinking about happiness—as the greatest pleasure that money can give us is to make it unnecessary to think about money" (Lewis 2007: 93). And apropos to the subject of this book, Lewis used pre-university (school) and religious education to illustrate the paradox of hedonism:

> The good results which I think I can trace to my first school would not have come about if its vile procedure had been intended to produce them. They were all by-products thrown off by a wicked old man's desire to make as much as he could out of deluded parents and to give as little as he could in return. That is the point. While we are

planning the education of the future we can be rid of the illusion that we shall ever replace destiny. Make the plans as good as you can, of course. But be sure that the deep and final effect on every single boy will be something you never envisaged and will spring from little free movements in your machine which neither your blueprint nor your working model gave any hint of.

(Lewis [1943] in 1986a: 26)

I have now to tell you how [Malvern College] made me a prig ... A prefect called Blugg or Glubb or some such name stood opposite me, belching in my face, giving me some order ... What pushed me over the edge into pure priggery was his face—the puffy bloated cheeks, the thick, moist, sagging lower lip, the yokel blend of drowsiness and cunning. "The lout!" I thought. "The clod! The dull, crass clown! For all his powers and privileges, I would not be he." I had become a Prig, a Highbrow.

The interesting thing is that the public-school system had thus produced the very thing which it was advertised to prevent or cure. For you must understand (if you have not been dipped in that tradition yourself) that the whole thing was devised to "knock the nonsense" out of the smaller boys and "put them in their place." ...

It was, of course, to turn us into public-school boys that my father had sent us [Lewis and his brother, Warren] to [Malvern College]; the finished product appalled him. It is a familiar tragicomedy ...

(Lewis 1955: 101, 104–5, 127)

[R]emember how much religious education has exactly the opposite effect to that [which] was intended, how many hard atheists come from pious homes.

(Lewis 2007: 507)

Lewis regarded the paradox of hedonism as an instance of a more general "curious and unhappy psychological law" that our psychological "attitudes often inhibit the very thing they are intended to facilitate ... [For example], a couple never felt less in love than on their wedding day, many a man never felt less merry than at Christmas dinner, and when at a lecture we say 'I *must* attend', attention instantly vanishes" (Lewis 2007: 1023). And again, "[t]he dutiful effort prevents the spontaneous feeling; just as if you say to an old friend during a brief reunion 'Now let's have a good talk' both suddenly find themselves with nothing to say" (Lewis 2007: 1075). "Even in social life, you will never make a good impression on other people until you stop thinking about what sort of impression you are making" (Lewis 2001b [1952]: 226). As a final example of this curious and unhappy psychological law, Lewis wrote about a British novelist and aesthete that "his taste [in books] was excellent as long as he did not think about it. To the present day one meets men, great readers, who write admirably until the fatal moment when they remember that they are writing" (Lewis 1954: 151).

The Pleasure of Intellectual Activity

It has been necessary to present the foregoing fairly detailed treatment of the concepts of pleasure and happiness because Lewis thought about the purpose of higher education against the background of his more general views about the nature of pleasure, happiness, and the fact that God created us for the purpose that we be perfectly happy. It would be plausible to think that if everyone had a natural right to happiness, and higher education is one, if not the best, path to happiness, then all might or should choose to spend at least some time in higher education. But as we have seen in this chapter, Lewis did not believe in the natural right to happiness. Hence, he did not embrace the idea that all persons might or should choose to go to university for the purpose of experiencing the happiness that is theirs by right. Nevertheless, he believed some people, even without a right to happiness, as a matter of fact discover that they experience pleasure from intellectual activity. And Lewis maintained that it is the experience of pleasure from advanced intellectual activity that provides the explanation for the existence of higher education.

Addendum

In recommending this manuscript for publication, a reviewer wrote that because Lewis did not write at length in one place about pleasure and happiness, there will be some concern that I am proof-texting Lewis's work, and perhaps getting Lewis to say something with which Lewis himself might not agree. In addition, the reviewer suggested I provide some treatment of the ontology of goodness, especially within the broad tradition of moral objectivism which Lewis defends, especially in *The Abolition of Man*.

What I have said about Lewis's view of pleasure and happiness is what Lewis said. That is one of my two reasons, which I stated in the Introduction, for my quoting him *ad nauseum*. In terms of the ontology of goodness, I am not sure what else can be said relative to the topic of this book beyond what I say in the text of this chapter and below in endnote 2. As a hedonist about pleasure and happiness, Lewis's view is straightforward: an experience of pleasure is a psychological event which exhibits the property of being good intrinsically, period, and God has nothing to say about the matter of pleasure's goodness (see endnote 2). For more expanded treatments of Lewis's view in terms of his contemporaries' beliefs about values and the meaning of life, readers can see Goetz 2018a. If readers are interested in how Lewis's understanding of pleasure and happiness differs from that of the Aristotelian Thomas Aquinas, they can look at Goetz 2015a.

The reviewer just mentioned goes on to point out that within the broad Christian tradition which affirms objectivism about value, goodness is identified with God (e.g., Boethius's *Consolation of Philosophy*). The reviewer is concerned that I pick only one aspect of goodness found in Lewis' writings (i.e., pleasure) and make that the sole focus of Lewis's view of an ontology of goodness. In the broad Christian tradition, the reviewer adds, the *summum bonum* for human beings seems to be one of relationship to God (e.g., the doctrine of *theosis*) in the beatific vision. "So, pleasure seems to be a part of this, but may only be a part of a much larger wholistic understanding of an ontology of goodness."

I do make pleasure's intrinsic goodness the sole focus of my treatment of Lewis's understanding of value because Lewis thought it provides the primary purpose of higher education, which is the subject of this book. Moreover, higher education occurs in this world; the *summum bonum* in another world. What the latter is like in terms of a person's relationship to God is beyond the scope of this book. Indeed, Lewis would have held it is beyond the scope of any book because we know next to nothing about it, beyond that the joys of heaven must be an essential part of a Christian solution to the problem of pain in this life (Lewis 2001f [1940], 148). Lewis wrote that "either there is 'pie in the sky' or there is not. If there is not, then Christianity is false, for this doctrine is woven into its whole fabric" (Lewis 2001f [1940]: 149). Moreover, Lewis believed we all desire heaven (perfect happiness) and thought this desire provided an argument for the existence of the afterlife and God (see Goetz 2018a: 78–84).

2

The Pleasure of Higher Education

Enjoyment

C. S. Lewis believed the purpose of life is that we be perfectly happy. At the same time, he recognized that the highest degree of happiness available in this life is far from perfect: "Not to get ... what one wants is not a disease that can be cured, but the normal condition of man" (Lewis 2007: 1133). Though our happiness in this life is overall inescapably imperfect, we still wish to be as happy as is possible during our life on earth, and at times we are tempted to act in ways that we believe are immoral in order to make ourselves happier than we would otherwise be. Lewis maintained that while we often believe we could make ourselves happier by acting immorally, we nevertheless ought to refrain from choosing to act on our belief. We ought to choose morally. Lewis believed that provided we are committed to not acting immorally to make ourselves happy, it is permissible to satisfy our desire for happiness in appropriate ways.

Lewis was also convinced that our human nature dictates to us more than a little of what we do. We know that we experience pain if we lack adequate food, drink, clothing, and shelter. Thus, we justifiably seek to procure these requisite basic instrumental goods through gainful means, and it would be best in terms of our own happiness if we could provide for our basic needs through employment that we find enjoyable.[1] It is here that Lewis believed we bump up against the paradox of hedonism discussed at the end of the last chapter. There is not only no guarantee that the effort we put into finding a job that is a source of pleasure will be successful, but also we might end up making ourselves unhappier than we would have been otherwise.

While recognizing the paradox of hedonism, Lewis believed we sometimes discover, without purposefully trying, that something we do makes us happy. Perhaps as adults we stumble on an occupation that is a source of pleasure. Perhaps our parents introduced us at a young age to a sport, hobby, or trade that we found and continue to find makes us happy. As a boy, Lewis realized that reading books and thinking about them made him happy. He described his discovery of imaginative literature in the following way: "Boys at school were taught to read Latin and Greek poetry by the [disciplinary] birch, and discovered the English poets as accidentally and naturally as they now discover the local cinema. Most of my own generation ... tumbled into literature in that fashion. Of each of us some great poet made a rape when we still wore Eton collars" (Lewis 1939a: 113). Lewis added that he was helped along his literary path by his father's love of books:

> I am a product of long corridors, empty sunlit rooms, upstairs indoor silences, attics explored in solitude, distant noises of gurgling cisterns and pipes, and the noise of wind under the tiles. Also, of endless books. My father bought all the books he read and never got rid of any of them. There were books in the study, books in the drawing room, books in the cloakroom, books (two deep) in the great bookcase on the landing, books in a bedroom, books piled as high as my shoulder in the cistern attic, books of all kinds reflecting every transient stage of my parents' interest, books readable and unreadable, books suitable for a child and books most emphatically not. Nothing was forbidden me. In the seemingly endless rainy afternoons I took volume after volume from the shelves. I had always the same certainty of finding a book that was new to me as a man who walks into a field has of finding a new blade of grass.
>
> (Lewis 1955: 10)[2]

By his later teens, Lewis had concluded that a job in the academy would most likely be the best way for him to sustain the happiness he experienced from advanced intellectual activity. But before we turn to Lewis's thoughts about the purpose of higher education, it is helpful to consider briefly what he thought about school or pre-university education; in particular, its demand for equality, where "what is possible for some ought to be (and therefore is) possible to all" (Lewis 1988 [1960]: 74).

Excellence and Envy

Why insist on equality in school? Lewis thought two psychological states, one noble and one ignoble, base, or dishonorable, explain the demand. The noble psychological state is the desire for fair play. In school, this desire translates into every young person being offered the opportunity to do, provided they are able, "sums and grammar" (Lewis [1944c] in 1986a: 34–5). However, Lewis reminded his readers that while not all children delight in learning, some young people will want to know: "The lazy boy will try to learn [a proposition in geometry] by heart because, for the moment, that needs less effort. But six months later, when they are preparing for an exam, that lazy boy is doing hours and hours of miserable drudgery over things the other boy understands, and positively enjoys, in a few minutes" (Lewis 2001b [1952]: 197). Against this backdrop of difference in likes, the ignoble demand for equality, which is itself a dislike of intellectual excellence that if unchecked hardens into a hatred, manifests itself and results in a system of schooling in which no student is allowed to excel in intellectual activity beyond his or her peers. Anyone who supports such excellence with its resultant inequality will be labeled, wrote Lewis, as "'high-brow', 'up-stage', 'old school tie', 'academic', 'smug', and 'complacent'. These words, as used today, are sores: one feels the poison throbbing in them" (Lewis [1944c] in 1986a: 33). When Lewis discussed affection as a kind of love, he pointed out how change threatens personal relations. For example, members of a "low-brow" family can become fiercely jealous of a family member who shows signs of becoming an intellectual and breaking the familial bonds. Lewis pointed out that a counterpart to this familial jealousy is sometimes manifested at the national level in a kind of education that "keeps back the promising child because the idlers and dunces might be 'hurt' if it [the promising child] were undemocratically moved into a higher [group] than themselves" (Lewis 1988 [1960]: 48).

Lewis described how, when he was in public school, a boy who was good in classics did almost nothing but classics. He thought this was wise because "[n]o one has time to do more than a very few things well before he is twenty, and when we force a boy to be a mediocrity in a dozen subjects we destroy his standards, perhaps for life" (Lewis 1955: 113). Moreover, he believed in grouping students according to ability. While some people who affirm the grouping of students according to their ability might have an elitist motivation, he justified his belief in this kind of grouping in terms of the happiness of the students. Those who derive pleasure from a certain level of intellectual activity will enjoy learning less or not at all if they are made to learn alongside others who are either uninterested or interested but not as advanced intellectually.[3] Lewis did not shy away from pointing out that some people genuinely dislike intellectual excellence, and he insisted there is no appeasing this dislike when it is fueled by an instance of envy which "is insatiable. The more you concede to it the more it will demand" (Lewis [1944c] in 1986a: 34). He wrote that "in every institution, there is something which sooner or later works against the very purpose for which it came into existence" (Lewis 1992a [1963]: 43). In the case of institutional schooling, Lewis was convinced that the ignoble demand for equality works against the progress of those students who are academically capable and desire more rigorous intellectual activity.

Lewis illustrated what he believed is the undesirable result of the dishonorable desire for equality in terms of a growing demand in pre-university education that subjects in which some students "do very much better than others should not be compulsory. Yesterday it was Latin; today ... it is Mathematics. Both these subjects give an 'unfair advantage' to boys of a certain type" (Lewis [1944c] in 1986a: 32). Lewis maintained that "to abolish that advantage" by rendering the subjects non-compulsory is "in one sense democratic" (Lewis [1944c] in 1986a: 32). But, he continued, to be consistent the abolition cannot stop with Latin and Mathematics. It has to be extended to all compulsory subjects so that any student can find something at which he or she has a chance of doing well:

> Even the boy who can't or won't learn his alphabet can be praised and petted for *something*—handicrafts or gymnastics, moral leadership or deportment, citizenship or the care of guinea-pigs, "hobbies" or musical appreciation—anything he likes. Then no boy, and no boy's parents, need feel inferior.
>
> (Lewis [1944c] in 1986a: 33)

> The basic principle of the new education is to be that dunces and idlers must not be made to feel inferior to intelligent and industrious pupils. That would be "undemocratic." These differences between the pupils— for they are obviously and nakedly *individual* [as opposed to group] differences—must be disguised.
>
> (Lewis 1961b: 166–7)

Lewis opposed the ignoble motivation for equality in school, the sphere of mental training, just as he believed people would rightly oppose the base motivation were it invoked in the sphere of virtue (no one could reasonably be opposed to the fact that some people are more virtuous than others on the grounds that they were superior in that regard). "Equality (outside mathematics) is a purely social conception. It applies to man as a political and economic animal. It has no place in the world of the mind" (Lewis [1944c] in 1986a: 34). Pre-university education, Lewis maintained, should be non-democratic and aristocratic in nature. It should be "shamelessly 'high-brow'" (Lewis [1944c] in 1986a: 34) for the sake of the young person who desires to excel and is able to do so. Democratizing education negatively impacts those children who are capable of moving ahead at a quicker pace:

> Children who are fit to proceed to a higher class may be artificially kept back, because the others would get a *trauma* ... by being left behind. The bright pupil thus remains democratically fettered to his own age group throughout his school career, and a boy who would be capable

of tackling Aeschylus or Dante sits listening to his coeval's attempts to spell out A CAT SAT ON A MAT ... The few who might want to learn will be prevented; who are they to overtop their fellows?

(Lewis 1961b: 167–8)

And what about those who would be "left behind" under this aristocratic conception of schooling? According to Lewis, "[t]he stupid [dull] boy, nearly always, is the boy who does not *want* to know" (Lewis [1944c] in 1986a: 34). Is he, then, to be brutally sacrificed to other people's children who enjoy intellectual activity? Lewis answered that this objection presupposes a misunderstanding of what the dull boy desires. When he grows up, there will be many jobs for him in which he himself will be happy and useful to others, and from which he will earn more money than "intellectual" employment. And he will not care that he is not an "intellectual" because he never wanted to be one (Lewis [1944c] in 1986a: 35).

In summary, Lewis's belief about the effects of the dishonorable motivation for equality on the happiness of young people in school seems to have been the following: while we do not know how to guarantee the future happiness of young people by means of a particular kind of vocation or job, we do know how to guarantee the present unhappiness of some school students: make sure they are not allowed, in the name of equality, to derive pleasure from doing what they desire and are able to do.[4]

Higher Education: Fulfillment of the Desire to Know

Lewis maintained that the ignoble desire for equality in pre-university education also has negative effects on the process of qualifying to attend university: "Entrance examinations must be framed so that all, or nearly all, citizens can go to universities, whether they have any power (or wish) to profit by higher education or not" (Lewis 1961b: 167). But, thought Lewis, before trying to make sure everyone can go to college, it is prudent to make sure every person will profit from attending university. And to make sure of this, it is necessary to understand what higher education is for. As Lewis wrote,

> [t]he first qualification for judging any piece of workmanship from a corkscrew to a cathedral is to know *what* it is—what it was intended to do and how it is meant to be used ... [A]s long as you think the corkscrew was meant for opening tins or the cathedral for entertaining tourists you can say nothing to the purpose about them.
>
> (Lewis 1942: 1)

Just as Lewis knew there are those who think a corkscrew is for opening tins and a cathedral is for entertaining tourists, so also he understood that there are people who think higher education is for something that it is not.

Lewis maintained that one purpose for which higher education does not exist is to make a student a good man, a man with well-developed appreciation for thought, imagination, art, etc., a man of good taste and good feeling (Lewis 1939a: 81).[5] He believed that if all things educational went as they ideally should, the goal of making a good man is achieved at the pre-university level, so that "the university student is essentially a different person from the school pupil. He is not a candidate for humanity, he is, in theory, already human" (Lewis 1939a: 85).[6] With the purpose of education in the form of schooling accomplished, Lewis maintained a person with the desire for advanced intellectual activity was ready for the university which provides the physical space and intellectual comradery in which to satisfy that desire. Lewis's philosophy tutor at Oxford wrote about Lewis that "[h]e has ... real enthusiasm for knowledge, as distinct from its emoluments [gains or revenues]" (Lewis 2004a: 618), and Lewis believed that he was like others in this regard:

> Among ... men ... there are some who desire to know. Or rather, all desire to know, but some desire it more fervently than the majority and are ready to make greater sacrifices for it. The things they want to know may be quite different. One may want to know what happened

a million years ago, another, what happens a million light-years away, a third, what is happening in his own table on the microscopic level. What is common to them all is the thirst for knowledge.

(Lewis 1939a: 84)

Lewis added that it might have happened that people with the desire to know were left in civil societies to satisfy their desire for higher-level intellectual activity on their own. However, he went on to suggest that civil societies have often concluded that those with the desire to know should be provided the opportunity to associate together in a more formal context. Thus, civil societies aided the formation of universities to help those with the desire to know satisfy their desire, where that satisfaction is "good in itself besides being always honourable and sometimes useful to the whole society" (Lewis 1939a: 84). For example, Oxford colleges were not formed to teach the young but to support those who desired knowledge for its own sake. Lewis pointed out that their original nature was confirmed by the fact that hardly any college in Oxford was financially dependent on undergraduate fees: "A school without pupils would cease to be a school; a college without undergraduates would be as much a college as ever, would perhaps be more a college" (Lewis 1939a: 85). Given the shared desire to know, Lewis encouraged his friend Arthur Greeves to apply for admission to Oxford because he "would find an enormous choice of congenial friends, and you can have no idea how the constant friction with other and different minds improves one" (Lewis 2004a: 481). Lewis wrote that as an undergraduate at Oxford "I fell among a set of young men ... who were sufficiently close to me in intellect and imagination to secure immediate intimacy ..." (Lewis 2001f [1940]: 29). His Oxford colleague Nevill Coghill wrote that as undergraduates together at Oxford he and Lewis

> were both members of a discussion-class ... in the Michaelmas Term of 1922 ... The class read papers to itself every week and presently it was Lewis's turn. He chose for his subject *The Faerie Queene* ... Lewis seemed to carry the class with him in his combative pleasure ... We

were soon acquainted ... [and we] were uninhibitably happy in our work ... [W]e used to ... go off for country walks together in endless but excited talk about what we had been reading ... and what we thought about it ... This kind of walk must be among the commonest, perhaps among the best, of undergraduate experiences.

(Coghill 1965: 51, 52, 54)

As a faculty member at Oxford Lewis was the central figure in a group known as the Inklings whose members, which included friends and fellow academics Coghill, Hugo Dyson, and J. R. R. Tolkien, met voluntarily to read and critique each other's written work and discuss ideas more generally (see Carpenter 1997; Zaleski and Zaleski 2015).

Given that a university student is in the academy because he enjoys higher-level intellectual activity,[7] he is, Lewis believed, attached to his tutor as to an older student to learn what he can, not to be taught: "If we [university teachers] are any good we must always be working towards the moment at which our pupils are fit to become our critics and rivals. We should be delighted when it arrives ..." (Lewis 1988 [1960]: 51). When it arrives, the tutor and tutee are really fellow students. Neither thinks about the other but about the subject (Lewis 1939a: 85). In this way, they are equals. Derek Brewer, a former tutee of Lewis's, described Lewis in terms of the ideal Oxford tutor:

He was an unusually good example of the ideal. The ideal itself was very much of its own time and place ... It conceived of learning as a way of life, exemplified by the bachelor fellows who normally lived in the college. They read books in their own rooms, where they lived, not in "offices"; they had no secretaries. Their reading, thinking, and writing were part of a unified life, neither "job" nor "recreation," because they were both. And the fellows included, *mutatis mutandis*, scientists as well as arts-men.

They did not, strictly speaking, "teach." In the mornings and evenings of term, they were visited in their rooms by arrangement by their pupils, who "read the subject with them". It was not exactly an egalitarian society, but there was a sense of fundamental equality and unity, divided into ranks and stages. I had no doubt, at the age of eighteen, that for all the differences of temperament, intelligence, ability, learning, repute, and age between me and this distinguished, jolly man, we were nevertheless of the same kind, engaged in the same pursuit ... I was not a schoolboy to be taught and disciplined, not a "student", but a "man" in his college, who came to "read with him", and he treated me more or less as an equal without thinking about it.

(Brewer 2005: 116)[8]

Brewer went on to point out that Lewis approximated an ideal that gradual changes in "university, in society, and in the Western world and the developing professionalism and fragmentation of literary studies on the model of science have eroded" (Brewer 2005: 117). And Lewis agreed. Despite his egalitarian relationship with tutees like Brewer, transformations were occurring in Oxford as it became more and more a place for teaching a pupil. One result of these changes was that undergraduates often entered the university with the idea of completing their pre-university education, of completing the process of becoming a good man or woman and citizen with an expanded mind, and not of entering a society devoted to the pursuit of the pleasure of learning for its own sake (as opposed to preparation for a job, improvement in social standing, social justice, etc.). Nevertheless, Lewis continued to insist that the university student should immerse himself in the life of learning as best as he can (get as much enjoyment out of it as he can), while at the same time pointing out that a temporary immersion in the life of learning "can be used educationally by those who do not propose to pursue learning all their lives" (Lewis 1939a, 86). Lewis believed there is nothing odd about the existence of such a by-product and had the following advice for those entering Oxford undergraduate life:

> Games are essentially for pleasure, but they happen to produce health. They are not likely, however, to produce health if they are played for the sake of it. Play to win and you will find yourself taking violent exercise; play because it is good for you and you will not. In the same way, though you may have come here only to be educated, you will never receive that precise educational gift which a university has to

give you unless you can at least *pretend*, so long as you are with us, that you are concerned not with education but with knowledge for its own sake. And we, on our part, can do very little for you if we aim directly at your education. We assume that you are already human, already good men; that you have the specifically human virtues and above all the great virtue of curiosity. We are not going to try to improve you; we have fulfilled our whole function if we help you to *see* some given tract of reality ... The proper question for a freshman is not "What will do me most good?" but "What do I most want to know?" For nothing that we have to offer will do him good unless he can be persuaded to forget all about self-improvement for three or four years, and to absorb himself in getting to know some part of reality, as it is in itself.

(Lewis 1939a: 86–7)[9,10]

Lewis's emphasis on getting to know reality as it is in itself makes clear that in affirming that the purpose of higher education is the experience of pleasure that accompanies advanced intellectual activity, Lewis was thinking of higher-level intellectual activity in terms of the desire to know, because apprehending the way things are can be an unending source of pleasure. In contrast, Lewis believed it is modern humanity's preoccupation with what is practical that is in opposition to concern about knowledge of what is true. Thus, in describing the categories of thought of the modern mind in the context of a consideration of the truth of Christianity, he wrote that

[m]an is becoming as narrowly "practical" as the irrational animals. In lecturing to popular audiences I have repeatedly found it almost impossible to make them understand that I recommended Christianity because I thought its affirmations to be objectively *true*. They are simply not interested in the question of truth or falsehood. They only want to know if it will be comforting, or "inspiring", or socially useful.

(Lewis [1946b] in 1986a: 65)

Lewis believed this narrowly instrumentalist attitude toward Christianity was also directed at higher education. People interested in higher education were increasingly interested in whether it was useful for finding a good job, sustaining a more comfortable life, and bettering society. The idea that those in the academy are individuals engaged in advanced intellectual activity for the purpose of experiencing the pleasure that comes with knowing the truth was becoming of less and less interest to those who were considering attending and working in the university.

Knowledge Is Not Intrinsically Good

In the previous section, I quoted Lewis's statement that the satisfaction of the desire to know is "good in itself" (Lewis 1939a: 84). Did he believe that knowledge is, like pleasure, strictly speaking, intrinsically good? There are three reasons to maintain that he did not believe this.

The first reason for thinking Lewis believed knowledge (intellectual activity as satisfaction of the desire to know) is not, strictly speaking, intrinsically good is that when he asserted knowledge is good for its own sake, his point was contrastive in nature: knowledge is good regardless of whether it leads to a further end such as employment, social mobility, or financial enrichment. That is, the proper aim of higher education is not the achievement of such future goods, even if what one learns at university might prove useful in terms of the pursuit of such goods. In claiming knowledge is good for its own sake, Lewis was not thinking of knowledge as good in itself in contrast with its pursuit for the purpose of experiencing pleasure.

A second reason for claiming that Lewis believed knowledge itself is not intrinsically good was his belief that those who were outside higher education could be just as happy as those inside higher education. If Lewis had believed that advanced intellectual activity is, like pleasure, an intrinsic good and a component of happiness, then one would reasonably have expected him to claim that those outside higher education, because they lack the intrinsic good that is higher-level intellectual activity, could not be as happy as those inside the academy. But one does not find him claiming this. Indeed, one finds him saying things that suggest knowledge, unlike happiness, is not the ultimate end of life. He wrote that "[w]hatever else the human race was made for, it at least was not made to know" (Lewis 2004a: 640). And he made clear that while he was "all for a planet without aches or pains," he doubted if he would "care for one of pure intelligence" (Lewis 2007: 623).

A third consideration that supports the view that Lewis believed knowledge is not, strictly speaking, intrinsically good is found in his thoughts about the value of culture, where culture is "intellectual and aesthetic activity" (Lewis [1940] in 1967: 12). Within his discussion of culture, Lewis shared his thoughts about John Henry Newman's mid-nineteenth-century lectures on university education that are contained in Newman's *The Idea of a University*. Newman claimed that the cultivation of the intellect or liberal knowledge is an end in itself and makes "the gentleman" (Lewis [1940] in 1967: 18). Newman added that the exercise of the intellect "has its own perfection. Things animate, inanimate, visible, invisible, all are good in their kind, and have a *best* of themselves, which is an object of pursuit" (Lewis [1940] in 1967: 18). So intellectual activity perfects the mind. But Newman stressed that perfecting the mind is neither a moral virtue that makes the person better (Lewis [1940] in 1967: 19) nor "has any tendency to make us pleasing to our Maker" (Lewis [1940] in 1967: 18).

Newman's view of the purpose of higher education might initially be regarded as eudaimonist in nature (see Chapter 1) insofar as it takes the purpose of a university education to be the advanced activity of the intellect (intellectual virtue), where this activity perfects a person as a human being and, presumably, constitutes his happiness (intellectual virtue is happiness). However, Newman seems not to have espoused the eudaimonist view of higher education. In *The Idea of a University*, he hardly mentions happiness in his defense of the intrinsic goodness of liberal education. When he does mention happiness, it is seemingly as something that is distinct from but can be brought about by learning. "[T]raining of the intellect," wrote Newman, is best for the individual ... If then a practical end must be assigned to a University course, I say it is that of training good members of society ... [The good member of society, the gentleman] has the repose of a mind which lives in itself, while it lives in the world, and which has resources for its happiness at home when it cannot go abroad.

(Newman 1996: 125, 126)

Perhaps, however, in contrast with the eudaimonist idea that happiness is made up of intellectual virtue, Newman believed happiness is composed of moral virtue. If he did believe this, he also made clear he believed intellectual virtue is not sufficient for morally virtuous activity (and, thereby, happiness):

Knowledge is one thing, virtue is another ... Philosophy, however enlightened, however profound, gives no command over the passions, no influential motives, no vivifying principles ... [Intellectual virtues such as] a cultivated intellect, a delicate taste, a candid, equitable, dispassionate mind ... are the objects of a University ... [B]ut still, I repeat, they are no guarantee for sanctity or even for conscientiousness, they may attach to the man of the world, to the profligate, to the heartless.

(Newman 1996: 89)

Whatever Newman's view of happiness was (and it is not at all clear from these passages), Lewis remained unpersuaded that learning is, as Newman thought, an end in itself. "I have not," wrote Lewis, "been able to make Newman's conclusion my own" (Lewis [1940] in 1967: 18–19).[11] He went on to state that he "well understood that there is a kind of goodness which is not moral [in nature]" (Lewis [1940] in 1967: 19). In terms of Newman's view, Lewis conceded that "a clever man is 'better' than a dull one" (Lewis [1940] in 1967: 19), just as a "well-grown healthy toad is 'better' or 'more perfect' than a three-legged toad" (Lewis [1940] in 1967: 19). But why is it important to spend time perfecting our nature in this sense, wondered Lewis, if doing so is not a direct or indirect source of the nonmoral goodness of pleasure (and/or the elimination of pain)?

Lewis pointed out, as I have already indicated, that Newman believed cultivation of the intellect makes a man a gentleman and, thereby, a good member of society, though it does not place us in better standing with God. Lewis was convinced that culture, of which higher education is an instance, neither necessarily makes a person a better member of society nor puts us in a better relationship with the divine:

> What, exactly, is the evidence that *culture* produces among those who share it a sensitive and enriching social life? If by "sensitive" we mean "sensitive to real or imagined affronts," a case could be made out. Horace noted long ago that "bards are a touchy lot." ... But *sensitive* in that meaning cannot be combined with *enriching*. Competitive and resentful egoisms can only impoverish social life. The sensitivity that enriches must be of the sort that guards a man from wounding others, not of the sort that makes him ready to feel wounded himself ...
>
> Let us be honest. I claim to be one of the cultured myself ... I gladly admit that we number among us men and women whose modesty, courtesy, fair-mindedness, patience in disputation and readiness to see an antagonist's point of view, are wholly admirable. I am fortunate to have known them. But we must also admit that we show as high a percentage as any group whatever of bullies, paranoiacs, and poltroons, of backbiters, exhibitionists, mopes, milksops, and world-without-end bores. The loutishness that turns every argument into a quarrel is really no rarer among us than among the sub-literate ...
>
> It is then (at best) extremely doubtful whether *culture* produces any of those qualities which will enable people to associate with one another graciously, loyally, understandingly, and with permanent delight.
>
> (Lewis [1955] in 1987: 35–6, 37)

> I reject at once an idea which lingers in the mind of some modern people that cultural activities are in their own right spiritual and meritorious—as though scholars and poets were intrinsically more pleasing to God than scavengers and bootblacks. I think it was Matthew Arnold who first used the English word *spiritual* in the sense of the German *geistlich*, and so inaugurated this most dangerous and most anti-Christian error. Let us clear it forever from our minds.
>
> (Lewis [1939a] in 2001g: 55)

Some of the modern people Lewis had in mind who believed cultural activities are spiritual and meritorious included, as just quoted, Matthew Arnold, a Victorian poet and cultural critic, and F. R. Leavis, a Cambridge academic and English literary critic. Arnold wrote that "culture [is] a pursuit of our total perfection by means of getting to know, on all the matters which most concern us, the best which has been thought and said in the world" (Arnold 2006: 5), and Leavis believed in "a necessary relationship between the quality of the individual's response to art [an aspect of culture] and his general fitness for humane living" (Lewis [1940] in 1967: 13). Lewis believed there was no connection between involvement with culture and spiritual maturity, and he maintained that Arnold's and Leavis's views were a gross exaggeration of culture's importance (Lewis [1940] in 1967: 12): "[T]he whole modern world," wrote Lewis, "ludicrously over-values books and learning and what (I loathe the word) they call 'culture'. And of course 'culture' itself is the greatest sufferer by this error: for second things are always corrupted when they are put first" (Lewis 2007: 733).[12] Concerning literature, Lewis maintained that "[t]he real frivolity, the solemn vacuity, is all with those who make [it] a self-existent thing to be valued for its own sake" (Lewis 1939a: 196).

The belief that cultural activities have spiritual value not surprisingly is expressed in the related idea that higher education has spiritual value. Andrew Delbanco writes that college "education is a mysterious process and ... we should be slow to assume that any student is beyond its saving power" (Delbanco 2012: 171). Delbanco does not go on to make explicitly clear from what the power of education saves its students. His book as a whole suggests that it is something like the lack of a virtuous character. Regardless, were Lewis to have been alive today and have read these words, he would surely have suggested that the sense of Delbanco's comments grossly exaggerates the importance of higher education. Like culture more generally, at best, higher education is of no more than secondary significance (if it even rises to that level of importance).

Knowledge Is Extrinsically (Instrumentally) Good

If Lewis believed knowledge is not, strictly speaking, intrinsically good, what did he mean when he said that it is so? Most plausibly, as already suggested at the beginning of the previous section, he described knowledge as intrinsically good in contrast with its being useful for the pursuit of other future goods such as procuring a job and attaining social status. But though it is good independent of its relationship to these considerations, Lewis believed it is still no more than instrumentally good as a source of pleasure. One of Lewis's favorite authors was Richard Hooker, a sixteenth-century clergyman who wrote in defense of the Church of England. Lewis found in Hooker someone for whom knowledge for its own sake meant knowledge for the sake of the delight that comes from knowing. Lewis wrote the following about Hooker's *Laws of Ecclesiastical Polity* in which Hooker spoke of man's delight with contemplation "for mere knowledge and understanding's sake":

> In the first place the [*Laws of Ecclesiastical*] *Polity* marks a revolution in the art of controversy ... He has also provided a model for all who in any age have to answer similar ready-made recipes for setting the world right in five weeks ... Truths unfold themselves, quietly and in due order, as if Hooker were developing—nay, we are sure that he is developing—his own philosophy for its own sake, because "the mind of man" is "by nature speculative and delighted with contemplation ... for mere knowledge and understanding's sake" (I.viii.5). Thus the refutation of the enemy comes in the end to seem a very small thing, a by-product.
>
> (Lewis 1954: 459)

Similar support for the view that Lewis thought of knowledge for its own sake as knowledge as a source of pleasure is found in a short paper entitled "Is History Bunk?" (Lewis [1957] in 1986a). In this piece, Lewis begins by pointing out that the historical impulse, which he defines as curiosity about what people thought, did, and suffered in the past, while not shared by everyone, is nevertheless longstanding. He then asks about the explanation for this enduring curiosity: "A very simple one is that offered in [John] Barbour's [fourteenth-century narrative poem about the actions of Robert the Bruce in the Scottish Wars of Independence and entitled *The*] *Bruce*; [which is that] exciting stories are in any case 'delitabill' [delightful] and if they happen to be true as well then we shall get a 'doubill pleasance' [double pleasure]" (Lewis [1957] in 1986a: 100). In Lewis's own words about Barbour's view, "[s]tories, even when untrue, give pleasure. But, if so, true stories well told ... ought to give a double pleasure; pleasure in the ... narrative as such, and pleasure in learning what really happened" (Lewis 1964: 177).

The simple explanation for historical curiosity is that proposed by *The Bruce*: there is the experience of pleasure that comes from knowing about the past. Lewis goes on to point out that there are "graver motives": a knowledge of history "is defended as instructive or exemplary: either ethically (the lasting fame or infamy which historians confer upon the dead will teach us to mind our morals) or politically (by seeing how national disasters were brought on in the past we may learn how to avoid them in the future)" (Lewis [1957] in 1986a: 100). In other words, the pursuit of historical knowledge is useful. However, Lewis believed it is not nearly as useful as some people might think because the lessons of history that are supposedly applicable to contemporary life become less obvious the more we know about the uniqueness of each historical situation. Thus, most people with an interest in history "find it safer and franker to admit that they are seeking knowledge of the past ... for its own sake [not for historical lessons from which they might learn]; that they are gratifying a 'liberal' curiosity" (Lewis [1957] in 1986a: 100). Here, "knowledge of the past for its own sake" is equivalent to *The Bruce's* simple explanation for satisfying the curiosity about history— the resultant experiences of pleasure.

After making his point about *The Bruce*, Lewis went on to credit Aristotle for providing us with the conception of a "liberal" curiosity that fuels the existence of the "liberal" studies which comprise not a small part "of the activities we carry on at universities" (Lewis [1957] in 1986a: 101). Lewis added that "[o]f course this conception ... has always been baffling and repellent to certain minds" (Lewis [1957] in 1986a: 101) which regard liberal curiosity as a waste of time. He responded that while we who are in universities do not demand that everyone should share the liberal curiosity that supplies our interests, "[w]e cannot ... let pass the assumption that [liberal studies are] to be condemned unless [they] can deliver some sort of 'goods' [other than pleasure] for present use" (Lewis [1957] in 1986a: 104). In other words, the simple explanation for liberal curiosity, which is that it provides those who possess the curiosity with experiences of pleasure, warrants defending.[13]

We come closest to Lewis maintaining the view that, strictly speaking, we desire to know for its own sake in a passage like the following:

> I am a man as well as a lover of poetry: being human, I am inquisitive, I want to know as well as enjoy. But even if enjoyment alone were my aim I should still choose this way, for I should hope to be led by it to newer and fresher enjoyments, things I could never have met in my own period, modes of feeling, flavours, atmospheres, nowhere accessible but by a mental journey into the real past. I have lived nearly sixty years with myself and my own century and am not so enamoured of either as to desire no glimpse of a world beyond them.
>
> (Lewis [n.d.] in 2005: 3–4)

Even in this passage, Lewis does not explicitly say he would desire to know without any experience of enjoyment. As is typical, when he discusses the desire to know he includes comments about enjoyment or pleasure. In this case, he directly states that were his desire only for enjoyment, he should still prefer historical knowledge as the way to that enjoyment, which implies that at present he recognizes it as his preferred means to experiencing pleasure. Hedonists about happiness standardly maintain that once we recognize that something serves as a reliable way to pleasure, the desire for pleasure for its own sake reproduces itself in the form of a desire for the means for its own sake (Silverstein 2000). Thus, it is plausible to affirm that it is because

Lewis was a hedonist about happiness and believed that the desire for knowledge is ultimately explained by the desire for pleasure that we find him regularly supplementing assertions about the desire to know with comments about enjoyment and pleasure.

Additional support for the view that Lewis believed it is experiences of pleasure that are ultimately good for a person, and that other goods like knowledge are no more than instrumental to pleasure, is found in his correspondence entitled *De Bono et Malo* (*Concerning Good and Evil*) with his good friend Owen Barfield in 1930. Therein, Lewis made the interesting comment that pleasure is an individual's particular good and what he (the individual) regards as his purpose (end). Presumably, Lewis believed the individual regards the experience of pleasure as his good and purpose, because pleasure is intrinsically good and, as such, perfects him in the sense that it achieves the purpose for which he exists.

> For if we ask a man why he is hurrying and he replies "To catch a train": and we ask him again "Why" and so on: in the end he is bound to answer *either* "Because this is my duty" *or* "Because this is my pleasure": that is either "This is the manifestation of universal good demanded by my time and place—in willing this I will as spirit" *or* "This is my particular good—this is what I as soul regard as my end." And if you asked him why he ought to do his duty, or why he liked pleasure, he would justly leave you unanswered as a fool. There is no answer to the ultimate [grounding,] but our inability to answer (as in the face of an axiom) is not ignorance but knowledge for we see ... why there is no answer.
>
> (Lewis 1930: 8)

Given the idea that the experience of pleasure, because of its intrinsic goodness, perfects the person having it, it is relevant to note that Lewis believed an individual's experience of happiness, which is constituted by experiences of pleasure, both pleases and glorifies God. "God," re-quoting Lewis, "not only understands but *shares* the desire ... for complete and ecstatic happiness" (Lewis 2004b: 123). And the experience of pleasure has "the smell of Deity" about it (Lewis 1992a

[1963]: 90). It follows then that to enjoy God, to experience pleasure in relationship with God, is to glorify God: "The Scotch [Westminster] catechism says that man's chief end is 'to glorify God and enjoy Him forever'. But we shall then know that these are the same thing. Fully to enjoy is to glorify. In commanding us to glorify Him, God is inviting us to enjoy Him" (Lewis 1986b [1958]: 96–7).

A Brief Digression: The Discarded Image

In addition to being philosophically educated, Lewis was professionally a tutor in medieval and Renaissance literature. As part of his learning on the topic, he developed a love for the medieval synthesis of theology, science, and history, which was a highly detailed and organized model of the universe. He occasionally gave a course of lectures at Oxford on the "Model," and his book *The Discarded Image* is the substance of those talks.

Toward the end of *The Discarded Image*, Lewis points out that anyone who has read the higher kinds of medieval and Renaissance poetry has not failed to take note of the amount of science, philosophy, and history that they contain. He writes that the commonest method used by writers for presenting information on these topics was digression. But why, asks Lewis, present such information in the first place? "At first one suspects pedantry, but that can hardly be the true explanation" because "[m]uch ... of the knowledge was too common to reflect any particular distinction on an author" (Lewis 1964: 199). Lewis's conclusion about the correct explanation is interesting: "One gets the impression that medieval people, like Professor Tolkien's Hobbits, enjoyed books which told them what they already knew" (Lewis 1964: 200). If all the "digressions are filled with a certain sort of matter, this must be because writers and their audience liked it" (Lewis 1964: 200–1). Thus,

> [t]he simplest explanation is, I believe, the true one. Poets and other artists depicted these things because their minds loved to dwell on them ... The medieval and Renaissance delight in the universe was,

> I think, [something] spontaneous and aesthetic ... [W]here Homer rejoiced in the particulars [of human life and the labours of men] the later [medieval] artist rejoiced also in that great imagined structure which gave them all their place. Every particular fact and story became more interesting and more pleasurable if, by being properly fitted in, it carried one's mind back to the Model as a whole.
>
> (Lewis 1964: 202–3)

The cosmological part of the Model to which Lewis refers included a conception of the sky in which the seven luminous planets (the Moon, Mercury, Venus, the Sun, Mars, Jupiter, and Saturn) were individually affixed in their respective spheres, where each sphere was larger than the one below it, and moved along with the rotational motion of its sphere. At the outermost reaches of the material universe was a sphere called "the First Movable or *Primum Mobile*. This, since it carries no luminous body, gives no evidence of itself to our senses; its existence was inferred to account for the motions of all the others" (Lewis 1964: 96). Associated with the *Primum Mobile* was an Intelligence with its intellectual desire, which Lewis described as follows:

> I am thinking in particular of one picture which represents the Intelligence of the Primum Mobile itself. It is of course wholly symbolical; they [the medievals] knew perfectly well that such a creature—it had no body—could not be literally depicted at all. But the symbol chosen is delightfully significant. It is a picture of a girl dancing and playing a tambourine; a picture of gaiety, almost of frolic. And why not? These spheres are moved by love, by intellectual desire ... Their existence is thus one of delight. The motions of the universe are to be conceived not as those of a machine or even an army, but rather as a dance, a festival, a symphony, a ritual, a carnival, or all these in one.
>
> (Lewis [1956] in 2005: 60)

I have digressed for a moment to describe Lewis's treatment of the medieval Model of the universe. He did not believe it to be true (Lewis 1964: 216, 222),[14] but he knew in great detail that some of the Model's parts were described as experiencing great joy, and also that those who wrote the descriptions took great pleasure in the science, philosophy, and history which infused that Model. Lewis was well acquainted with others who found pleasure in intellectual activity, and this helps to make clear that his view of the purpose of higher education did not come to be in a vacuum.

The overwhelming evidence from Lewis's writings, then, supports the view that he sought the life of higher education because he derived pleasure from higher-level learning and knowing. It was the pleasure which he received from intellectual activity in the forms of thinking, reading, and writing that was sought for its own sake, not the knowledge. Were he not to have enjoyed higher-level intellectual activity, and absent what he believed to be a specific calling or command of God to be a member of the academy, he would not have had a justification for a life in higher education except in terms of its usefulness for things like employment and social status, where the employment and social recognition by others would themselves be sources of pleasure.

The Purpose of Higher Education: Its Relationship to the Present and the Future

When we ask about the purpose of something, we are essentially concerned about the *future* and often with what is nonexistent and might be brought into reality. For example, if you believe the purpose of higher education is that you obtain a good job in order to earn more money, the job and money are future goods that you do not presently possess and are seeking to bring into existence through the earning of a college degree. However, when Lewis maintained the purpose of higher education is experiencing pleasure, he was usually not thinking about bringing about a future good for yourself that you do not presently possess. Rather, he was thinking about *sustaining* into the future the thinking and learning and accompanying pleasure that you *presently* engage in and experience. In extended comments that reflect his hedonistic understanding of happiness and awareness of the paradox of hedonism, Lewis cautioned against a future-oriented attitude toward culture and, by extension, higher education, as opposed to resting content with present, spontaneously arising, intellectual pleasures:

> To be constantly engaged with the idea of *culture*, and (above all) of *culture* as something enviable, or meritorious, or something that confers prestige, seems to me to endanger those very "enjoyments" for whose sake we chiefly value it. If we encourage others, or ourselves, to hear, see, or read great art on the ground that it is a *cultured* thing to do, we call into play precisely those elements in us which must be in abeyance before we can enjoy art at all. We are calling up the desire for self-improvement, the desire for distinction, the desire to revolt (from one group) and to agree (with another), and a dozen busy passions which, whether good or bad in themselves, are, in relation to the arts, simply a blinding and paralysing distraction.
>
> At this point some may protest that by *culture* they do not mean the "enjoyments" themselves, but the whole habit of mind which such experiences, re-acting upon one another, and reflected on, build up as a permanent possession. And some will wish to include the sensitive and enriching social life which, they think, will arise among groups of people who share this habit of mind ... I can well imagine a lifetime of such enjoyments leading a man to such a habit of mind, but on one condition; namely, that he went to the arts for no such purpose ... For the true enjoyments must be spontaneous and compulsive and look to no remoter end ... The desirable habit of mind, if it is to come at all, must come as a by-product, unsought.
>
> (Lewis [1955] in 1987: 34–5)[15]

As I will explain in the next chapter, Lewis believed one of the problems with justifying higher education in terms of the acquisition of qualifications for getting a good job and earning more money is that it conveys to people the erroneous idea that happiness is something that is not and cannot be experienced now but only in the future. The "in-order-to-get-a-job" justification of the academy nourishes the idea that higher education is something to be endured as opposed to enjoyed.

In Lewis's mind, the correct justification of higher education is one that conjoins enjoyment in the present with enjoyment in the future. God, wrote Lewis, "wants [human beings] to attend chiefly to two things, to eternity itself and to that point of time which they call the Present. For the Present is the point at which time touches eternity. Of the present moment, and of it only, humans have an experience" (Lewis 1961b: 67–8). Lewis thought that because only the present or "the now" is real, we should

> [n]ever … commit [our] … happiness to the future. Happy work is best done by the man who takes his long-term plans somewhat lightly and works from moment to moment 'as to the Lord.' It is only our *daily* bread that we are encouraged to ask for. The present is the only time in which … any grace [can be] received.
> (Lewis [1939a] in 2001g: 61)

"*[E]njoy* the present pleasure …" (Lewis 2007: 1183). As a lover of animals, Lewis thought we should be mindful of the sub-human world of the beasts who live in the present because they can live nowhere else:

> We all at times feel somewhat painfully our human isolation from the sub-human world—the atrophy of instinct which our intelligence entails, our excessive self-consciousness, the innumerable complexities of our situation, our inability to live in the present. If only we could shuffle it all off! We must not—and incidentally we can't—become beasts. But we can be *with* a beast.
> (Lewis 1988 [1960]: 52)

Can a Christian Be in Higher Education?

The reasonable conclusion to draw from Lewis's thoughts about the value of intellectual activity is that he believed knowledge is not, strictly speaking, intrinsically good. It is the pleasure that one derives from more advanced intellectual activity that is intrinsically good. This intellectual activity is never more than an extrinsic, instrumental good. Lewis held his view of the purpose of higher education as a Christian. But there were concerns he had to address before he could be intellectually comfortable with being a Christian in the academy. These concerns are the subject of the next chapter.

Addendum

In a paper read to the English Society at Oxford (seemingly in the 1930s), Lewis was concerned with the distinction many people (but not he) make between what he called "highbrow" (superior and literary) and "lowbrow" (inferior and non-literary) books. In trying to make sense of the distinction, which he thought could not be done, Lewis wrote about changes that were occurring in education in the UK:

> The growth of English Schools at Universities, the School Certificate [an educational attainment qualification exam, established in 1918, and usually taken by students at age 16] and the Educational Ladder—all excellent things—may yet produce unexpected results. I foresee the growth of a new race of readers and critics to whom, from the very outset, good literature will be an accomplishment rather than a delight, and who will always feel, beneath the acquired taste, the backward tug of something else which they feel merit in resisting. Such people will not be content to say that some books are bad or not very good; they will make a special class of "lowbrow" art which is to be vilified, mocked, quarantined, and sometimes (when they are sick or tired) enjoyed ... They will have no conception, because they have had no experience, of spontaneous delight in excellence. Their "good" taste will have been acquired by the sweat of their brows, its acquisition will often (and legitimately) have coincided with advancement in the social and economic scale, and they will hold it with uneasy intensity. As they will be contemptuous of popular books, so they will be naïvely tolerant of dullness and difficulty in any quack or sloven who comes before them with lofty pretensions; *all* literature having been as hard to them as that, so much an acquired taste, they will not see the difference. They will be angry with a true lover of literature ... and call him a *dilettante*.
>
> (Lewis 1939a: 113–15)

If I have read Lewis correctly, his thoughts about literature are almost prophetically mirrored in and fulfilled by what has occurred in contemporary higher education. If we replace "a new race of readers and critics" with "a new race of cultural elites," "good literature" with "a college degree," and "lowbrow art" with "skilled trades" or "blue-collar work," then higher education will be considered an accomplishment rather than a delight, and those who successfully complete it will be members of a social and economic class which vilifies and mocks those who occupy positions in the skilled trades. If readers believe I am being overly harsh at this point, they should read Michael Sandel's book *The Tyranny of Merit* (Sandel 2020) and Adrian Wooldridge's *The Aristocracy of Talent* (Wooldridge 2021).

The association of cultural elitism with higher education is not surprising, given a eudaimonistic conception of human happiness that is widely accepted by those in the academy. Given an eudaimonistic understanding of human well-being, it is natural to conclude that advanced intellectual activity perfects human nature in the sense that it makes those in the academy happier, with the result that those who, for whatever reason, are on the outside of higher education are less happy than those who are on the inside. As I have made clear above, Lewis rejected an eudaimonistic view of happiness. Thus, it is not surprising to read in Justin Dyer's and Micah Watson's *C. S. Lewis on Politics and the Natural Law* (Dyer and Watson 2016) that Lewis did not believe the ancient and classical eudaimonist view that government exists for the purpose of promoting, through active intervention, the perfection of its citizens. Dyer and Watson make clear (Dyer and Watson 2016: 116–23) that Lewis believed government is justified in interfering with the liberty and interests of its citizens on the grounds of the harm principle of the philosopher John Stuart Mill who was a hedonist about happiness. According to the harm principle, the state can justifiably interfere with the interests of a citizen if the actions he takes in promoting his happiness adversely and unjustly affect the actual or potential happiness of others. Given the lack of such unjust actions, a citizen should be free to experience the pleasure that accompanies his actions. "The State," wrote Lewis, exists simply to promote and to protect the ordinary happiness of human beings in this life. A husband and wife chatting over a fire, a couple of friends having a game of darts in a pub, a man reading a book in his own room or digging in his own garden—that is what the State is there for. And unless they are helping to increase and prolong and protect such moments, all the laws, parliaments, armies, courts, police, economics, etc., are simply a waste of time.

(Lewis 2001b [1952]: 199)

Most generally, Lewis was suspicious of political power:

I fully embrace the maxim ... that "all power corrupts." I would go further. The loftier the pretensions of the power, the more meddlesome, inhuman, and oppressive it will be ... All political power is at best a necessary evil: but it is least evil when its sanctions are most modest and commonplace, when it claims no more than to be useful or convenient and sets itself strictly limited objectives. Anything transcendental or spiritual, or even anything very strongly ethical, in its pretensions is dangerous and encourages it to meddle with our private lives.

(Lewis [1955] in 1987: 40)

And, finally, Lewis warned about the use of education in school and the inculcation of the party line as a means of access to the "managerial class":

[E]ducation is increasingly the means of access to the Managerial Class ... The boy will not get good marks (which means, in the long run, that he will not get into the Managerial Class) unless he produces the kind of responses, and the kind of analytic method, which commend themselves to his teacher ...

Thus to say that, under the nascent régime, education alone will get you into the ruling class, may not mean simply that the failure to acquire certain knowledge and to reach a certain level of intellectual competence will exclude you. That would be reasonable enough. But it may come to mean, perhaps means already, something more. It means that you cannot get in without becoming, or without making your masters believe that you have become, a very specific kind of person, one who makes the right responses to the right authors. In fact, you can get in only by becoming, in the modern sense of the word, *cultured* ... Every boy or girl who is born is presented with the choice: "Read the poets whom we, the *cultured*, approve, and say the sort of things we say about them, or be a prole." ...

Culture is a bad qualification for a ruling class because it does not qualify men to rule. The things we really need in our rulers—mercy, financial integrity, practical intelligence, hard work, and the like—are no more likely to be found in cultured persons than in anyone else.

(Lewis [1955] in 1987: 41, 43, 44, 46–7)

As the university has become more and more an extension of secondary school in our day, so has it become more and more a necessary condition of membership in, in Lewis's words, the managerial class.

3

Higher Education and Being a Christian

Intellectual Activity and God

Though C. S. Lewis was a Christian, his conception of the purpose of higher education was not theistic and Christian in the sense that acceptance of higher education's purpose requires a belief in the existence of God and the death and resurrection of Jesus of Nazareth. Neither was his idea about the purpose of higher education atheistic or non-Christian in the sense that acceptance of it requires a denial that God exists and that Jesus was resurrected. Lewis believed higher-level intellectual activity, like eating and drinking, is a natural human activity that can be accompanied by experiences of pleasure. He thought we are directly aware of both the activity and its accompanying pleasure at the time of their occurrence. However, while Lewis held that we might be aware of our advanced intellectual activity and its accompanying experiences of pleasure which are intrinsically good without a belief in God's existence, the intrinsically good pleasure and intellectual activity are ultimately not possible without the creative and sustaining activity of God.

Living in the Present

Lewis believed that an experience of pleasure is intrinsically good and that some people derive experiences of pleasure in the here and now through involvement in higher education. He maintained the university is first and foremost for individuals who are happy in the present moment reading books, writing papers, doing research, devising and conducting experiments, and most generally sharing the life of the mind with others who also derive pleasure from these intellectual activities. While he recognized that people need jobs, and obtaining one can be a result of involvement in the university as a student, he consistently maintained that it is wrong to think of the justification for the academy's existence in terms of satisfying this need for future employment.

I once had a conversation with the spouse of one of my colleagues about how frustrating it was for her to have spent years "grinding it out" in higher education, as an undergraduate in college and a graduate in law school, then to have passed the bar exam and gained employment with a firm, and finally to have become a partner in the firm, only to discover, as she told me, that in the end she was not at all happy in her work. She had followed the culturally prescribed educational and professional plan to the letter with the belief that her happiness down the road was assured, only to discover in the end that it was not to be had.

Lewis believed that, like my colleague's spouse, those who go to college primarily for the purpose of getting a job misguidedly focus their attention on something in the too-distant future. They play a risky high-stakes game, even if the ending of their story happens through good fortune to be happier than the one just described. For these individuals, life in the academy is typically endured with the expectation that there is something much better down the road after graduation. Lewis thought this approach to higher education an instance of a more general and deeply flawed approach to life, and he used the devilish Screwtape in *The Screwtape Letters and Screwtape Proposes a Toast* to describe and promote this general way of living. As we have already seen, Lewis believed God wants people mainly to focus on two things: eternity, where everything will always be present, and the present moment in this life which mirrors the eternal "now" (Lewis 1961b: 68). The devil's business is about getting persons to be primarily focused on the mid-range future, that which is between eternity and the present. "To be sure," wrote Lewis, God wants people "to think of the Future too—just so much as is necessary for *now* planning the acts of justice or charity which will probably be their duty tomorrow. The duty of planning the morrow's work is *today's* duty; though its material is borrowed from the future, the duty, like all duties, is in the Present" (Lewis 1961b: 69). However, Lewis made clear that drawing our attention to the real demands of morality in the context of thinking about whether you can guarantee yourself happiness in this world misses the point. What God is opposed to is the idea of a person giving his or her heart to the Future in the sense of thinking that, if I do this and that, I can guarantee the realization of my own happiness in the months and years ahead. Thus, Lewis depicted the devil and his minions working to encourage people to choose a way of life in which they devote their fullest attention to producing a possible future happiness at the expense of enjoying the present:

> [T]hought about the Future inflames hope and fear. Also, it is unknown to [people], so that in making them think about it we make them think of unrealities ... [W]e want a man hagridden by the Future—haunted by visions of an imminent heaven or hell upon earth— ... dependent for his faith on the success or failure of schemes whose end he will not live to see. We want a whole race perpetually in pursuit of the rainbow's end ... [and not] happy *now*, but always using as mere fuel wherewith to heap the altar of the Future every real gift which is offered to them in the Present ... [A man] may be untroubled about the Future ... because he has persuaded himself that the Future is going to be agreeable. As long as that is the real course of his tranquillity, his tranquillity ... is only piling up more disappointment ... for him when his false hopes are dashed ... [A man must not be allowed to concern] himself with the Present because there, and there alone, all duty, all grace, all knowledge, and all pleasure dwell ...
>
> (Lewis 1961b: 68, 69–70)

Pleasure, Lewis stressed, is only experienced in the present moment and as such is a mirror of eternity, and he added that God wants us not to live overly much in the future at the expense of the present. Some who share Lewis's belief about the importance of living in the present moment disagree with his claim that the now of pleasure is a mirror of eternity. Indeed, they maintain we could not act in the present and thereby experience pleasure, if we were to believe that we will exist for eternity. According to them, we must believe that we die and there is no afterlife in order to be able to act at all, because if we were to believe that we will exist forever we could and would always put off until tomorrow what we can do today. For example, Julian Baggini, a proponent of living in the present, writes that

> [a]n eternal life might turn out to be the most meaningless of all. What would be the point of doing anything today if you could just as easily do it tomorrow? As Albert Camus put it in *The Plague*, "The order of the world is shaped by death." The very fact that one day life will end is what propels us to act at all ... [T]he promise of eventual death is necessary to make any action worthwhile at all.
>
> (Baggini 2004: 54, 55)

> Moments of pleasure are precious *because* they pass, because we cannot make them last any longer than they do.
>
> (Baggini 2004: 133)

While Baggini states his argument in terms of our death being our final end and a necessary condition of our acting in the present, presumably he thinks we must *believe* that our deaths are our final end in order for us to act now. To the best of my knowledge, Lewis never addressed the argument that our activity in the present requires the belief that our futures are ultimately finite in duration. However, given what he thought about the intrinsic goodness of pleasure, he most certainly would have maintained that a belief that our existence permanently ends at death is not needed in order either for us to act in the present or for that action to be worthwhile. A veritable host of people down through the ages have believed they will exist forever and still were able to act, and Lewis would have insisted that they were able to act because the intrinsic goodness of pleasure provided them with a reason to perform an action that leads to that pleasure. Given a belief that pleasure is intrinsically good, people are attracted to it and need a reason not to pursue it. Absent such a reason, they will act with the expectation and/or hope that they will experience the pleasure they desire. And, Lewis would have added, moments of pleasure are not precious because they pass, as Baggini claims, but because they are intrinsically good. And given that they are intrinsically good, people at least hope, even if they do not believe, that they will exist forever to experience pleasure.

Lewis maintained that because experiences of pleasure are intrinsically good, we should enjoy the present and not always be thinking about tomorrow. To elucidate his belief about living life in the present as it relates to life in the academy, it is helpful to consider his thoughts about higher education in the light of his conviction that we are immortal beings whom God creates for the purpose of being perfectly happy.

Higher Education as Service to God

When C. S. Lewis entered Oxford as a student in early 1917 he was an atheist, and he did not believe in the existence of God when he began his tutorial work as a don at Magdalen College, Oxford in 1925. However, within about six years of accepting his appointment at Magdalen, Lewis had become first a theist (a person who believes that God exists) and then a Christian (it was a two-step process for Lewis). Once he had become a Christian, Lewis was concerned with whether being a Christian presents problems all its own for being a member of the academy.

Perhaps surprisingly, Lewis's concern about being a Christian and devoting himself to higher-level intellectual activity arose out of his belief that God created us for perfect happiness, which is a happiness that, once experienced, never ends. God's purpose in creating us for perfect happiness implies that we are immortal beings in the sense that we are made to exist forever. Lewis believed, in his own words, that "[t]here are no *ordinary* people. You have never talked to a mere mortal. Nations, cultures, arts, civilisations—these are mortal, and their life is to ours as the life of a gnat. But it is immortals whom we joke with, work with, marry, snub, and exploit" (Lewis [1941] in 2001g: 46). Moreover, Lewis thought that all of us, as immortals, "are every moment advancing either to Heaven or to hell" (Lewis [1939a] in 2001g: 48–9). Furthermore, he thought we are advancing toward heaven or hell *freely* in the sense that we indeterministically choose how we will live our lives, where our alternatives are two in number. We can either choose a life of renunciation of unethical means pursued in an effort to make ourselves happy in this life, which he regarded as a life of death to self and advancing toward heaven, or choose a life of autonomy in which we use whatever means we want, including those which we believe are immoral to make ourselves happy, which he regarded as a life of self and advancing toward hell. Lewis wrote that "[i]t's not a question of God "sending" us to Hell. In each of us there is something growing up which will of itself *be Hell* unless it is nipped in the bud" (Lewis [1948b] in 1970: 155).

The idea of self-renunciation was of serious interest to Lewis in his early twenties when he did not believe in God. At that time, he considered the idea as it is presented in Buddhism and found it wanting because Buddhism wrongly applied it to the very existence of the self or I (the "Atman"). In a letter to his friend Leo Baker in 1921, who had provided him with a copy of *The Gospel of the Buddha according to Old Records*, Lewis wrote the following:

> [T]hanks for the Gospel of Buddha: in so far as it is a gospel, an exposition of ethics etc, it has not perhaps added much to what I know of the subject, tho' it has been very pleasant reading. On the metaphysical presuppositions of Buddhism, it has given me new light: I did not realize, before, his denial of the Atman: that is very interesting. I cannot at present believe it—to me the Self, as really existing, seems involved in everything we think. No use to talk of "a bundle of thoughts" etc for, as you know, I always have to ask "who thinks?" Indeed Buddhism itself does not seem to make much use

of the non-Atman doctrine, once it has been stated: and it is only by torture that the theory of re-birth is made compatible with it. Perhaps he has confused a moral truth with a metaphysical fallacy? One sees, of course, its inferiority to Christianity—at any rate as a creed for ordinary men: and though I sometimes feel that complete abnegation is the only real refuge, in my healthier moments I hope that there is something better. This minute I can pine for Nirvana, but when the sky clears I shall prefer something with more positive joy.

(Lewis 2004a: 567)

What Lewis said he learned from reading *The Gospel of the Buddha* was that Buddhism denies the existence of the atman or self as a substance or thing which thinks, experiences pleasure, and persists through time in this life and can survive into the afterlife. Lewis concluded that Buddhism confused the denial of the self in the form of ethical self-restraint that is required in the pursuit of pleasure with the metaphysical denial of the self as an entity which makes all of ordinary life possible. Christianity is more reasonable because it affirms the existence of the atman and, thereby, makes intelligible the possibility of experiencing perfect happiness in the afterlife and the actuality of happiness in this life whose less-than-perfect nature is in part accounted for by the exercise of ethical self-restraint.

As an atheist student in Oxford, Lewis had concluded Christianity provides a better understanding of the self and its desire for happiness than Buddhism. However, as a Christian don in Oxford he worried about whether he could justify continuing his work in higher education. Given he believed there is so much at stake concerning the everlasting happiness of immortal individuals, Lewis wondered whether a Christian can legitimately find his or her vocation in this life deriving pleasure from thinking, reading and writing books, papers, and articles, discussing ideas with others, mentoring and collaborating with students, etc. Should not a Christian focus solely on "the salvation of human souls?" (Lewis [1940] in 1967: 14).

Lewis, however, reasoned that if salvation is salvation for perfect happiness, then there must not be anything in principle wrong with experiencing happiness in this life. True, given the purpose for which we are created, we must not take the things which provide for our happiness in this life too seriously. But given our capacity for happiness in this life, our enjoyment of it is perfectly reasonable, provided we are not enjoying it as the fruit of immoral acts. In some reflections on Christianity and its relationship to literature, Lewis wrote that "[t]he Christian will take literature a little less seriously than the cultured Pagan: he will feel less uneasy with a purely hedonistic standard for at least many kinds of [literary] work ... We can play, as we can eat, to the Glory of God" (Lewis 1939a: 195–6). However, because we often play with others, we should always be mindful that "our merriment must be of that kind (and it is, in fact, the merriest kind) which exists between people who have, from the outset, taken each other seriously—no flippancy, no superiority, no presumption ... Next to the Blessed Sacrament [the Eucharist] itself, your neighbor is the holiest object presented to your senses" (Lewis [1941] in 2001g: 46).

Thus, while Lewis initially thought a happy life in the academy might be hard or impossible to justify in the face of matters of the immortal afterlife, he concluded a Christian can reasonably be at home with others in higher education which, as an instance of culture, is mortal. After all, God creates us with a human nature that includes the desire to know and to experience beauty, just as it includes the desires for food, drink, sex, friendship, etc., where all of these things are desired as means to experiences of pleasure and mitigations of experiences of pain. Lewis added that "God makes no appetite in vain" (Lewis [1939a] in 2001g: 56), by which he in part meant that it would make no sense for God to endow us with the stated desires and then in principle forbid us to pursue their fulfillment in any and all situations. Hence, "it is clear that Christianity does not exclude any of the ordinary human activities" ((Lewis [1939a] in 2001g: 54).[1]

In Lewis's estimation, then, Christians who are members of the academy because they enjoy it are engaging in a form of play. But he believed that involvement in higher education, as a form of play with its pleasure that is a ray of divine glory (Lewis 1992a [1963]: 89), should also be part of a life that in every respect is devoted to God and, in that sense, is spiritual or religious in nature. In Lewis's mind, there is no essential conflict between activities grounded in desires for the satisfaction of natural human needs such as food, water, shelter, and sex and the spiritual life: "There is no essential quarrel between the spiritual life and the human activities as such" (Lewis [1939a] in 2001g: 55). Lewis insisted that any natural human activity which is done in obedience to and for the glory of God is acceptable: "Christianity does not simply replace our natural life and substitute a new one; it is rather a new organisation which exploits, to its own supernatural ends, these natural materials" (Lewis [1939a] in 2001g: 54).[2] Lewis reminded his readers that Jesus attended a wedding (John 2:1-11), and the apostle Paul instructed people to get on with their work and not be idle (Ephesians 4:28; I Thessalonians 4:11; 2 Thessalonians 3:10) (Lewis [1939a] in 2001g: 54; [1940] in 1967: 20). With respect to his own employment, Lewis wrote "[m]y own professional work, though conditioned by tastes and talents, is immediately motivated by the need for earning my living. And on earning one's living I was relieved to note that Christianity … can be delightfully humdrum" (Lewis [1940] in 1967: 20). Given that he had to earn a living, he concluded he might as well, if he had the opportunity, earn it by doing what he enjoyed. More generally, Lewis was surprised to discover that his later life as a Christian was not all that different from his earlier life as an atheist in terms of required daily activities: "Before I became a Christian I do not think I fully realised that one's life, after conversion, would inevitably consist in doing most of the same things one had been doing before, one hopes, in a new spirit [to the glory of God], but still the same things" (Lewis [1939a] in 2001g: 51).

Lewis concluded there is no reason for a Christian to think that involvement in higher education is not itself a form of activity that can fulfill our nature and make us to some degree happy in this life, and when pursued morally to the glory of God is perfectly acceptable to Him. A life of higher-level intellectual activity can legitimately be pursued as an instance of the principle of living in the present as opposed to the future. It is not a matter of whether but of how we enjoy happiness in this life that will determine if we enjoy the perfect happiness of the afterlife for which we are made.

Higher Education in Wartime

As a person who lived much of his life during the first half of the twentieth century, Lewis was, like so many other young men of his generation, no stranger to large and awful human conflicts. In the midst of the First World War, he had enlisted and been sent to the trenches in France where he was wounded by what today is euphemistically termed "friendly fire." During the Second World War, he was in the middle of his academic career but nevertheless devoted much of his time to the war effort by patrolling the streets of Oxford at night as a member of the Home Guard, giving talks about Christian theology to young men in the Royal Air Force, and addressing the British nation in BBC radio talks whose contents are found today in the book *Mere Christianity*.[3]

At the outset of the Second World War in late 1939, Lewis delivered an evensong address, "Learning in Wartime," about the moral permissibility of a Christian's involvement in academic life. How, with the Nazis militarily taking over continental Europe and threatening to bring England to its knees, could a Christian continue to take seriously the pursuit of learning? Is there "really any legitimate place for the activities of the scholar in a world such as this?" (Lewis [1939a] in 2001g: 50)? Is this "not like fiddling while Rome burns?" (Lewis [1939a] in 2001g: 47). True, the British government was allowing young men to attend university, so there was no legal problem with involvement in higher education during the war. But there was still the additional question: How is it morally permissible or even psychologically possible for a Christian to retain his interest in learning in a university under the huge shadow of a rapidly spreading and horrific human conflict? (Lewis [1939a] in 2001g: 48–9).

Lewis understood all too well what higher education had done for him in terms of providing him with much pleasure. He also believed as a Christian that his need for gainful employment justified his life in the academy. Why not, then, be gainfully employed doing that which gave him and others like him pleasure? As we saw in the previous sections, Lewis concluded his involvement in higher education could be justified in peacetime. But at the outset of a great war between his and another nation? Should not he and other Christians in higher education be devoting all of their time, whether as civilians or as members of the military, to the war effort? Lewis considered and answered this question in light of his belief, which I have already explained, that human persons were immortals who are at every moment advancing toward or away from heaven and perfect happiness. If in peacetime Christians did not have to devote their lives completely to evangelizing those who have lost their way on such a consequential journey, then "[the European] war [against Hitler] creates no absolutely new situation; it simply aggravates the permanent human situation so that we can no longer ignore it. Human life has always been lived on the edge of a precipice. Human culture has always had to exist under the shadow of something infinitely more important than itself" (Lewis [1939a] in 2001g: 49). If enjoying the pleasures of higher-level learning can be justified against the backdrop of matters of eternal destiny, heaven and hell, then it can most certainly be justified against the backdrop of a great war.

Lewis pointed out that there has never been a lack of reasons for delaying advanced learning "until some imminent danger has been averted or some crying injustice put right" (Lewis [1939a] in 2001g: 50).[4] In the face of these reasons, he reminded his listeners that if higher education (culture or learning) had to be postponed until all individuals in this life were secure in the sense that they faced no dangers or injustices of any kind, then no higher-level learning would occur this side of the grave. As a matter of fact, human beings have rightly not postponed such learning until there is heaven on earth, despite all of the reasons for doing so: "They propound mathematical theorems in beleaguered cities, conduct metaphysical arguments in condemned cells, make jokes on scaffolds, discuss the last new poem while advancing to the wall of Quebec, and comb their hair at Thermopylae. This is not *panache*; this is our nature" (Lewis [1939a] in 2001g: 50). Alexander Wolff writes in his book *Endpapers: A Family Story of Books, War, Escape, and Home* that after the end of the First World War, his grandfather, the publisher Kurt Wolff, "brought out several books … Foremost was Heinrich Mann's novel *Der Untertan* (literally, 'The Underling') … Kurt read the manuscript while serving on the Western Front" (Wolff 2021: 43). In a review of *Endpapers*, Benjamin Balint writes that "[e]ven while serving in the trenches of the Western Front, Kurt continued to solicit and read manuscripts, including Kafka's 'Metamorphosis,' which he brought out during the war" (Balint 2021). Lewis added his own reflections about literary work in war from his own experiences in the trenches in France during the Great War:

> Before I went to the last war I certainly expected that my life in the trenches would, in some mysterious sense, be all war. In fact, I found that the nearer you got to the front line the less everyone spoke and thought of the allied cause and the progress of the campaign; and I am pleased to find that Tolstoi, in the greatest war book ever written, records the same thing—and so, in its own way, does the *Iliad* … [E]nlistment in the army is [not] really going to obliterate our human life … The war will fail to absorb our whole attention because it is a finite object and, therefore, intrinsically unfitted to support the whole attention of a human soul.
>
> (Lewis [1939a] in 2001g: 51–2)

A Christian understands that learning can be justified in wartime, given that it can be justified in the face of the fact that people are making decisions in this life that will determine whether they will or will not enjoy in the afterlife the perfect happiness for which they are created. And given that people serving on the front lines of war can reasonably seek to fulfill their desire to engage in intellectual activity, they (and others) can also reasonably seek to fulfill this desire in a time of peace. It is for such people that Lewis thought higher education primarily exists.

The Need for Christians in the Secular Academy

Lewis understood that Christians, like anyone else, need employment, and he concluded that those Christians who derive pleasure from advanced learning can reasonably be employed in the secular academy. He also pointed out that while culture, which includes higher education, might at times be an innocent, instrumental good, it might also at times be instrumentally bad/evil, and therefore "[i]t is ... probably better that the ranks of the 'culture-sellers' should include some Christians ... It may even be the duty of some Christians to be culture-sellers ... [I]f the abuse [of culture] is common, the task of resisting that abuse might be not only lawful but obligatory" (Lewis [1940] in 1967: 20).

As in Lewis's day, so also in our own, higher education is often home to those who deny the possibility of knowledge about anything, including the existence of God, objective values, and purposeful action. Lewis thought that because Christians believe in these things, "[t]he mere presence of Christians in the ranks of culture-sellers will inevitably provide an antidote" (Lewis [1940] in 1967: 21) to these other individuals and their views. But what Christians must not do, Lewis maintained, is use their work as a platform to market their religious convictions. He stressed that Christians in the secular academy should stick to their subject matter and not take money for "supply[ing] a quite different thing (homiletics and apologetics). That is stealing" (Lewis [1940] in 1967: 21). Given "we mustn't take money for doing a thing and then secretly do something quite different" (Lewis 1994 [1966]: 46), Lewis insisted that if you are paid, as he was, to teach English literature, then you are morally obligated to teach English literature, period. Christians were needed in the secular university, not that they could proselytize for their Christian convictions but because, with their presumed moral integrity, they would teach what they were paid to teach. In a letter to Mary van Deusen about the views of the theologian Paul Tillich with whose views she disagreed, Lewis wrote that "[i]t is not horrible that you [should] grant him his ideas: it [would] be horrible if you did not" (Lewis 2007: 1012). Lewis showed this respect for the views of others in his tutoring of students. A former tutee of Lewis's, George Sayer, recalls that "[e]xcept in the pursuit of accuracy, he tried to avoid impressing his pupils with his own views. Thus, I was his pupil for two years before I realized that he was a Christian ..." (Sayer 2015: 176). John Lawlor, another pupil of Lewis's, writes that there was

> [o]ne thing Lewis never did [in his tutorials], in all my recollection of him. He never imposed his Christianity on the argument. If it was there already (and the great majority of writers we were dealing with were Christian in their cast of mind if not always in any direct allegiance) he would take up the point and develop it. But never would he obtrude his beliefs. Here ... he was reserved to an almost fantastic degree.
> (Lawlor 1965: 72)

Lawlor goes on to point out that "[l]ike any good tutor he showed me how the case I had sketched could be made stronger, introducing me to an area of criticism, which, while it gave comforting support to my argument, seemed to him largely misconceived" (Lawlor 1965: 75). However, Lewis believed a discussion of one's own religious convictions could, in the right context and for the right reason, occur. As he wrote in one letter to Rhona Bodle, "I quite agree with you about not using one's job for propaganda, but once the pupil raises the question I think one has a free hand" (Lewis 2004b: 941). And in another letter to Bodle he wrote that "as a child, I [should] have been very allured and impressed by the discovery—which must be made when questions are asked—that the teacher believed firmly in a whole mass of things he wasn't allowed to teach! Let them give us the charm of mystery if they please" (Lewis 2007: 332). Lewis's perspective as a child in this regard carried over into his adulthood.

Undermining Christianity and Intellectual Activity

"The teacher believed firmly in a whole mass of things he wasn't allowed to teach." As I briefly indicated above, Lewis was aware that many of his colleagues believed in a whole mass of things they were allowed to and often did teach but which, if true, undermined the knowledge of the truth of Christianity and anything else. Indeed, these things, if true, undermined the reality of advanced intellectual activity itself and, thereby, the purpose for the existence of higher education. The things believed and taught by these colleagues of Lewis were subsumed under the philosophical view known as *naturalism*. It is time to set out what Lewis had to say about it.

4

Higher Education and Naturalism

A Well-Kept Secret

When people today talk about ideological views impacting higher education, they frequently mention such things as political correctness, cancel culture, de-platforming, diversity, equity, inclusion, and "wokeism," each of which often leads to people self-censoring—not sharing what they believe with others. However, there is another ideological view that bears on higher education that is equally if not more widely espoused among members of the professoriate, yet it moves under the proverbial radar. Few people outside the academy are aware of this view, but C. S. Lewis believed that if it is true it undermines the existence of higher education because it implies we cannot reason and experience the pleasure which provides the purpose for the existence of the university. And the view? The philosophical doctrine known as *naturalism*. The philosopher Timothy Williamson writes that "[m]any contemporary philosophers describe themselves as naturalists" (Williamson 2011). Another philosopher Barry Stroud states that "'Naturalism' seems to me ... rather like 'World Peace.' Almost everyone swears allegiance to it, and is willing to march under its banner" (Stroud 2004: 22). And the philosopher Peter van Inwagen acknowledges that "Naturalism was a popular doctrine (popular among scientifically-minded philosophers and philosophically-minded scientists) in the 1940s when Lewis devised his argument against it, and it is if anything even more popular today" (van Inwagen 2011: 28). What, then, is naturalism?

Naturalism and Reasoning: Lewis's Argument from Reason

Naturalism in its most austere or strict form, which is the form with which Lewis was concerned, is the doctrine that in principle *any* event that occurs in our world is *completely* explicable in terms of what is non-mental in nature. For example, the naturalist David Armstrong maintains that "if the principles involved [in analyzing the single, all-embracing spatiotemporal system that is reality] were completely different from current principles of physics, in particular if they involved appeal to mental entities ... we might then count the analysis as a falsification of Naturalism" (Armstrong 1978: 262). Another naturalist David Papineau writes that "[w]e may not know enough about physics to know exactly what a complete 'physics' might include. But as long as we are confident that whatever it includes, it will have no ineliminable need for any distinctively mental categorizations, we can be confident that mental properties [and events] must be identical with (or realized by) certain non-mentally identifiable properties [and events]" (Papineau 2002: 41). According to Papineau, because mental events are identical with physical events (e.g., neuron firings), the explanations of these events must ultimately be non-psychological (non-mental) in nature:

> When I say that a complete physics excludes psychology, and that psychological [mental] antecedents are therefore never needed to explain physical effects, the emphasis here is on "needed." I am quite happy to allow that psychological categories *can* be used to explain physical [and mental] effects, as when I tell you that my arm rose because I wanted to lift it. My claim is only that in all such cases an alternative specification of a sufficient antecedent, which does not mention psychological categories, will also be available.
>
> (Papineau 1993: 31 n. 26)

But what is a non-mental explanation? Because "non-mental" is just the negation of "mental," an understanding of the former presupposes an understanding of the latter. The latter can be elucidated by revisiting and slightly expanding upon the issue of mental attitudes and their contents which was set forth in Chapter 1. Consider thinking. You can think about taking a walk this afternoon, listening to some music, watching a football game, etc. In these cases of thinking, there is the attitude of thinking and the content that is apprehended, which is respectively "that I will take a walk this afternoon," "that I will listen to some music," and "that I will watch a football game."

However, thinking is not the only mental attitude with content. For example, consider the mental attitudes of believing that you are experiencing pleasure and desiring that you have a pint of beer. In the case of believing that you are experiencing pleasure, believing is the attitude and "that I am experiencing pleasure" is the apprehended content. Similarly, with desiring that you have a pint of beer, desiring is the attitude and "that I have a pint of beer" is the content that is apprehended. It is in virtue of their contents that attitudes like thinking, believing, and desiring (and choosing, hoping, fearing, etc.) refer to or are about (you might say the attitudes have intentionality or "aboutness") actual or possible events/things in the world. For instance, with believing that I am experiencing pleasure and desiring that I have a pint of beer, the events in the world referred to by the contents are an actual experience of pleasure and a possible drinking of a beer.

Given this definition of a mental event, it follows that an explanation that is non-mental in nature is one that does not involve a mental attitude with content. Lewis was convinced that if naturalism were true, then we could not reason because reasoning in principle involves causation of one mental event *by another mental event*. And if naturalism excludes reasoning *per se*, then it excludes reasoning in higher education and the pleasure that accompanies it.[1]

Lewis set forth what is now known as his "argument from reason" against naturalism in terms of a consideration of the nature of a deductive argument, where a deductive argument consists of statements called "premises" which are supposed to support what is termed the "conclusion." In a good deductive argument, the premises are such that if they are true, then the conclusion must also be true. One form of deductive argument, which is known as *modus ponens*, is as follows:

If P, then Q
P
Therefore, Q

With this argument, given it is the case that "if P, then Q," and "P" are both true, then "Q" must also be true. "P" and "Q" are variables for which any content can be substituted. As an example, consider a football game between the New Orleans Saints and the Tampa Bay Buccaneers. If the Tampa Bay Buccaneers score more points than the New Orleans Saints, then the Tampa Bay Buccaneers will win the game (If P, then Q). The Tampa Bay Buccaneers scored more points than the New Orleans Saints (P). Therefore, the Tampa Bay Buccaneers won the game (Q).

Lewis believed that when we focus our attention on and understand the premises of a deductive argument and arrive at the conclusion, we are engaged in reasoning. Moreover, when we reason we are passive. We are patients. For example, when I focus my attention on tomorrow's weather and think that "If it will be sunny tomorrow, then I will head to the beach," and after looking at the weather report think "It will be sunny tomorrow," then, from my grasping of these premises, I cannot help but reach (provided I do not suffer a heart attack and die, get knocked unconscious, etc.) the conclusion "I will head to the beach." Lewis maintained that I cannot help inferring the conclusion "I will head to the beach" because given what I am aware of in terms of the premises of this argument, I am *causally determined* by my awareness to infer the conclusion, regardless of whether I desire to or not. Or consider the "greater-than" relation in "If A is greater than B and B is greater than C, then A is greater than C." Lewis wrote "I am quite convinced that my acts of thought ... are not free but determined. [For example], if the truths A [is greater than] > B and B [is greater than] > C are both present to my mind I *must* think A [is greater than] > C. I have no choice" (Lewis 2007: 1351). Lewis pointed out that if naturalism is true, then no one can inferentially believe (reason to a belief) in naturalism: "Any thing [such as naturalism] which professes to explain our reasoning fully without introducing an act of knowing [believing] thus solely [causally] determined by what is known, is really a theory that there is no reasoning" (Lewis 2001c [1960 rev. ed.]: 27).[2]

It is important to make clear that Lewis understood that there is a difference between apprehending or understanding content and believing that content. Thus he did not maintain that a person who deterministically infers "Q" from his apprehension of "If P, then Q" and "P" must also *believe* "Q" is true. For example, Lewis would have maintained that an atheist who reads a *modus-ponens* argument where "Q" is "God exists" can be causally determined to think "God exists" without believing "God exists." Given the atheist thinks "God exists" is false, he will conclude that one or more of the premises he apprehends in a *modus-ponens* argument whose conclusion is "God exists" must be false.

Naturalism and Purposes as Explanations

Lewis believed that if there is no reasoning, then a central source of experiences of pleasure in higher education does not exist. Lewis thought naturalism undermines the existence of higher education in an additional way. Though he did not explicitly set forth the main point of this section in terms of higher education, it is implied by his treatment of the topic of miracles in his book *Miracles* (see Lewis 2001c [1960 rev. ed.]) and Goetz 2018a: Chapter 5).

According to Lewis, higher education exists for a purpose. However, a purpose is something mental in nature insofar as it consists of content. For example, Lewis believed that the purpose for the existence of the university is that those involved in higher education experience pleasure from advanced intellectual activity. "That those involved in higher education experience pleasure from advanced intellectual activity" is content that refers to a state of affairs in the world. Yet naturalism, because it maintains that any event in this world in principle has a complete explanation in non-mental terms, entails that higher education cannot exist for this or any other purpose, because a purpose is an explanation that is mental in nature.

In *That Hideous Strength*, the last book in his space trilogy, Lewis has the naturalist psychology professor, Frost, say that "[i]n the light of what we now know, all history will have to be rewritten. The real causes of all the principal events are quite unknown to historians; that, indeed, is why history has not yet succeeded in becoming a science" (Lewis 2003b [1945]: 254). Echoing Lewis's character Frost, the real-life naturalist philosopher Alex Rosenberg has recently written books in which he claims that history gets things wrong because it explains events in terms of purposes:

> Our conscious thoughts are very crude indicators of what is going on in our brain. We fool ourselves into treating these conscious markers as thoughts about what we want and about how to achieve it, about plans and purposes. We are even tricked into thinking they somehow bring about behavior. We are mistaken about all of these things ... You cannot treat the interpretation of behavior in terms of purposes ... as conveying real understanding ... [T]he individual acts of human beings [are] unguided by purpose ... What individuals do, alone or together, over a moment or a month or a lifetime is really just the product of the process of blind variation and environmental filtration operating on neural circuits in their heads.
>
> (Rosenberg 2011: 210, 213, 244, 255)

Rosenberg recounts how the French diplomat Talleyrand spoke with other statesmen at the Congress of Vienna in 1815, which followed the defeat of Napoléon at Waterloo. Though the Congress was seemingly convened for the purpose of achieving a stable European order, Rosenberg maintains that

> [i]t had no purpose, and neither did the machinations of any of its participants. In fact, none of them—not Metternich [of Austria], not Talleyrand [of France], not Castlereagh [of Britain], and not Tsar Alexander [of Russia]—came to the Congress with any purpose. There

weren't and indeed aren't any purposes ... [though there] was and is the appearance of purpose.

(Rosenberg 2018: 231)

What explained the deliberations and negotiations of these individuals with each other at the Congress? Rosenberg writes about Talleyrand that there were

> firings in his hippocampus ... sending sharp wave ripples out across his neo-cortex, where they stimulated one neural circuit after another, until combined with firings from the pre-frontal cortex and ventral striatum, and doubtless a half dozen or more other regions of Talleyrand's brain, causing his throat, tongue, and lips to move and him to speak. No [purposeful] narrative to report here—just one damn electrochemical process after another.

(Rosenberg 2018: 160)

According to Rosenberg, then,

> human behaviors aren't really driven [explained] by purposes, ends, or goals ... Every behavior that looks like it's driven by a purpose is just the result of physical processes, like those of blind variation and natural selection uncovered by Darwin ...

(Rosenberg 2018: 206)

Readers might be thinking "This is crazy! Surely Rosenberg is not representative of a view held by other people in higher education. Are there really other individuals in the academy who believe what Rosenberg believes?"[3] Yes, there are. For example, another prominent naturalist, Richard Dawkins, explains how there can be no supernatural explanation of anything that occurs in our world:

> Indeed, to claim a supernatural explanation of something is not to explain it at all, even worse, to rule out any possibility of its ever being explained. Why do I say that? Because anything "supernatural" must by definition be beyond the reach of a natural explanation. It must be beyond the reach of science and the well-established, tried and tested scientific method. To say that something happened supernaturally is not just to say "We don't understand it" but to say "We will never

understand it, so don't even try." ... The whole history of science shows us that things once thought to be the result of the supernatural—caused by the gods (both happy and angry), demons, witches, spirits, curses, and spells—actually do have natural explanations: explanations that we can understand and test and have confidence in. There is absolutely no reason to believe that those things for which science does not *yet* have natural explanations will turn out to be of supernatural origin.

(Dawkins 2012: 21–2)

One might reasonably wonder what Dawkins believes a supernatural, as opposed to a non-supernatural or natural, explanation is. He provides an idea of what he thinks the difference is between them in the following comments:

People sometimes say, "Everything happens for a reason." In one sense this is true. Everything does happen for a reason—which is to say that events have causes, and the cause always comes before the event ... That is the true sense in which "everything happens for a reason", the sense in which "reason" means "past cause". But people sometimes use reason in a very different sense, to mean something like "purpose". They will say something like "The tsunami was punishment for our sins" or "The reason for the tsunami was to destroy the strip clubs and discos and bars and other sinful places." It is amazing how often people resort to this kind of nonsense.

(Dawkins 2012: 223)

In light of these two quotes, it is reasonable to conclude that Dawkins believes a supernatural explanation is an explanation in the form of a purpose, which is a species of mental explanation. By contrast, a natural explanation is a physical causal explanation, where a physical causal explanation is the kind of explanation typically sought in the physical sciences in terms of one non-mental event causally producing or necessitating another non-mental event.

If we conjoin these thoughts of Dawkins about the nature of a supernatural explanation with those of Rosenberg quoted above, it follows that naturalists believe that just as there cannot be divine purposeful supernatural explanations of events in our world, so also there cannot be human purposeful supernatural explanations of events in our world. Lewis was thoroughly aware of the implications of the truth of naturalism for purposeful explanations. In *That Hideous Strength*, Lewis has professor Frost make clear that

> [m]otives [purposes] are not causes [explanations] of action but its by-products. You are merely wasting your time by considering them. When you have attained real objectivity you will recognize, not *some* motives, but *all* motives are merely animal, subjective epiphenomena [real but having no explanatory relevance]. You will then have no motives and you will find that you do not need them [to explain bodily movements]. Their place will be supplied by something else which you will presently understand better than you do now.
>
> (Lewis 2003b [1945]: 293)

Elsewhere, Lewis described the implications of naturalism for purposeful explanations in terms of scientific determinism. According to scientific determinism, none of our behavior is originated by us for purposes but is instead the effect of purposeless mechanistic causes:

> Determinism does not deny the existence of human behaviour. It rejects as an illusion our spontaneous conviction that our behaviour has its ultimate origin in ourselves. What I call "my act" is the conduit-pipe through which the torrent of the universal process passes, and was bound to pass, at a particular time and place. The distinction between what we call the "voluntary" and the "involuntary" movements of our own bodies is not obliterated, but turns out ... to be not exactly the sort of difference we supposed. What I call the "involuntary" movements necessarily—and, if we know enough, predictably—result from mechanical causes outside my body or from pathological or organic processes within it. The "voluntary" ones result from conscious psychological factors which themselves result from unconscious psychological factors dependent on my economic situation, my infantile and pre-natal experience, my heredity ... and so on back to the beginnings of organic life and beyond. I am a conductor, not a source. I never made an original contribution to the world-process.
>
> (Lewis 1992a [1963]: 36–7)

Lewis made clear that the naturalist's insistence on the universal impotence of explanatory purposes and the efficacy of causal explanations alone implies that there is no place for either praising or condemning human actions (Lewis 2003b: 292). Lewis maintained that many of those who embrace naturalism fail to understand its implications, but, when they do, they find them incredible. But why should they? asked Lewis. "What should they find incredible, since they [believe] no longer in a rational universe?" (Lewis 2003b [1945]: 200).

Higher Education and Thinking about Naturalism

Lewis believed that (i) people in higher education derive pleasure from reasoning, (ii) reasoning is a form of higher-level intellectual activity that involves mental causal explanations, and, therefore, (iii) the occurrence of reasoning that takes place in higher education provides one way in which the existence of the academy falsifies naturalism. Moreover, the fact that people are involved in higher education for a purpose also falsifies naturalism. Thus, both the occurrence of reasoning in higher education and the explanation for membership in the academy are evidence for the existence of what Dawkins calls supernatural explanations, where a supernatural explanation is a mental explanation of an effect event, whether that effect event is mental or physical in nature.

Given that the existence of higher education falsifies naturalism, would Lewis have concluded that naturalism itself is not worth thinking and reasoning about? Not in the least. He believed that any position in which people are interested is open for thoughtful consideration, even if the truth of the position being considered implies that it cannot be considered (reasoned about). One can discern Lewis's intellectual openness to ideas and arguments in some comments he made about the Oxford Socratic Club, of which he was the president for many years. Lewis wrote in 1942–3 that the Club was established for the purpose of providing

> an arena specially devoted to the conflict between Christian and unbeliever ... Its value from a merely cultural point of view is very great. In any fairly large and talkative community such as a university, there is always the danger that those who think alike should gravitate together into *coteries* where they will henceforth encounter opposition only in the emasculated form of rumour that the outsiders say thus and thus. The absent are easily refuted, complacent dogmatism thrives, and differences of opinion are embittered by group hostility. Each group hears not the best, but the worst, that the other group can say ... At the very least we helped to civilize one another; sometimes we ventured to hope that if our Athenian patron were allowed to be present, unseen, at our meetings he might not have found the atmosphere wholly alien ... Those who founded it do not for one moment pretend to be neutral ... We never claimed to be impartial. But argument is. It has a life of its own. No man can tell where it will go. We expose ourselves ... to your fire no less than you are exposed to ours ... The arena is common to both parties and cannot finally be cheated.
>
> (quoted in Hooper in Como 2005: 243–4)

Lewis's comments imply that if naturalistic guests (or critics of his argument from reason against naturalism[4]) at the Socratic Club got the better of the argument, the Club's existence could no longer be justified. A good argument has a life of its own, and those who are aware of its course cannot help but believe its conclusion follows from its premises. Lewis would have affirmed that the university, like the Oxford Socratic Club, is not neutral. Its very existence entails the falsity of naturalism. Nevertheless, the best arguments for naturalism can be studied and debated, because those in the university get pleasure from thinking and reasoning about ideas and viewpoints and understanding their implications. Lewis believed that, were members of the university to come to believe that naturalism is true (though he was convinced they could not reason their way to this belief), then the university would cease to have a Dawkinsian supernatural explanation for its existence. It would not exist for a purpose. As Alex Rosenberg suggests above about the explanation for the presence of the attendees at the Congress of Vienna, the explanation for the presence of human beings in and as members of the university would be just one damn electrochemical process blindly causally producing another.

Naturalism and Experiences of Pleasure

Up to now in this chapter, I have focused on Lewis's beliefs about the implications of naturalism for the explanatory relevance of the mental in reasoning and acting. Lewis believed naturalism also undercuts the rationale for the existence of higher education for another reason: it eliminates the experiences of pleasure (and pain), period.

An experience of pleasure is what philosophers term a *quale* (plural *qualia*), which is the Latin name for a quality or that which is qualitative in nature. Lewis wrote about the importance of the qualitative for himself when he discussed the role of mental images (images that are located in the mind and have aboutness) in his life:

> I doubt if any act of will or thought or emotion occurs in me without them ... [I]n their total effect, they do mediate to me something very important. It is always something qualitative—more like an adjective than a noun. That, for me, gives it the impact of reality. For I think we respect nouns (and what we think they stand for) too much. All my deepest, and certainly all my earliest, experiences seem to be of sheer quality. The terrible and the lovely are older and solider than terrible and lovely things. If a musical phrase could be translated into words at all it would become an adjective. A great lyric is very like a long, utterly adequate, adjective. Plato was not so silly as the Moderns think when he elevated abstract nouns—that is, adjectives disguised as nouns—into the supreme realities—the Forms.
>
> (Lewis 1992a [1963]: 86)

Lewis stated that the Moderns think Plato was silly. The Moderns include naturalists who dismiss the reality of the qualitative that was so important to Lewis and most, if not all, people. For example, the naturalistic philosopher Jaegwon Kim has pointed out the inferior status of consciousness more generally and experiences of pleasure more particularly, if physicalism (and, by implication, naturalism) is true. I quote Kim at length:

> For most of us, there is no need to belabor the centrality of consciousness to our conception of ourselves as creatures with minds. But I want to point to the ambivalent, almost paradoxical, attitude that philosophers [read "naturalists"] have displayed toward consciousness ... [C]onsciousness had been virtually banished from the philosophical and scientific scene for much of the last century, and consciousness-bashing still goes on in some quarters, with some reputable philosophers arguing that phenomenal consciousness, or "qualia," is a fiction of bad philosophy. And there are philosophers ... who, while they recognize phenomenal consciousness as something real, do not believe that a complete science of human behavior, including cognitive psychology and neuroscience, has a place for consciousness ... in an explanatory/predictive theory of cognition and behavior [read "there is no place for mental-to-physical explanation"] ...
>
> Contrast this lowly status of consciousness in science and metaphysics with its lofty standing in moral philosophy and value theory. When philosophers discuss the nature of the intrinsic good, or what is worthy of our desire and volition for its own sake, the most prominently mentioned candidates are things like pleasure, absence of pain, enjoyment, and happiness ... To most of us, a fulfilling life, a life worth living, is one that is rich and full in qualitative consciousness. We would regard life as impoverished and not fully satisfying if it never included experiences of things like the smell of the sea in a cool morning breeze, the lambent play of sunlight on brilliant autumn foliage, the fragrance of a field of lavender in bloom, and the vibrant, layered soundscape projected by a string quartet ... It is an ironic fact that the felt qualities of conscious experience, perhaps the only things that ultimately matter to us, are often relegated in the rest of

philosophy to the status of "secondary qualities," in the shadowy zone between the real and the unreal, or even jettisoned outright as artifacts of confused minds.

(Kim 2005: 10, 11, 12)

In other words, naturalists are committed to denying a real and primary status to pleasures because *qualia* in general are not "at home" in a naturalistic world. They do not "fit" in it. Anyone who knows anything about the contemporary philosophy of mind understands this all too well. The most widely accepted naturalistic view of the mind in recent years has been what is known as *functionalism* according to which a state of mind is what it is in virtue of its causal role in a flow chart irrespective of its qualitative nature. For example, under functionalism pain is a state that is brought about by tissue damage or pressure or extremes of temperature and produces certain outputs or responses (cringes, the utterances of expletives, etc.). As the philosopher of mind John Heil points out, when you are in pain there are no doubt certain inputs that cause the pain and certain outputs that occur because of the pain. "But," writes Heil,

> could this be *all there is* to your being in pain? Surely, when you experience pain, your experience has a characteristic qualitative *feel*—a raw feel ... [T]here is "something it is like" to be in pain ... And this 'what it is like', the *qualitative aspect* of pain, seems conspicuously absent from the functionalist story ... The reason a state of pain leads you to whimper ... is that it is *painful*!
>
> (Heil 2020: 199)

Lewis agreed. He held that experiences of pleasure (and pain) "are unmistakably real, and therefore, as far as they go, give the man who feels them a touchstone of reality" (Lewis 1961b: 58). Moreover, he insisted that experiences of pleasure are bearers of real, positive, objective intrinsic value. But as we have seen, on the naturalistic view of reality all the explanatory work concerning events in this world must be done by what is non-mental in nature. Hence, naturalism implies that an experience of pleasure with its intrinsic goodness is explanatorily superfluous. Better to explain away, if possible, the reality of pleasure with its goodness than admit its existence. This is the position of naturalists, and Lewis, had he been a naturalist, would have concurred.

Lewis pointed out to his readers that naturalists often use science to justify the identification and, ultimately, elimination of pleasures and pains. He used what he called the distinction between "looking along" and "looking at" to illustrate the naturalist's "scientific" treatment of *qualia*:

> I was standing today in the dark toolshed. The sun was shining outside and through the crack at the top of the door there came a sunbeam. From where I stood that beam of light, with the specks of dust floating in it, was the most striking thing in the place. Everything else was almost pitch-black. I was seeing the beam, not seeing things by it.
>
> Then I moved, so that the beam fell on my eyes. Instantly the whole previous picture vanished. I saw no toolshed, and (above all) no beam. Instead I saw, framed in the irregular cranny at the top of the door, green leaves moving on the branches of a tree outside and beyond that, 90 odd million miles away, the sun. Looking along the beam [the latter experience], and looking at the beam [the former experience] are very different experiences.
>
> (Lewis [1945b] in 1970: 212)

Lewis applied the distinction between looking along and looking at to cerebral physiologists who study the human brain with its neural events and their relationship to human experiences. He believed a physiologist can look at neural events and learn about the correlations between them and experiences of pleasure only because the physiologist has first looked along pleasure by experiencing it. Lewis believed the naturalist uses this knowledge of the relevant correlations discovered by science to maintain erroneously the philosophical thesis that an experience of pleasure just is the same thing as an occurrence of the correlative neural events. He made the same point about correlations between what is looked at and what is looked along with respect to neural events and thinking. He emphasized that when we think, we are looking along mental events that are correlated with the neural events that a cerebral physiologist is looking at. Lewis insisted that events of thought that are looked along are not, contrary to what naturalists claim, identical with physical events that are looked at:

> The cerebral physiologist may say, if he chooses, that the mathematician's thought is "only" tiny physical movements of the grey matter. But then what about the cerebral physiologist's own thought at that very moment? A second physiologist, looking at it, could pronounce it also to be only tiny physical movements in the first physiologist's skull. Where is the rot to end?
>
> The answer is that we must never allow the rot to begin. We must, on pain of idiocy, deny from the very outset the idea that looking *at* is, by its own nature, intrinsically truer or better than looking *along*.
>
> (Lewis [1945b] in 1970: 215)

Lewis believed that what a physiologist sees when looking at a mathematician's brain is not the thinking that the mathematician looks along. The events looked at and along are at most correlated but not identical with each other. However, Lewis maintained that at some point causal interactions between the two occur. For example, Lewis believed that on occasions when we reason there is mental-to-physical causation: "Nature (at any rate on the surface of our own planet) is perforated or pock-marked all over by little orifices at each of which something of a different kind from herself—namely reason—can do things to her" (Lewis 2001c [1960 rev. ed.]: 40). In other words, it is the case that "whenever we think rationally we are, by direct spiritual [mental] power, forcing certain atoms in our brain ... to do what they would never have done if left to Nature" (Lewis 2001c [1960 rev. ed.]: 205). Similarly, he believed that when we choose to act for a purpose what ultimately explains the movements of our physical bodies is that purpose.

Purpose Is Not Pleasure

Lewis believed that experiences of pleasure and purposeful explanations of actions both falsify naturalism, but it is also important to make clear that he also would have insisted that purposefully explained intellectual activity is no guarantee of experiences of pleasure. For example, in his article entitled "The Power of Purpose-Driven Schools," Mark Oppenheimer describes how purpose in education can help sustain what is boring: "[E]ven when a student is not naturally drawn to a task—learning grammar, say, or trigonometry—she may perform better when she believes that being good at the task will help her make a difference in the world down the road" (Oppenheimer 2021). But, adds Oppenheimer, "finding higher purpose helps one endure the work, not love it" (Oppenheimer 2021). Lewis would have agreed, and while he would have conceded to Oppenheimer that purposefully pursued schoolwork might make that work endurable, higher education ideally should not involve work that is merely to be endured, even if purposefully. The purpose of higher-level intellectual activity is the experience of pleasure that comes from that activity.

Outstanding Issues

I have discussed at length Lewis's views of higher education in this and the preceding chapters. However, there are issues of import related to higher education that I have not treated because Lewis did not explicitly address them. In the next chapter, I consider a few of these topics. Given what Lewis did say, it is reasonable to think we can reliably construct a Lewisian position concerning them.

Addendum

Lewis recognized that we sometimes reason wrongly or incorrectly because of things like mental fatigue and inattention (Lewis [1939–1945?] in 1967: 63, 67–8). When we reason wrongly in these cases, a thinking of the conclusion has a mental cause other than the apprehensions of contents of premises and a valid inference (good reasoning) to a conclusion. "To be caused," wrote Lewis, "is not to be proved" (Lewis 2001c [1960 rev. ed.]: 24). Lewis also cited prejudice and wishful thinking as examples of non-rational mental causes that do not justify (properly cause) thinking of conclusions (Lewis 2001c [1960 rev. ed.]: 24). For example, we sometimes hear charges that a person believes in pacifism because he is afraid to fight, or that an individual believes in corporeal punishment because he or she enjoys seeing others experience pain (Lewis 2001c [1960 rev. ed.]: 55). These charges presuppose we know the distinction between a mental-to-mental causal explanation that justifies the inferring of a conclusion and one that does not. So, Lewis believed even reasoning wrongly falsifies naturalism.

5

Lewis and Higher Education Today

Contemporary Voices

C. S. Lewis believed in a utilitarian (instrumentalist) justification for higher education where the academy primarily exists for the purpose of experiencing the pleasure that comes with higher-level intellectual activity. Before addressing some additional questions that his view raises, it is helpful to elucidate Lewis's view of the purpose of the academy by considering two individuals' recent comments about the current state of higher education as it occurs in institutional universities.

In a monologue on his weekly television show on HBO, American political commentator and comedian Bill Maher recently took aim at higher education:

> [L]et's talk about what higher education in America really is: a racket that sells you a very expensive ticket to the upper-middle class. President Biden's American Families Plan asks the American taxpayers to pony up hundreds of billions so that everyone can go to college ... We imagine going to college is the way to fight income inequality, but actually it does the reverse ... I know that free college is a leftwing thing, but is it really liberal for someone who doesn't go to college and makes less money to pay for people who do go and make more? ... Colleges are businesses selling a consumer product for hundreds of thousands of dollars [all for a] magical piece of paper called a diploma ... I've heard this from so many nurses and teachers and administrators rolling their eyes when relating how they needed to take some bulls—course in order to advance in the field when really they've already learned what they need by working the job ... The answer isn't to make college free, the answer is to make it more unnecessary, which it is for most jobs.

So that the two-thirds of Americans who either can't afford to or just don't want to go don't feel shut out because the system we have sets up this winner-loser dynamic and breeds resentment ... and that in turn feeds into our widening political division.

(Maher 2021)

What might Lewis have said in response to Maher's comments? He likely would have answered that if the primary purpose of higher education is, as he (Lewis) believed, the experience of pleasure, then those who do not enjoy advanced intellectual activity have an excellent reason for not going to college. Given that many people do not derive pleasure from such intellectual activity, Lewis would have made clear that people who maintain that everyone should go to college are mistaken. Moreover, he would have made clear that an institution which exists for the purpose of training persons to be nurses or administrators is a vocational school, not a university. He would have added that the skills taught in a vocational school prepare people for work that is thoroughly honorable in nature. Individuals who are in higher education are different from those who are not, but this is not a difference that implies that the former are morally better, or more fully human, than the latter.

In a recent article, Allysia Finley describes how Linfield University in McMinnville, Oregon has sought to remain relevant to seekers of a college degree:

> Linfield ... resembles other small private colleges across the country struggling with financial pressures. Except its president, Miles K. Davis, isn't the typical ivory-tower intellectual.
>
> Mr. Davis, 61, has been pushing to change Linfield's institutionally stodgy and politically progressive academic culture, in part by placing an increased emphasis on career education. He's expanded his college's nursing and business programs and eliminated more than a dozen tenured faculty positions in liberal-arts disciplines. His efforts are a case study in the obstacles to change in the long-cosseted world of American higher education.
>
> "The academic world has become increasingly disconnected from the applied world," says Mr. Davis, the university's first black president,

in a Zoom interview. His effort to counter that trend provoked an ugly rebellion from the liberal-arts faculty. The usually sleepy college, established in 1858, has made national news as Linfield faculty rallied support from academics across the country in their campaign to drive Mr. Davis out.

"If you're not in the news, then you're probably not doing enough to adapt in this changing environment," says Mr. Davis ... Most colleges "were not set up to have people like me here," Mr. Davis says. "They were founded by the elite, often by religious orders or wealthy landowners to educate their children. Now, as society has changed and as we have increased the need for credentialing in society, a lot of people are coming into institutions who look more like me."

"[P]eople want a return on their investment," Mr. Davis says. "So the age in which we were able to offer education for the sake of inquiry has passed. It's passed because we priced ourselves out of that market."

Students nowadays "want clear career paths," and he set about reorganizing Linfield to meet that demand ... Linfield offered buyouts to 13 professors in liberal-arts programs with shrinking enrollment. "I know it's unpopular to talk about this in education these days, but you just can't keep offering things from a 'field of dreams' perspective—that if you build it, they'll come," he says. "You have to be aware of changing needs in society in order to develop relevant programs that people are willing to pay for" ... Mr. Davis pressed to expand the nursing and business programs, which are more remunerative. The average annual salary of a recent graduate of Linfield's nursing program is $83,349, vs. $20,140 for a Linfield psychology degree.

(Finley 2021)

The assumptions motivating Davis's presidency of Linfield University are those of many people today. One assumption is that higher education exists for the purpose of credentialing people to get a job that pays well, supplanting the bygone purpose of education, in Davis's words, "for the sake of inquiry." Another assumption is that institutions of higher learning that exist for some non-credentialing purposes (e.g., the pleasure of higher-level intellectual activity) are elitist and inaccessible to certain segments of society.

We know that Lewis would have answered Davis that the primary purpose of higher education is not inquiry (higher-level intellectual activity). Lewis believed the pleasure many individuals experience from advanced intellectual activity in the form of inquiry is what justifies the existence of the academy. Moreover, Lewis believed the pursuit of higher-level intellectual activity for the sake of pleasure is not inherently elitist in nature. He held that no one is morally better as a human being, or more spiritual and pleasing to God, simply in virtue of being a member of the academy for the purpose of experiencing the pleasure of that intellectual activity.

Davis and others who share his belief about what justifies the existence of higher education might respond that Lewis was simply denying the truth if he believed his understanding of the purpose of higher education did not necessarily arise out of and sustain an elitist motivation. Did Lewis really believe that those in higher education for the pleasure of advanced intellectual activity do not inevitably treat those outside the university as inferior human beings, and did he really fail to understand that those who enjoy involvement in higher education in many instances also achieve a better standard of living than those who are outside the academy?

As we have seen in previous chapters, Lewis understood the problem of elitism all too well, but he would have insisted that people in higher education are not, simply because of their involvement, elitists. If they are elitists it is because of their immoral choice to treat those outside the academy as second- or third-rate human beings. Lewis believed we should not be surprised that these people in higher education choose as they do because the human race is composed, in theological terms, of fallen people, and fallen people have the freedom to choose wrongly to mistreat their fellow human beings. Lewis reminded his readers of the fallen nature of the human race in terms of what might happen if humans were to encounter another form of rational species in the universe:

> I have no pleasure in looking forward to a meeting between humanity and any alien rational species. I observe how the white man has

hitherto treated the black, and how, even among civilized men, the stronger have treated the weaker. If we encounter in the depth of space a race, however innocent and amiable, which is technologically weaker than ourselves, I do not doubt that the same revolting story will be repeated. We shall enslave, deceive, exploit or exterminate; at the very least we shall corrupt it with our vices and infect it with our diseases.

(Lewis [1963b] in 1967: 173)

We know what our race does to strangers. Man destroys or enslaves every species he can. Civilized man murders, enslaves, cheats, and corrupts savage man. Even inanimate nature he turns into dust bowls and slag-heaps. There are individuals who don't. But they are not the sort who are likely to be our pioneers in space. Our ambassador to new worlds will be the needy and greedy adventurer or the ruthless technical expert. They will do as their kind has always done. What that will be if they meet things weaker than themselves, the black man and the red man can tell.

(Lewis [1958b] in 1987: 89)

Davis clearly thinks of people interested in the liberal arts (which, for our purposes, is higher-level intellectual activity) as not only elitist but also stodgy individuals with a "field-of-dreams" or ivory-tower perspective. In his mind, these persons have intellectual interests that prove not to be relevant for the economic market place. It is reasonable to hold that Lewis would have responded to Davis that those who are in higher education for the right reason are experiencing pleasure at the only time it can be experienced, which is in the present. They take their long-term plans somewhat lightly and enjoy the daily bread which they have been given and for which they are encouraged to pray. Lewis would have added that the paradox of hedonism suggests that those enjoy the liberal arts without a concern for their future employment in the economic market place will more often than not land on their feet in work outside the walls of the academy. They will land on their feet because they enjoy the life of higher-level intellectual activity, and advanced intellectual activity is the heart and soul of, or important to, professions in the economic market place such as medicine, computer science, biotechnology, engineering, aerospace, teaching, library science, clergy work, and on and on. And, Lewis would have stressed, it is a matter of common sense that employers like to hire people who enjoy their work, because individuals who enjoy what they do tend to do it well.

Let's Be Reasonable

In his book entitled *Let's Be Reasonable*, Jonathan Marks claims that "our colleges and universities [should be] communities of students and faculty who [consider] it a disgrace not to listen to reason ... If universities, distracted by other things, fail [at the work of cultivating ... reason, and pride in being reasonable], students and graduates marching under those other banners are unlikely to do themselves or others much good" (Marks 2021a: 6). Marks maintains that "the shaping of [reasonable people is] liberal education's aim" (Marks 2021a: 12). He adds that the goal of professors is "to cultivate in our students an experience of and a taste for reflecting on fundamental questions, for following arguments where they lead, and for shaping their thoughts and actions in accordance with what they can learn from those activities" (Marks 2021a: 15).

Lewis shared Marks' belief in the importance of reason (higher-level intellectual activity) in the purpose of the academy, but would have disagreed with Marks' explanation of that importance. Lewis believed higher education, if it is fulfilling its purpose, does not have to be concerned about the disgrace of students and faculty not listening to reason because they are in higher education for the pleasure that comes from listening to reason. They desire to listen to reason because doing so is enjoyable. Lewis thought that a person in higher education would need a reason not to listen to reason. True, an individual might lose his desire for and interest in higher-level intellectual activity. However, if that were to happen, Lewis would have maintained the person would have an excellent reason to leave higher education because he no longer derived pleasure from it. And there would be no disgrace in leaving, because advanced intellectual activity is not virtuous activity whose absence leaves a person less perfected as a human being.

With regard to Marks' idea of "shaping" reasonable people, Lewis likely would have said there are two senses of "reasonable" which are relevant in the current context and they should be clearly distinguished. In the first sense of "reasonable," a person is reasonable who, once having apprehended the premises of a good deductive argument, cannot help but infer its conclusion (see Chapter 4). The individual's awareness of the argument's premises "shapes," in conformity with the rule of inference, his arrival at the conclusion by causally determining his awareness of the conclusion. Marks writes a good bit about constructively shaming (Marks 2021a: 68–72) those who do not follow reason: "[S]ince we regularly fail to follow arguments where they lead, fail to persist in thinking when thinking gets hard, and fail to stick with arguments that threaten our self-confidence, good teachers have to make us feel these vices" (Marks 2021a: 70). Lewis would have recognized that a person might find it hard to follow an argument. But if an individual cannot, after trying, understand an argument's premises or its logical structure, then that is not his fault and he should not, Lewis believed, be shamed for not being able to do so. Furthermore, Lewis would have held that if a person gets pleasure from reasoning, then he will stick with it when it becomes difficult so long as he continues to experience pleasure (or believes he will eventually experience pleasure) from doing so. If at some point he no longer derives pleasure from his effort to understand the premises, then he will recognize that he gave his best effort and there is nothing about which to be ashamed. His self-confidence might be shaken, but Lewis would have said that this is a psychological issue which each of us has to learn to face and address. But it is not an issue for which shaming is appropriate.

In the second sense of "reasonable," a person who is reasonable acts in accordance with what he finds it reasonable (e.g., virtuous) to do. Lewis believed higher education is not the place to learn to be reasonable in this sense. Reasonable behavior is supposed to be learned in primary and secondary school. Those in higher education simply assume that people who are there are reasonable in the sense that concerns their actions.

Secular or Naturalist Universities?

George M. Marsden, a historian of American higher education, defines "secular activities" as "activities ... conducted without direct religious reference," though those activities are not "necessarily antireligious" (Marsden 2014: 104–5). If, with Marsden, we think of secular activities as those that are not done for a religious purpose, then Lewis believed higher-level intellectual activity that is pursued exclusively for the purpose of experiencing pleasure is secular in nature. Though he believed a Christian who derives pleasure from such intellectual activity can and should also pursue it to the glory of God (see the following section), Lewis also thought a person can derive pleasure from being intellectually engaged with biology, chemistry, English, history, politics, philosophy, and physics without doing so for an additional religious reason.

What Lewis believed is inconsistent with advanced intellectual activity is not secularism but naturalism. As we have seen (see Chapter 4), he thought naturalism undermines all intellectual activity, and it does so because it denies the reality of mental explanations of some events in this world (arriving at conclusions in reasoning and certain motions of our physical bodies brought about for purposes) as well as the reality of experiences of pleasure (and pain). In short, while Lewis believed there is conceptual space for secular colleges and universities, he thought there is no such space for colleges and universities espousing naturalism.

Christian Universities

Lewis was a Christian for about the last thirty-two years of his life, and he taught during those years at Oxford and Cambridge universities whose original colleges (Oxford and Cambridge are made up of individual colleges) were Christian. But what, one might ask, makes higher education Christian in nature? Lewis would have made clear that Christian higher education believes in the reality of mental explanations of some events in this world (e.g., going to college for the purpose of experiencing pleasure; the apprehension of premises of an argument causally determining the apprehension of the argument's conclusion), while also affirming non-mental, physical explanations of other events (e.g., a virus causing a sore throat and cold; lightning striking a tree and causing its fall). He would have reminded people that the reality of mental explanations is no small matter for the existence of higher education itself. Most people, including Christians, believe the existence of higher education is explained in terms of a purpose. These individuals often disagree about what that purpose is, but they, unlike naturalists, agree that the existence of the university has a purposeful explanation.

But while Lewis would have insisted acknowledging the reality of mental explanations of some events is a necessary condition of higher education that is Christian, it is not a sufficient condition because someone (e.g., Jews, Muslims, some secularists) can affirm the reality of mental explanations of some events in our world without being Christian. What, then, in addition to the acknowledgment of mental explanations is required to make higher education Christian in nature? I am not aware of any place where Lewis explicitly answered this question. However, I believe it is reasonable to maintain that he would have affirmed some version of his thoughts about "mere Christianity" in answer to the question. He stated in the Preface to *Mere Christianity* that

> [e]ver since I became a Christian I have thought that the best, perhaps the only, service I could do for my unbelieving neighbours was to explain and defend the belief that has been common to nearly all

> Christians at all times ... [T]he questions which divide Christians from one another often involve points of high Theology or even of ecclesiastical history ... I think we must admit that the discussion of these disputed points has no tendency at all to bring an outsider into the Christian fold ... [I have written] in the defence of what Baxter calls "mere" Christianity.
>
> (Lewis 2001b [1952]: viii–ix)

In another place, Lewis wrote about mere Christianity that

> if any man is tempted to think—as one might be tempted who read[s] only contemporaries—that "Christianity" is a word of so many meanings that it means nothing at all, he can learn beyond all doubt, by stepping out of his own century, that this is not so. Measured against the ages "mere Christianity" turns out to be no insipid interdenominational transparency, but something positive, self-consistent, and inexhaustible.
>
> (Lewis [1944e] in 1970: 203)

What, then, is common to the belief of Christians of all times and places? With guidance from the Apostles' Creed, I think Lewis would have claimed that higher education that is "mere Christian" in nature must affirm the existence of God as Creator of heaven and earth and everything contained therein, the Incarnation, life, death, and Resurrection of Jesus Christ, the forgiveness of sins, and the resurrection of the body and everlasting life (perfect happiness, beatitude). It also seems reasonable to maintain that Lewis's belief about the primary purpose of higher education entails he would have insisted that a university's Christian nature cannot rightly provide the primary explanation for its (the university's) existence. As an institution of higher education, a Christian university's existence, like any other university's existence, must be fundamentally explained in terms of the pleasure that comes from advanced intellectual activity.

As I alluded to in Chapter 2, Lewis believed that experiences of pleasure with their goodness are reminders of or messages from God:

> We can't—or I can't—hear the song of a bird simply as a sound. Its meaning or message ("That's a bird") comes with it inevitably—just as

one can't see a familiar word in print as a merely visual pattern. The reading is as involuntary as the seeing. When the wind roars I don't just hear the roar; I "hear the wind" ... [T]o receive [pleasure] and to recognise its divine source are a single experience. This heavenly fruit is instantly redolent of the orchard where it grew. The sweet air whispers of the country from whence it blows. It is a message ... One could, if one practised, hear simply a roar and not the roaring-of-the-wind. In the same way, only far too easily, one can concentrate on the pleasure as an event in one's own nervous system—subjectify it—and ignore the smell of Deity that hangs about it.

(Lewis 1992a [1963]: 89–90)

Lewis thought that the pleasure that accompanies advanced intellectual activity has the smell of deity about it, and presumably he would have maintained that the recognition of this "message" of deity is, or at least can be, a source of a justification for a university being theistic in nature. Lewis also wrote about what he termed "appreciative pleasures," which are pleasures experienced with the understanding that the object that is the source of the pleasure deserves to be appreciated, where this understanding presupposes a judgment about the object's goodness:

> This judgment that the object is very good, this attention (almost homage) offered to it as a kind of debt, this wish that it should be and should continue being what it is even if we were never to enjoy it, can go out not only to things but to persons. When it is offered to a woman we call it admiration; when to a man, hero-worship; when to God, worship simply.
>
> (Lewis 1988 [1960]: 16–17)

In other words, Lewis believed that the appreciation of pleasurable intellectual activity naturally leads to the worship of God as the object which ultimately provides the experience of pleasure. And he thought that the experience of pleasure also flows over into praise which is itself accompanied by pleasure:

> [A]ll enjoyment spontaneously overflows into praise unless (sometimes even if) shyness or the fear of boring others is deliberately brought in to

check it. The world rings with praise—lovers praising their mistresses, readers their favorite poet, walkers praising the countryside ... I had not noticed how the humblest, and at the same time most balanced and capacious, minds, praised most ... I had not noticed either that just as men spontaneously praise whatever they value, so they spontaneously urge us to join them in praising it ... The Psalmists in telling everyone to praise God are doing what all men do when they speak of what they care about ... [W]e delight to praise what we enjoy because the praise not merely expresses but completes the enjoyment; it is its appointed consummation ... [T]he delight is incomplete till it is expressed.

(Lewis 1986b [1958]: 94–5)

It is reasonable to conclude that Lewis would have found the idea of worship and praise of God at a Christian university in no way incompatible with the advanced intellectual activity and accompanying pleasure that justifies its pursuit, but rather a thoroughly appropriate completion of that pleasurable activity. And he would have added that all of this redounds to the glory of God, which he thought of in terms of brightness, splendor, or luminosity (Lewis [1941] in 2001g: 42).

Furthermore, Lewis believed higher-level intellectual activity and the experiences of pleasure that accompany it are events which occur in souls which are entities (substances) that are distinct from their physical bodies (what philosophers term "soul-body substance dualism"). Lewis wrote that "we ourselves and all that we most care about seem to come in the class 'concrete (that is, individual) and insensible.' If reality consists of nothing but physical objects and abstract concepts, then reality has, in the last resort, nothing to say to us" (Lewis 1992a [1963]: 114). When asked "*What is a soul*?," Lewis answered "I am. (This is the only possible answer: or expanded, 'A soul is that which can say I am')" (Lewis 2007: 10).[1] Hence, he would have thought it appropriate for members of a Christian university to affirm the existence of the soul as an entity that is a substance in its own right and separable from its physical body. Many members of universities today, because they are naturalists, deny not only the reality of reasoning and the explanatory efficacy of purposes but also soul-body dualism. For example, the naturalistic psychologist Paul

Bloom points out that while all of us initially believe in the existence of the soul as a substance that is distinct from its physical body, "[o]ne of the first things an undergraduate learns in an introduction to psychology class is that substance dualism is mistaken" (Bloom 2007: 149). But given Lewis believed there are no good reasons to be a naturalist and deny mental explanations (see Goetz 2018a: Chapters 2 and 5), he would have also insisted there are no good reasons not to affirm soul-body dualism.

In light of these thoughts about the relationships between pleasure, appreciation, worship, and a Christian university, what might Lewis have believed leads someone to (want to) become a member of such an intellectual community? I think he would have answered that what first and foremost leads a person to have an interest in being a member of a Christian university is the "What?-You-too?" experience (see the Introduction) which those who love the same thing share as a basis of friendship.

Lewis, as I have said, was an advocate for what he termed "mere Christianity." For those Christian universities which desire and/or believe they need to be more than merely Christian, Lewis would probably have recognized the legitimacy of adding further theological statements for affirmation by their members, which would amount to those individuals leaving the main hallway of mere Christianity and entering a denominational room with its more specific theological distinctions (Lewis 2001b [1952]: xv–xvi).

"Faith-Based" Higher Education?

In describing Lewis's view of higher education as it relates to Christian universities, I have purposefully not used the terms "faith-based universities" or "faith-based colleges." The reason for my avoiding these terms is that they suggest that the foundation of a Christian university is the Christian faith of the persons who belong. Lewis would have objected to this idea for the reason I have already mentioned in the previous section, which is that a Christian university is first and foremost a university. The university's being Christian makes it a species of a genus, where what defines the genus is the occurrence of advanced intellectual activity.

Where, if at all, one might ask, do seminaries (theological colleges), with their goal of training people to serve as clergy in a church or parish ministry, fit into this discussion of the idea of a Christian university? It is plausible to think Lewis would have believed that a seminary, like a law or medical school, is an institution with a vocational purpose. He would have maintained that ideally a person in clerical vocational training will derive pleasure from the higher-level intellectual activity that is needed for it. And perhaps the charter of a seminary includes a purpose statement to the effect that the advanced intellectual activity that is required for church work should be enjoyed.[2] But the main point for Lewis would have been that the justification for the existence of the higher-level intellectual activity in a seminary is not the pleasure that comes from intellectual activity but the vocational goal of developing a person for work in an ecclesiastical setting.[3]

And what about Bible colleges? If the advanced intellectual activity that takes place therein is for the purpose of promoting spiritual growth through instruction in and study of the Bible, then Lewis would likely have maintained that Bible colleges have a purpose that, while it requires higher-level intellectual activity, makes them more akin to primary and secondary schools with their eudaimonistic (virtuous) aims.

Lewis believed that few people read the Bible unless they regard it as a sacred text that provides religious instruction. In an essay entitled "The Literary Impact of the Authorized Version," Lewis stated that he thought "it very unlikely that the Bible will return as a book [that is read] unless it returns as a sacred book ... among the believing minority who read it to be instructed and get literary enjoyment as a by-product" (Lewis [1950] in 1969: 144–5). But might not people generally, whether or not they are in the believing minority, read the Bible for the purpose of literary pleasure? Lewis conceded they might. However, he was convinced not many would:

The Bible ... considered ... as a single book, has been read for almost every purpose more diligently than for literary pleasure ... I cannot help suspecting ... that those who read the Bible as literature do not read the Bible ... You can read it as literature only by a *tour de force.* You are cutting the wood against the grain, using the tool for a purpose it was not intended to serve. It demands incessantly to be taken on its own terms: it will not continue to give literary delight [pleasure] very long except to those who go to it for something quite different.

(Lewis [1950] in 1969: 127, 142, 144)

Lewis did acknowledge that if the Bible were read neither as a sacred book nor as literature, it might still be the subject of "the specialist's study" (Lewis [1950] in 1969: 145). Here, I think he meant that the Bible could be read and studied by academicians such as anthropologists, sociologists, and historians. In this case, it would be read to learn about the lifestyle and history of the nation of Israel and the early Christian church in the same way that Herodotus, Thucydides, Seutonius, and Pliny are read and studied to learn about the classical Greeks and Romans. Those who read the Bible in this way would be reading it as a form of advanced intellectual activity and for the pleasure that comes from so reading it. They would be reading it as members of the university read it.

Who Decides What Is Studied in Higher Education?

The fact that there are many areas of study through which to satisfy the desire for the pleasure of higher-level intellectual activity raises the question "Who determines the subject matter (curriculum) in higher education?" It is plausible to hold that Lewis would have answered, "The individuals inside higher education with their intellectual interests." In light of his belief in the reality of the "What?-You-too?" experience, Lewis believed people with the same or similar intellectual interests will naturally seek out membership in academic settings which are populated with people who share, and courses of study and research that match, their own academic tastes. Lewis would likely have insisted that those inside the academy should not accommodate the demand of those outside who mandate that this or that subject be included in a university's list of subjects for study. Potential members of the academy, whether teachers or pupils, should be allowed to vote with their feet in the sense that they should be permitted to seek to become members of (or associated with) institutions or groups of higher learning whose intellectual ethos best matches and nurtures their own intellectual interests from which they derive pleasure.

It is worth emphasizing that Lewis believed membership in an institution of higher learning whose intellectual ethos best matches your own academic interests which are pursued for pleasure does not mean membership in an institution where you read, talk, write, reason about, and come to understand only those views with which you agree. Quite the contrary. He repeatedly wrote about the pleasure that comes with seeing the world and things in it through the eyes of others with different perspectives. Lewis referred to the impulse

> to go out of the self, to correct its provincialism and heal its loneliness. In love, in virtue, in the pursuit of knowledge, and in the reception of the arts, we are doing this. Obviously this process can be described either as an enlargement or as a temporary annihilation of the self. But that is an old paradox; "he that loseth his life shall save it".
>
> We therefore delight to enter into other men's beliefs ... even though we think them untrue. And into their passions, though we think them depraved ... And also into their imaginations, though they lack all realism of content.
>
> (Lewis 1961a: 138–9)[4]

Thus, Lewis believed that people who are not naturalists can, if they desire, read, write, and talk about the works of naturalists, and individuals who are Christians can, if they desire, read and study the works of non-Christians. As someone who enjoyed reading and thinking about different points of view, Lewis would have reminded people that if it should turn out that Christianity is false, then so much the worse for Christian universities: "If Christianity is untrue, then no honest man will want to believe it, however helpful it might be ..." (Lewis [1946?] in 1970: 108-9). And while Lewis believed naturalism is false, he would have insisted that if naturalism is true, then so much the worse for higher education.

What would Lewis have thought about what in America are termed "great books" curricula? Roosevelt Montás, the director of Columbia University's Center for the Core Curriculum from 2008 to 2018, describes how the Core Curriculum is composed of required humanities courses which present, in chronological order, major texts in literature, ethics and politics, visual art, and music (Montás 2021: 210-13). Montás discusses the Core Curriculum's focus on the Western tradition and those persons who criticize this emphasis in terms of its lack of inclusivity, diversity, and representation. Montás believes such criticism is inherent and integral to the liberal education which the Core Curriculum provides. He adds that sadly the faculty and administrators at most institutions of higher learning have concluded that arguments and defenses for core curricula are not worth the trouble, and they have supplanted such curricula with distribution requirements, or no requirements at all, which allows faculty and students "to stay within their intellectual comfort zones" (Montás 2021: 215). While Montás says this abandonment of the idea of a core curriculum is understandable, it is "one that shirks a basic responsibility of the faculty and which, in the long run, does a disservice to the students, to the institution, and to society" (Montás 2021: 215). Montás writes that

> the underlying force driving the disintegration of undergraduate curricula is not a passion for student choice or a commitment to diversity, but a crisis of consensus among academic humanists about what things are most worth *knowing*. And because debates about curricula are likely to be had in moral terms—not between what is educationally good or bad but between what is ethically pure or corrupt—it is simply easier for colleges to avoid having them altogether.
> (Montás 2021: 74)

Lewis would likely have made the following two points in response to Montás. First, he would have maintained that the place for a core curriculum, which is analogous to "[Matthew] Arnold's ideal—'the best that is known and thought in the world'" (Lewis 1939a: 75), is the pre-university school, not higher education. He wrote that the best of what is known and thought "may train your mind and make you in the Aristotelian sense a better man; but are you [students in the university] not old enough now to cease being trained?" (Lewis 1939a: 89).[5] Lewis believed that higher education is the place where a student should be "turned loose on some tract of reality as it is" (Lewis 1939a: 88), a tract of reality "he [the student] is interested in" (Lewis 1939a: 61), which will provide him with pleasure. Lewis thought, using the words of Montás, that permitting a student in higher education to focus on a specific place, idea, or issue is not a matter of allowing him or her to stay in his or her comfort zone, but a matter of what provides him or her with the pleasure of higher-level intellectual activity. True, focusing on some tract of reality is a matter of increasing specialization, and "specialization suggests narrowing and narrowing suggests confinement ... [T]here is, of course, an obvious sense in which the specialist is narrower than the man reading a selection of 'great literatures'. But is there not a sense in which he is freer?" (Lewis 1939a: 75). Montás mentions how he resented people's expectations at Columbia concerning "what [he] was supposed to like ... what classes and topics [he] was supposed to be interested in" (Montás 2021: 112). Lewis likely would have maintained that Montás's resentment makes perfect sense at the level of higher education because the purpose for being a member of the university is to engage in the intellectual activity which provides you with experiences of pleasure.

Second, Lewis probably would have reminded us that when Montás refers to "what things are most worth *knowing*" (Montás 2021: 74), the reference to worth is a reference to value, and he (Lewis) believed the most fundamental value is the nonmoral goodness of the pleasure that in the case of higher education accompanies intellectual activity. On Lewis's view, what is most worth knowing for persons in the academy is the topic, idea, or tract of reality which gives them pleasure. Amartya Sen writes that when he was a graduate student at Cambridge University and searching for a research topic for his doctoral thesis, a faculty member, Joan Robinson, "wanted me to join her in doing capital theory. She told me, 'This is where really original work can be done,' adding, 'let us together put the last nail in the coffin of neoclassical economics.'" Sen says that "[w]hen I told Maurice Dobb [another faculty member] about Joan's advice, he responded, 'Leave the nailing to her, and do whatever interests you most'" (Sen 2021: 294). Lewis would have seconded Dobb's advice.

Did Lewis think *any* topic could legitimately be on the table for advanced thought, study, and discussion, or did he believe that certain topics were out of bounds? Asked slightly differently, given Lewis believed morality puts constraints on the ways we choose to seek bodily pleasures, say the pleasures of sex and drink, did he also believe morality constrains the ways we choose to pursue higher-level intellectual pleasures?

Lewis most certainly would have acknowledged constraints on the choices we might make to pursue pleasures of the intellect. While discussing forgiveness, Lewis wrote the following:

> Suppose one reads a story of filthy atrocities in the paper. Then suppose that something turns up suggesting that the story might not be quite true, or not quite so bad as it was made out. Is one's first feeling, "Thank God, even they aren't quite so bad as that," or is it a feeling of disappointment, and even a determination to cling to the first story for the sheer pleasure of thinking your enemies as bad as possible? If it is the second then it is, I am afraid, the first step in a process which, if followed to the end, will make us into devils. You see, one is beginning to wish that black was a little blacker. If we give that wish its head, later on we shall wish to see grey as black, and then to see white itself as black. Finally, we shall insist on seeing everything— God and our friends and ourselves included—as bad, and not be able to stop doing it: we shall be fixed for ever in a universe of pure hatred.
> (Lewis 2001b [1952]: 118)

Similarly, Lewis would have found a choice to dwell in thought on the unjust misfortunes of others you dislike or of whom you are jealous for the purpose of experiencing pleasure morally objectionable. And he would have insisted that choosing higher-level intellectual activity directed at, say, developing ways to experiment on or harm the innocent for the sake of pleasure, is morally reprehensible. Most generally, Lewis believed the moral status of an action, its being moral or immoral, is determined by the purpose for which the choice to perform the action is made (see Goetz 2018a: 98–102), and he believed this principle is just as true of advanced intellectual activity that is chosen as it is true of chosen bodily activity. However, he would have insisted that many instances of advanced intellectual activity pursued for the purpose of experiencing pleasure, including the intellectual activity of thinking and writing about the purpose of higher education itself, are morally innocent.[6]

But what about higher-level intellectual activity concerning a contentious topic like an individual's race and its relationship to that person's interest and success in higher education? What did or would Lewis have thought about a choice to engage in intellectual activity concerning it? Here, I must plead ignorance: I am unaware of any place where Lewis explicitly answered this question, or one like it, about higher-level intellectual activity and race. However, from reading and rereading his works I am convinced he would have maintained that consideration of race in higher education can be morally innocent. Thus, I think he would have maintained that if you have a desire for and derive pleasure from reading and thinking about the notion of race and its relationship to interest and success in higher education, then you do nothing wrong in focusing on its relationship to these matters.

What if, however, you were interested in researching the issues of race and interest and success in higher education among different racial groups, and you knew in advance that you might discover that members of racial group A have more interest and success in higher education than members of racial group B? And what if you also were to believe that many people who have hostility to members of racial group A would feel bolstered by the finding that members of that group have, on average, lower interest and success in higher education than members of racial group B? Furthermore, what if you were to believe that the public dissemination of your finding would or might bring about serious harm to members of group A (it would or might subject them to racist abuse and discrimination)? Would Lewis have claimed your research would nevertheless be permissible?

I am convinced Lewis would have maintained that reading and thinking about the issues of race and its relationship to interest and success in higher education with respect to members of racial groups A and B would itself be morally innocent. However, it is plausible to think he would have said that given your belief about what others might do with the results of your research, your reason for choosing to publish them would be all important. If your reason for choosing to publish them were that you aid and abet those with the stated hostility, then your choice would be immoral. However, if your reason for choosing to publish them were, say, to increase interest and success in higher education for members of the racial group in question, then, depending upon whether you do or do not have a desire to publish the results of your research, your choice would be morally either innocent or commendable. Lewis often expressed his views about what is moral and immoral in terms of the idea of conscience. Thus, if you were to believe that it was wrong for you to choose to publish your results for the reason that you aid and abet the hostile group, and you nevertheless went ahead and chose to publish them for this reason, then he would have insisted that you chose immorally because you violated your conscience (see Goetz 2018a: 108–9).

Someone might respond that all of this is interesting, but would want to know whether Lewis was, as a matter of fact, interested in race as it relates to participation in higher education. As a subject for study in higher education, I suspect he was not interested. Were he to have been involved in the establishment of an institution of higher learning, I think he would not have included such a topic for intellectual consideration on the grounds that it did not pique his interest as a source of pleasure.[7] In saying this, I am in no way saying or implying that Lewis had no views about race. Lewis believed white people had badly mistreated non-whites, as I pointed out in the first section of this chapter with my mention of Lewis's belief about the fallen nature of human beings and what would happen if they were someday to meet non-human, rational creatures from other worlds in the universe: "Against [those creatures] we shall, if we can, commit all the crimes we have already committed against creatures certainly human but differing from us in features and pigmentation" (Lewis [1958b] in 1987: 89–90). In addition, Lewis believed Christian missionary work had not always been done in a virtuous way: "The missionary's holy desire to save souls has not always been kept quite distinct from the arrogant desire, the busybody's itch, to (as he calls it) 'civilize' (as he calls them) 'natives'" (Lewis [1958b] in 1987: 90). However, having a view about race is different from deriving pleasure from higher-level intellectual activity concerning it and related topics. And my sense is that Lewis for the most part, if not entirely, lacked the latter.

Higher Education: The Individual versus the State

Throughout this book, I have focused on what Lewis believed is the purpose of higher education from the perspective of the individual person, as opposed to the state, because Lewis thought the former, and not the latter, is what is ultimately important:

> If individuals live only seventy years, then a state, or a nation, or a civilisation, which may last for a thousand years, is more important than an individual. But if Christianity is true, then the individual is not only more important but incomparably more important, for he is everlasting and the life of a state or a civilisation, compared with his, is only a moment.
>
> (Lewis 2001b [1952]: 74–5)

While Lewis believed in the primary importance of the individual, he nevertheless recognized that the state has the power to affect positively the lives of individuals. Given this potential cause-effect relationship, it is only reasonable to think he believed it is important that the state make use of people who enable it to function efficiently on behalf of the individuals whose lives it impacts. If we ask "Who are the people most likely to be capable of contributing to this efficient functioning?", it is reasonable to conclude Lewis believed that those individuals who enjoy the higher-level intellectual activity that best suits the needs of the state are the persons most likely to facilitate its smooth functioning: "we do not want our rulers to be dunces" (Lewis [1955] in 1987: 41).[8]

However, Lewis understood all too well that the state, in an effort to satisfy its needs with the requisite people, will seek to increase its control over advanced intellectual activity. Thus, as Steven Loomis and Jacob Rodriguez argue in their book *C. S. Lewis: A Philosophy of Education* (Loomis and Rodriguez 2009), the modern western state is slowly but surely exerting more and more control over its citizens' lives. It is seeking to make higher education available to everyone (regardless of whether a person enjoys intellectual activity) and standardizing the curriculum so that those who complete it are prepared to get a job in the civic machine. According to Lewis's brother, Warren, whom I quoted in the Introduction, England was already in the days of their youth seeking to control education through the public schools with the goal of producing young men who would be replacement parts for its governmental machinery.

Loomis and Rodriguez also claim that because the modern western state is increasingly naturalistic in its outlook, it is supporting the exclusion of purposeful explanations of actions from academic disciplines in the academy. Psychology is being turned into neuroscience and politics into political science, with the belief that as our knowledge of biology, chemistry, and physics increases we will discover more of the physical laws according to which our human behavior is causally explained and determined. An additional point that Loomis and Rodriguez do not make is that if the state's educational apparatus is run by what Lewis called "Conditioners," people who deny any objective value, even though they are "motivated simply by their own pleasure" (Lewis 2001d [1944]: 65), then these individuals, because they do not believe pleasure is intrinsically good, will not hesitate to deny the freedom to pursue advanced intellectual activity for enjoyment. Given these points, it is reasonable to conclude Lewis thought that a person with his understanding of the purpose of higher education will find it increasingly difficult to secure a place and feel at home in contemporary western state-sponsored higher education.

Who Pays the Bill?

But, it will understandably be asked, given that a university education as Lewis conceived of it is rarely if ever free, who, besides the wealthy, can afford it? I think it is reasonable to say that Lewis did not know the answer to this question. Indeed, I believe he concluded that because we live in a fallen world there is no answer that provides results which are fair to everyone. I suspect he would have reminded us that the "system" of higher education as it presently operates has been unable to answer the affordability question in a fair way. In the United States, the cost of higher education has become unaffordable for too many people. Millions of individuals and families take out loans to pay for college, loans which they struggle to repay. Lewis would likely have added that what is especially disconcerting is that under the present system of higher education students (and/or parents) with little to no interest in higher-level intellectual activity end up heavily indebted. The advanced intellectual work bores them and is often unrelated to any job they might hold in the future. Instead of pressuring these students to indebt themselves to earn a college degree, Lewis would probably have encouraged them to pursue work in the trades and vocational professions which they hopefully enjoy and for which they are far better suited, and, most importantly, do not require a college degree. Like the school boys whom Lewis described (see Chapter 2), these persons of university age do not care that they are not "intellectuals" because they never wanted to be.

6

What Do I Think?

Pure Interpreter

In the previous chapters, I have devoted my attention exclusively to setting out Lewis's thoughts about pleasure and happiness, and their relationship to his belief about the purpose of higher education. Dorothy L. Sayers, who was a contemporary of Lewis's and widely read and respected as an author (for her Lord Peter Wimsey murder mysteries), playwright (for her Christian BBC productions and cathedral festival plays), and a translator of Dante's *Divine Comedy*, wrote the following to Lewis in 1948:

> There is to-day far too little straightforward interpretive criticism. Everybody insists on doing "creative" criticism—which means that the critic simply uses his author as a spring-board from which to leap off into an exposition of his own views about the universe ... [W]e need the pure interpreter, who will sit down before a poem, or whatever it is, with humility to it and charity to the reader, and begin by finding out and explaining what the author actually did say, before he starts to explain what the author ought to have said and would have said if he had been as enlightened a person as his critic. A friend of mine, after toiling through several unintelligible books about modern poetry, said plaintively: "I want a critic who will say: 'This is a poem about a bus; this is what the poem says about the bus; this is the conclusion the writer draws from his observation about the bus; I think he has said it well (beautifully, badly, etc.) for the following reason.' After that he can say what he likes, and I shall know where I am."
>
> (Lewis 2004b: 885)

I have tried to be a "pure interpreter" of Lewis's thought about higher education in the previous chapters. However, some readers of drafts of this book have asked what I, as someone who has spent most of his adult life in higher education, think about the purpose of the academy. My reaction to their query has been twofold. On the one hand, the fact that they could not ascertain what I think from what I have written about Lewis's views in the previous chapters has reassured me that I have not strayed from my purpose in writing this book. On the other hand, these readers have persuaded me that I should say something concerning what I think about the purpose of higher education. Therefore, in what follows I will cease to be a pure interpreter of Lewis and offer some thoughts of my own. Like Lewis, I am a Christian, so some of the issues I consider at the end of the chapter concern the purpose of higher-level intellectual activity conducted by Christians.

General Thoughts

While one can write a book about a person and his (or her) views of a topic and disagree with those views, I have written about Lewis as a kindred intellectual spirit in the sense that he and I share similar views about many of the topics discussed in this book, including the nature of pleasure and the purpose of higher education. Lewis and I agree: the experience of pleasure is intrinsically good and this goodness provides the primary justification for engaging in higher-level intellectual activity. So far as I know, only one contemporary writer concerned about the primary purpose of advanced intellectual activity even acknowledges the possibility that it might be the experience of pleasure (see Introduction, endnote 7).

However, even though the experience of pleasure is not on the list of purposes that contemporary writers on higher education consider for explaining involvement in the academy, it still might be what explains why some individuals are members of the academy.

For example, an interesting question is "How many students attend university for the purpose of experiencing pleasure?" From what I have been able to ascertain, the number of students attending university for the pleasure that comes from advanced intellectual activity varies from one institution to another. I usually find more students who enjoy intellectual activity at universities which are more selective with respect to their admission of students. It is true that not every student at these more highly selective universities is there for the enjoyment of higher-level intellectual activity, but my experience is that many more students at these universities are there for the pleasure that they derive from intellectual activity than students who are present at less highly selective institutions. Far more students at the less selective universities are there primarily or only because they and their parents accept the cultural message that people need to go to college to get a good job.

I am not criticizing students who attend university for the purpose of getting a good job. It is easy to understand why they are in higher education for this purpose. The culture in which they have grown up tells them that this is *the* path they must pursue in life in order to be happy in their adult years. It is unreasonable to blame them for believing this when they have heard nothing else from a very young age about why they should go to college.

Absurdly Utopian and Elitist

"But surely you cannot be serious. You really believe the purpose of higher education is the experience of pleasure? Such a view is absurdly utopian and unachievable."

Well, is the achievement of the purposes "universal social justice" and/or "good jobs" for all who pass through the halls of higher education any less utopian? Surely the aim of social justice for all will forever remain unrealized, as will good jobs for everyone. Yet few who promote these justifications of higher education abandon them because of their unattainable utopian nature. Why should things be different when it comes to justifying higher-level intellectual activity in terms of the experience of pleasure for all those who participate in it?

"Ok," you might say,

> Your purpose for being involved in higher education is no more utopian than these other aims. But surely it is elitist, whereas the other justifications are not. Those in higher education for the purpose of realizing social justice and/or good jobs have everyone in mind. You believe higher education is for the select few who derive pleasure from it. How can you honestly maintain that the creation of a space for higher-level intellectual activity without any further end than the experience of pleasure is anything other than proverbial ivory-tower privilege?

But what is meant by "elitist" in this criticism? The fact that higher education is for the few and not for the many does not entail that it is elitist in the sense that the relatively few people who are involved in it are better human beings in a moral sense, or happier, than those who do not participate in it. Those outside of the academy can be just as morally good as those within. In terms of happiness, the reality is simply that some people derive happiness from one activity, in this case higher-level intellectual activity, while others do not. True, those in higher education are likely better at thinking and reasoning about advanced intellectual topics, but, again, that does not guarantee that they are morally better or happier human beings than those who are not involved in higher education.

However, do not many of those in higher education think they are morally better or more virtuous than people who are not part of the academy? Are not academicians often snobbish and arrogant toward those on the outside? Most certainly they are. But the proper response to the snobs is not to deny that the purpose of higher education is the experience of pleasure. Rather, it is to inform them that they ought to look in the proverbial mirror to see how unacceptable their own behavior is toward the rest of humanity, the "everyone" crowd who need good jobs and equitable recognition.

Friendship with Others in the Professoriate

Friendships often form around shared pleasurable interests. For example, those who read and write about Lewis know that he was friends for about ten years with Charles Williams, who worked in London for Oxford University Press and derived much pleasure from his reading of literature, particularly poetry. Williams gave lectures on literature for years in London, and he both lectured and tutored for the English faculty in Oxford during the Second World War when the London offices of Oxford University Press were moved there. Just as those who knew Lewis were struck by his passion for higher-level intellectual activity (see the statements about Lewis at the head of the Introduction), so also those who knew Williams were similarly impressed. According to Williams's biographer Grevel Lindop, Williams's "enthusiasm [for poetry] seemed completely genuine. 'He was *really* interested, I think, in poetry', recalled [a] pupil. 'He was really interested in "How does the poet do this?"' And there was the stimulus of Williams's extraordinary presence" (Lindop 2015: 390). Another student of Williams stated, "I remember him saying—peering intensely at us—'My dear young ladies' (as he often called us) 'you must get poetry into your blood and your bones! And *especially* into your blood and bones!'" (Lindop 2015: 390). And yet another pupil of Williams said:

> The whole message of the way he taught was, that what was important was your response to the piece of literature that you were reading. Nothing else mattered, [...] not having read the accepted critics wouldn't matter, it wasn't the point. The point was, what is *your* response to it? And that has stayed with one all one's life and been a guiding principle.
>
> (Lindop 2015: 390)

From my years of interacting with and observing colleagues across many disciplines, I have concluded that for many of them it is their absorption in higher-level intellectual activity which they share with others, including students, that fundamentally explains their involvement in higher education. Indeed, many of my colleagues enjoy advanced intellectual activity so much that they accept far less money as remuneration for their work than they might earn doing something else for a living. My belief about the reason for my colleagues' involvement in higher education applies to many of those who maintain they are in higher education for ideological reasons, often political, but sometimes religious or philosophical. While these "ideologues" claim their goals are such things as a more just society, the salvation of souls, or metaphysical enlightenment, what seems actually to motivate them is their enjoyment of advanced intellectual activity in company with others of like mind. It is true that more than a few of these individuals seek to read, discuss, write about, and inculcate only the views with which they agree. Unlike Lewis, they seemingly derive no pleasure from and, therefore, have no interest in, seeing the world through the eyes of others. But this truth about them does not contradict the fact that they are involved in the academy for the pleasure they get from higher-level intellectual activity.

There is much discussion today about whether higher education can be effectively conducted online, remotely, or at a distance. The answer to this question is at least in part a function of what the purpose of higher education is. If it is to get a job, where the goal is fundamentally the imparting of certain information that never gets into, in Charles Williams's words, your blood and bones, then remote learning might, to some extent, succeed. However, from what I read, the completion rate for online courses is low, which suggests that a person must be highly motivated to stick with a course that is taught remotely.

"But," someone might respond, "those who are in higher education for the purpose of experiencing pleasure are highly motivated. Given this motivational advantage, an online model is more likely to work for them." Perhaps, but I doubt it. A significant part of the enjoyment that comes from higher-level intellectual activity is supplied by being in the same physical space as and interacting with others with whom you share the desire for that intellectual activity. Because of the pleasure this interaction provides, the shared physical space is instrumentally good. What must also be remembered is that many people who enjoy higher intellectual activity derive their pleasure from hard sciences like biology, chemistry, and physics. These sources of pleasure typically require the shared physical space of laboratories. This fact was impressed upon me by a physician with whom I spoke during the recent Covid-19 lockdowns. He shared with me his frustration about how his son, who is a pre-medical student, was taking his college chemistry courses remotely: "You can't do lab courses remotely! Lab work is hands-on! You need to gain experience with the physical instruments and materials!"

However, what if higher education does not involve course work, whether in the lab or not? What if it is largely or wholly comprised of independent research (without the need for in-class instruction or laboratories)? Might not an online model be more feasible? Again, perhaps, but I am skeptical. From over thirty years in higher education, I can say with some authority that the students who enjoyed their intellectual activity in college most, and who were usually my best students, were the ones who showed up for class every day, came to my office outside class to discuss ideas, and were actively involved with other students in discussions of their work. All of this was made possible by their presence in a common physical space. Nevertheless, it is important that I make clear that I would not insist that higher education requires a "one-model-fits-all" approach. Some people who enjoy higher-level intellectual activity might find that an online format is suitable for them, and it is not my purpose to deny them such a format.

Shared physical spaces, though by no means only shared physical spaces, create the possibility for what are commonly referred to as "cliques." Lewis knew all too well the ill effects of such groups. In various places, he wrote about what he called the "Inner Ring" (e.g.,

Lewis [1944f] in 2001g: 141–57), which he described in part as a group to which no one is ever formally or explicitly admitted:

> You discover gradually, in almost indefinable ways, that it exists and that you are outside it, and then later, perhaps, that you are inside it. There are what correspond to passwords, but they too are spontaneous and informal. A particular slang, the use of particular nicknames, an allusive manner of conversation are the marks. But it is not constant. It is not easy, even at a given moment, to say who is inside and who is outside. Some people are obviously in and some are obviously out, but there are always several on the border line ... There are no formal admissions or expulsions. People think they are in it after they have in fact been pushed out of it, or before they have been allowed in ... When it is very secure and comparatively stable in membership, it calls itself "we." When it has to be suddenly expanded to meet a particular emergency, it calls itself "all the sensible people at this place." From outside, if you have despaired of getting into it, you call it "that gang" or "they" or "so-and-so and his set" or "the Caucus" or "the Inner Ring." If you are a candidate for admission, you probably don't call it anything.
>
> (Lewis [1944f] in 2001g: 144–5)

According to Lewis, all of us at one time or another in our lives know of an Inner Ring and desire membership in it:

> I believe that in all men's lives at certain periods, and in many men's lives at all periods between infancy and extreme old age, one of the most dominant elements is the desire to be inside the local Ring and the terror of being left outside. This desire, in one of its forms, has indeed had ample justice done to it in literature. I mean, in the form of snobbery ... Often the desire conceals itself so well that we hardly recognize the pleasures of fruition.
>
> (Lewis [1944f] in 2001g: 146, 147)

Is the Inner Ring something evil? Not necessarily, thought Lewis:

> I am not going to say that the existence of Inner Rings is an evil. It is certainly unavoidable. There must be confidential discussions, and it

is not only not a bad thing, it is (in itself) a good thing that personal friendship should grow up between those who work together ... Let Inner Rings be an unavoidable and even an innocent feature of life, though certainly not a beautiful one; but what of our longing to enter them, our anguish when we are excluded, and the kind of pleasure when we get in? ... [T]his desire is one of the great permanent mainsprings of human action ... Unless you take measures to prevent it, this desire is going to be one of the chief motives of your life, from the first day on which you enter your profession until the day when you are too old to care ... [I]f all you want is to be in the know, your pleasure will be short-lived ... You were not looking for virtue or kindness or loyalty or humour or learning or wit or any of the things that can be really enjoyed. You merely wanted to be "in." And that is a pleasure that cannot last.

(Lewis [1944f] in 2001g: 148, 149, 151–2, 155)

Is the professoriate of contemporary higher education an Inner Ring? Many people probably think it is. There is no question that it exhibits some of the properties of an Inner Ring. Most certainly, there are people who want membership in it because they want the pleasure of being on the inside. There is definitely also, as I pointed out earlier in this chapter, an element of snobbery exhibited by far too many of those who are in higher education toward those who are not. In addition, there is often what Lewis called a password, which in contemporary academia is quite often either a naturalistic anti-theistic belief, particularly theistic belief as it is found in Christianity and Judaism, or a left-of-center political belief, though those in the professorial Inner Ring usually refuse to make the espousal of these naturalistic and leftist political beliefs a formal litmus test for membership in their institutions of higher learning. If you are in the professoriate you do not call it anything other than the professoriate.

But I believe there is also good reason to deny that the professoriate of higher education is an Inner Ring. Most importantly, many of those who are members are on the inside ultimately because they enjoy advanced intellectual activity. While there typically is formal admission to it by means of standardized tests, qualifying exams, credentialing in the form of masters and doctoral degrees, what ultimately motivates membership in it is more often than not a love of the pleasure that attends the life of the mind. It is this love which explains why members are good at what they do and enjoy the privilege of associating with others who are also good at what they do. They are, in Lewis's words, "sound craftsman, and other sound craftsmen ... know it" (Lewis [1944f] in 2001g: 156). Hence, they

> consort simply with the people [they] like, [they] ... find that [they] have come unawares to a real inside, that [they] are indeed snug and safe at the centre of something which, seen from without, would look exactly like an Inner Ring. But the difference is that its secrecy is accidental, and its exclusiveness a by-product, and no one was led thither by the lure of the esoteric ...
>
> (Lewis [1944f] in 2001g: 157)

However, it might be objected, even if the professoriate is not an Inner Ring, am I not turning a blind eye to the harmful effects of a significant segment of the professoriate whose members exclude people who disagree with their anti-theistic and left-of-center politics? While I believe this exclusion is taking place, I also cannot blame those with these points of view for taking pleasure in reading, thinking, writing about, and inculcating largely, if not only, the views with which they agree.[1] If this kind of higher-level intellectual activity is what gives them pleasure, so be it. Colleagues of mine sometimes suggest that the antidote to the lack of diversity in higher education, despite the hollow advocacy for diversity by those with the acceptable points of view, is the hiring of people with different (e.g., theistic and right-of-center political) points of view for which those individuals can advocate. I have long believed that this is not the best solution to the problem of a lack of variety of viewpoints in higher education, where the goal is a diversity of viewpoints. If one wants people who share the same physical space to consider a genuine multiplicity of views, then one can achieve this goal through the inclusion of people who derive pleasure from intellectual activity that is concerned with a variety of views, regardless of their own ideological persuasions. I pointed out in Chapter 2 how Lewis derived immense pleasure from intellectual activity concerned with medieval cosmology. Yet, he believed that cosmology was false (see Chapter 2). As someone who, like Lewis, derives pleasure from seeing the world through the eyes of people with whom I disagree, I have no problem fairly presenting views that I think are false (e.g., I expend much energy in my courses considering naturalism, yet I am not a naturalist). Indeed, if I err in my teaching, it is in focusing too much on viewpoints with which I disagree to the neglect of those with which I agree or, short of agreement, have sympathy. I tend to spend more time on perspectives which I think are mistaken because learning about them helps me to understand better the things I believe, where this understanding is a source of much pleasure.

But what if certain universities have reached or will reach a point where those who are naturalists and or politically "woke" purposefully exclude some or all of those persons who derive pleasure from reading, thinking, and writing about different points of view? If this has happened or will come to be, then it seems to me that those who enjoy intellectual activity concerned with different points of view will have to form their own institutions of higher education and let the public vote with their feet. "But," it will likely be retorted, "This takes money!" Yes, it does, but so does being associated with academic institutions that are not intellectually interested in diverse points of view. If your interest is pleasure from advanced intellectual activity that is concerned with a diversity of views, then you will pay, assuming payment is required, to be associated with people who derive pleasure from reading, thinking, writing about, and teaching different points of view.

I believe a fundamental issue in contemporary higher education is being clear about what kind of higher-level intellectual activity provides you with pleasure. If it is higher-level intellectual activity that is solely concerned with ideas with which you agree, then it is reasonable for you to read, think, write about, and teach that with which you agree to the exclusion of other viewpoints. However, if you derive pleasure from advanced intellectual activity that concerns itself with a diversity of viewpoints, regardless of whether or not you agree with them, then it is reasonable for you to read, think, write about, and teach different points of view. In terms of viewpoints, the most serious problem in higher education is the lack of truth-in-advertising. Too many institutions of higher learning misleadingly represent themselves as being concerned with a multiplicity of viewpoints when, as a matter of fact, they are only interested in inculcating perspectives with which they agree. Contemporary higher education is generally so lacking in truth-in-advertising that the catch-phrase "Diversity, Equity, and Inclusion" (DEI) is frequently code for uniformity, inequity, and exclusion. If members of a university desire to consider only one or a limited number of points of view, then in principle they should not be stopped from fulfilling their desire. What those on the outside who are interested in what takes place on the inside should demand is accurate descriptions of the academy's intellectual and cultural life.

However, what if the institutions of higher learning are publically funded with taxpayer dollars? Should they not be required to consider a diversity of viewpoints? For example, Michael R. Bloomberg, the mayor of New York City from 2002 to 2013, reminds his readers:

> Speakers over the past decade have regularly been disinvited, shouted down and even physically attacked by student activists unwilling to entertain different ideas and perspectives. This behavior is anathema to a university's mission and deeply damaging to our nation ... Free inquiry and discourse—including professing ideas and beliefs—lie at the heart of higher education and democratic society. In both the sciences and humanities, rigorous debates based on facts, data and reason allow ideas and theories to be evaluated and amended, adopted and discarded, in ways that promote understanding, advance knowledge, and teach responsible citizenship ... Higher education is rooted in intellectual exploration. Colleges that don't expose students to challenging and uncomfortable ideas fail their pupils.
>
> (Bloomberg 2022)

While I understand Bloomberg's concern, I disagree with his implied view that the primary purpose of higher education is inquiry that is free from unwarranted constraints. In agreement with Lewis, I believe the purpose is the pleasure that comes from higher-level intellectual activity. However, I am sympathetic with Bloomberg's belief that the good of a democratic polis is furthered by the unhindered exploration of different ideas and perspectives. What such a political state needs are professors and students who enjoy considering a variety of ideas and perspectives. If taxpayer-funded higher education fails to provide the requisite multiplicity of perspectives that a significant number of people desire, then they will have to make their dissatisfaction known.

But, as I have already stated, higher education as such does not require a consideration of a diversity of viewpoints. Some people enjoy advanced intellectual activity that focuses only on ideas with which they agree. "But," it might be objected, "if everyone is focusing only on what gives them pleasure, might certain legitimate and important topics be neglected?" Perhaps they will be neglected. But if people are concerned about what is being neglected, then they can choose to devote their time and effort to it, even if they derive no pleasure from doing so. "But what persons would do that, unless they were adequately compensated in some way?" Probably none. But that is my point. Ideally, any reasonable person would want someone who derives pleasure from an intellectual activity that concerns a certain subject matter to devote intellectual energy to it. But if no such person exists, then some other means of enticement, more often than not, money, will have to be developed to attract people to spend their time and effort on what for them is not a source of pleasure.

Being a Student for the Purpose of Getting a Job

I agree with Lewis that "in order to get a job" is a less-than-optimal reason for attending university as a student. Nevertheless, the majority of students whom I have taught over the years have attended college for this reason. I have watched as the vast majority of them have not enjoyed much of their academic experience. They have "gutted out" their time in college with the belief that the enjoyment they seek in life will be found in a job they obtain after graduation. I do not doubt that some of these individuals have found enjoyable employment upon graduating from the academy. But even for these persons, it would have been better had they also enjoyed their time while in college. I am convinced that the best approach to higher education is to enter it because you derive pleasure from advanced intellectual activity and to bracket the question of a job. If you enjoy this intellectual activity while in college, you will likely do well in terms of employment that you will enjoy when you graduate. And even if you do not find such enjoyable work, at least you will have enjoyed your time in higher education.

In his post-Second World War essay "Leisure the Basis of Culture," Josef Pieper made clear how, in Max Weber's terms, persons in the West have come to a point where they do not work to live but live to work for work's sake (Pieper 1964: 4–5). Pieper pointed out that reflective individuals down through the ages (Aristotle is his seminal example) thought that people work or are "unleisurely" in order that they might have leisure in the form of contemplation, which is a kind of intellectual activity, and Pieper pointed out to his readers that the Latin word for "work," *negotium*, is the negation of *otium*, which means "leisure" (Pieper 1964: 5). Similarly, Pieper called attention to the fact that the Latin word for "school," *schola*, means "leisure" (Pieper 1964: 4), but that "leisure" had become a word with unfavorable connotations:

> To those who live in a world of nothing but work, in what we might call the world of "total work," [leisure] presumably sounds immoral, as though directed at the very foundations of human society ... Leisure, from this point of view [of the world of "total work"], appears as something wholly fortuitous or strange, without rhyme or reason [and] another word for laziness, idleness and sloth.
>
> (Pieper 1964: 4, 24)

While Pieper's essay is illuminating and enjoyable to read, I must register one disagreement with it: I think his central claim that leisure is an end in itself is mistaken, if he meant that leisure as an end in itself is not pursued as a means to pleasure where pleasure is, strictly speaking, intrinsically good. Pieper regarded leisure as "a contemplative attitude" (Pieper 1964: 28), which reflected his close adherence to the philosophical view of Thomas Aquinas who, under the influence of Aristotle's philosophical thought, maintained both that the end of man is contemplation of God and that pleasure is not intrinsically good (see Goetz 2015a).

In contradistinction to Aquinas and Aristotle, I believe that the purpose for being involved in higher education is not that you engage in higher-level intellectual activity, period. The purpose for being involved in higher education is that you experience the pleasure that comes from this activity. Moreover, it is important for me to make clear that I believe that enjoyed intellectual activity can be useful for unforeseen vocational purposes. Lewis stressed the distinction between the intended and unforeseen consequences of what we do. When he was discussing an aspect of Alexander Pope's theological thought, he wrote that an implication of it

> is that there exists on the Divine level a distinction with which we are very familiar on our own: that between the plan (or the main plan) and its unintended but unavoidable by-products. Whatever we do, even if it achieves its object, will also scatter round it a spray of consequences which were not its object at all. This is so even in private life. I throw out crumbs for the birds and provide, incidentally, a breakfast for rats. Much more so in what may be called managerial life. The governing body of the college alters the time of dinner in hall; our object being to let the servants get home earlier. But by doing so we alter the daily pattern of life for every undergraduate. To some the new arrangement will be a convenience, to others the reverse. But we had no special favour for the first lot and no spite against the second. Our arrangement drags these unforeseen and undesired consequences after it. We can't help this.
>
> (Lewis 1992a [1963]: 53–4)

The opportunities for work after the intended and successful pursuit of higher education for pleasure, though in many cases unforeseen, might be neither unavoidable nor undesired. For example, if you enjoy advanced intellectual activity whose subject matter is chemistry, you might find you will enjoy this intellectual activity in chemical research with a pharmaceutical company. Or you might derive much pleasure from the study of languages and end up working in either the private or public sector in a foreign country. Similarly, if you enjoy higher-level intellectual activity whose subject matter is mathematics, you might find you will enjoy this intellectual activity in the aerospace industry and designing satellites, in code breaking, or in biology and the quantitative study of the material mechanisms of inheritance.[2] Were we to live in an ideal world, all of us would enjoy our "work" as a form of leisure because our work itself would be a source of pleasure. We would neither work in order to engage in leisure nor engage in leisure in order to work, but enjoy the pleasure of leisure without end. "But that is not our world!", my students often respond. Most assuredly it is not, but the fact that it is not in no way undermines the goodness of the ideal. It shows how less than ideal our world is.

However, cannot one pursue the pleasure of higher education when employment after college is regarded as more than just an unforeseen side effect of that pursuit? Cannot one pursue higher-level intellectual activity both for pleasure and for getting a job? Of course. But whenever there is more than one of something, in this case a purpose to act, the question arises about how the multiple things are related. I believe in the primacy of the purpose of experiencing pleasure. So long as a person in higher education acts primarily for this purpose, I can see no reason to exclude the possibility that an individual might also act for the purpose of getting a job that makes use of the intellectual activity which is pursued for the experience of pleasure. You potentially will be living the best of both worlds, experiencing pleasure in the academy and equipping yourself for work that you will enjoy, whether you know what that work will be during your university years or not.

The Curriculum

Roosevelt Montás of Columbia University writes that he has "heard college deans and presidents extoll the merits of low-requirement curricula and of student choice in designing their own courses of study. Why not let students pick for themselves what they find most relevant or appealing … ? Some schools even boast of having no requirements at all apart from completing a certain number of credits" (Montás 2021: 73). As a proponent of the idea of a core curriculum, Montás is deeply opposed to a low- or no-requirements curriculum.

In opposition to Montás, and in the spirit, if not the letter, of Lewis's comments which are relevant to the idea of a core curriculum (see Chapter 5), I am a minimalist when it comes to the issue of required courses. The only courses I would require of students are those which are essential for the study of what gives them pleasure. Montás observes that the Christian thinker St. Augustine "like all ascetics, had a strong weakness for pleasure, and he continually highlights the spiritual pleasures and ecstasies of his chosen life of abstinence. It struck me vividly," continues Montás, "that Augustine had not, in fact, given up pleasure when taking up celibacy and other monastic rigors. Instead, he traded one kind of pleasure for another" (Montás 2021: 45–6). Yet, adds Montás, "Augustine's strongest attachment was to truth and to the possibility of attaining it" (Montás 2021: 46), which, Montás seems to believe, entails a lack of interest in the experience of pleasure from knowing the truth. Assuming Montás does believe this, what is unclear to me is why he thinks the attachment to truth excludes attachment to pleasure as the explanation for the interest in the former. Like Lewis, "I'm all for a planet without aches or pains [and, experiences of pleasure] … but I doubt if I'd care for one of pure intelligence" (Lewis 2007: 623).

Most generally, when you are thinking about a curriculum (course of study) in higher education, you should always be clear about what you believe the purpose of higher education is. If you believe the purpose of higher education is the advancement of social justice, then presumably you will build a curriculum to serve that purpose. If you believe the purpose of higher education is the achievement of employment in certain occupations, then presumably you will construct a curriculum that promotes the procurement of jobs in those occupations. If you believe the purpose of higher education is the experience of pleasure, then you will put together a course of study whose contents provide you with enjoyment. Yet, different purposes might justify inclusion of the same disciplines in a curriculum. Thus, if the purpose of higher education is the experience of pleasure, then those who enjoy higher-level intellectual activity in the form of philosophy will include philosophy as one of the disciplines. Likewise, if the purpose of higher education is the eudaimonist aim of perfecting human nature and philosophy is believed to be helpful for this perfective enterprise, then philosophy will once again be included as one of the disciplines in the curriculum.

The Size and Geography of Higher Education

In 1930, C. S. Lewis wrote to his friend Arthur Greeves about how he (Lewis) and another friend, Owen Barfield, had

> read some Beowulf with a very remarkable young woman. She was a farmer's daughter who got a county scholarship and went up to London getting a good degree in English. Then—and here's the marvel—she settled down at home again and divides her time between milking the cows [and] taking occasional pupils, apparently contented in both. That's what we want, isn't it? *Emigration* from the uneducated class into ours only swells the intellectual unemployed: but to have education transforming people [and] yet leaving them with their roots in the earth ... is the way to make class disappear altogether.
>
> (Lewis 2004a: 915)

What Lewis described as the emigration of the uneducated class swelling the ranks of the intellectually unemployed mirrors what is happening today with the awarding of the Ph.D., which has become practically necessary for securing a position in higher education. The problem is that the number of Ph.D.'s that are awarded far exceeds the number of academic posts which are available in the academy with the result that those with a Ph.D. are swelling the ranks of the unemployed in higher education. Some people recommend limiting the number of Ph.D.'s that are awarded. However, this "solution" might be construed as an elitist way of preventing, in Lewis's terms, the uneducated class, some of whose members might be first-generation college students, from "swelling" the ranks of higher education.

For the sake of discussion, I will assume that the paucity of jobs in higher education relative to the number of people seeking employment therein is not as serious a problem for people who enjoy earning a Ph.D. and do so without unreasonably indebting themselves financially. These individuals are in higher education for the right reason, which is that they enjoy higher-level intellectual activity. True, it is still a problem for these persons that they cannot find the employment they desire in higher education, but at least they have not incurred unreasonable financial debt in enjoying advanced intellectual activity.[3] In what follows, I will assume that the problem is not that there are too many Ph.D.'s relative to available jobs, but that there are too many people who are taking on too much debt for the purpose of obtaining a job in higher education that they might not get.

The problem of too few jobs in higher education is hard to rectify because it is, on my view of the purpose of higher education, a function of how many people enjoy advanced intellectual activity. And the number of persons who enjoy higher-level intellectual activity is, relative to the size of the entire population, small. One way to try to create more jobs in higher education would be to increase the number of people who enjoy higher-level intellectual activity. However, as Lewis was all too aware, it is the pursuit of a goal that all too often undermines the achievement of it. Focus too much on having a good talk with an old friend and you will find yourself with nothing to say. Send your child to a Christian school so that he will embrace Christianity and he will end up rejecting the faith. But even if we could somehow successfully navigate our way through this paradox, we would still face the problem that it is all too easy to avoid higher-level intellectual activity. Some words of Lewis's about avoiding God are apropos for avoiding higher-level (and even lower-level) intellectual activity:

> Avoid silence, avoid solitude, avoid any train of thought that leads off the beaten track. Concentrate on money, sex, status, health and (above all) on your own grievances. Keep the radio on. Live in a crowd. Use plenty of sedation. If you must read books, select them very carefully. But you'd be safer to stick to the papers. You'll find the advertisements helpful; especially those with a sexy or a snobbish appeal.
>
> (Lewis [1963b] in 1967: 168–9)

In other words, if our goal is to see if we can create interest in advanced intellectual activity, then we should encourage people to cease focusing unnecessarily on money, material goods, and status; to turn off their radios, televisions, and streaming devices; to minimize their use of social media; and instead read a book and/or talk about ideas with others to see if these activities might be a source of pleasure.

While it is easy in today's world to avoid advanced intellectual activity, I doubt this is a new problem in terms of the limited number of people who are interested in higher education for the purpose of experiencing the pleasure of intellectual activity. From what I read, it seems that the number of people enjoying higher-level intellectual activity has always been small relative to the total population. Julie E. Reuben points out that in the early years of the twentieth century, "American universities and colleges had developed an elaborate array of extracurricular activities … [W]hile students cared little about their classes [advanced intellectual activity], they were ardently interested in these activities" (Reuben 1996: 255). This lack of interest on the part of students in their classes was, Reuben notes a few pages earlier, complemented by the belief of others that there was a "lack of inspirational teaching." Reuben quotes a statement of Robert C. Angell of the University of Michigan, made in 1928, about how this pedagogical problem undercut the influence of faculty:

> The failure of the students to respond more readily to intellectual stimulation is in some measure due to the personality and point of view of the faculty. No one can deny that professors are interested in their fields of study; but many believe that frequently they have little ability in, or enthusiasm for, imparting their knowledge and interest to immature undergraduates.
>
> (Reuben 1996: 249)

I readily acknowledge that there are uninspiring teachers and that their inability to instruct others might be responsible for the lack of interest in higher education on the part of some people. Perhaps better teaching would significantly grow the interest of people in advanced intellectually activity. However, it is equally important to make clear that if students were in college because they enjoyed advanced intellectual activity, then professors would not have to generate, in some cases *ex nihilo*, interest in a topic. The interest of professors in their topics would be matched by the interest of students in those topics. Throughout my years in higher education, not a few administrators have assumed that I, as professor, am responsible for ginning up student interest in what I teach. I remember the question on the student evaluation form about the professor's enthusiasm in teaching the class. Enthusiasm is important, but it is also the case that no amount of professorial enthusiasm can overcome the fact that many students in college derive little to no pleasure from higher-level intellectual activity.

Without either increasing the number of people who derive pleasure from higher-level intellectual activity or simply denying a lot of people who cannot afford a Ph.D. the opportunity to pursue it, the problem of too many people unreasonably indebting themselves financially for the purpose of being employed in higher education is not easy to solve. Some people (e.g., some politicians) recommend making higher education available to everyone free of charge. I believe this is utter foolishness, especially if higher education has as its proper goal advanced intellectual activity for the sake of pleasure. Most people are not interested in such intellectual activity because they do not derive pleasure from it. Anyone who advocates making higher education free for everyone should be made to teach those who enroll in university courses. It would be a pleasure to see how long those who advocate for cost-free higher education would remain in the teaching profession.

Given the reality that most people derive little or no pleasure from advanced intellectual activity, the Columbia University linguist John McWhorter is correct: "We must revise the notion that attending a four-year college is the mark of being a legitimate American, and return to truly valuing working-class jobs" (McWhorter 2021: 143). I would add that we must make clear that earning a four-year college degree is not only not the mark of being a legitimate citizen, but also it is not the mark of being a fulfilled human being. McWhorter also reminds his readers:

> Attending four years of college is a tough, expensive, and even unappealing proposition for many poor people (as well as middle-class and rich ones). Yet the left endlessly baits applause with calls for college to be made widely available and less expensive, with the idea that anyone who does not get a four-year college degree has been mired without opportunity.
>
> Yet people can, with up to two year's training at a vocational institution, make a solid living as electricians, plumbers, hospital technicians, cable television installers, body shop mechanics, and many other jobs. Across America, we must instill a sense that vocational school—not "college" in the traditional sense—is a valued option for people who want to get beyond what they grew up in.
>
> (McWhorter 2021: 143–4)

I agree with McWhorter (and others) who emphasizes that vocational training is a valued option, that a person is no less human or no less American (or no less whatever nationality) for working in the trades. However, I would stress that vocational training is a valued option for certain people not principally because it will enable them to get beyond where they grew up but because they can get pleasure from that kind of work. As McWhorter says, four years of college is not *appealing* to many people. Why, then, keep telling them that they must earn a four-year college degree? Why not tell them to forget going to college and instead explore a line of work that appeals to them and from which, as McWhorter intimates, they can earn a living?

Some individuals who attend what are known in America as Division I or Division II universities do so at no financial expense. These persons are commonly referred to as "student athletes." The truth is that in most cases these individuals are professional athletes who devote most of their waking hours to playing their sport. They have no time for advanced intellectual activity. If students at all, they are athlete-students. I understand that there are exceptions; there are some genuine student-athletes in higher education. But they are the exception to the rule. I believe the academy should stop serving as a support system for professional sports like football, both American and what others around the globe consider football (i.e., soccer), basketball, baseball, ice hockey, tennis, golf, etc. Those in higher education for the experience of pleasure from advanced intellectual activity can easily get their requisite exercise by playing a sport for fun. Indeed, what better reason is there to play it? Surely the majority of athlete-students play their sport because it is for them a source of pleasure. Why then burden them with the requirement of advanced intellectual activity from which they derive little to no pleasure, all so that they can play the sport which they do enjoy?

Higher-Level Intellectual Activity outside the Institutional University

Like many who write today about higher education, Lewis engaged in higher-level intellectual activity within the walls (many Oxford and Cambridge colleges are literally enclosed by medieval walls) of a residential university that awards degrees. However, advanced intellectual activity need not be restricted to such a physical space. It can take place in evening classes, continuing education programs, churches, community clubs, and online. Michael Sandel asks about civic education, "why assume that four-year colleges and universities have, or should have, a monopoly on this mission? A more capacious notion of educating citizens for democracy would resist the sequestration of civic education in universities" (Sandel 2020: 191–2). However, Sandel's point can be extended beyond educating citizens for democracy and applied to higher education that is pursued for pleasure. Why assume four-year universities have, or should have, a monopoly on it?

Sandel informs his readers that some of America's first labor unions demanded reading rooms in factories so that workers could educate themselves about public affairs. These unions, he says, saw no incompatibility between civic learning and work (Sandel 2020: 192). And Adrian Wooldridge, in his book *The Aristocracy of Talent: How Meritocracy Made the Modern World*, writes of the British working class at the beginning of the twentieth century that it

> contained large numbers of self-educated people who, thanks to their social backgrounds, didn't get a chance to go to university but nevertheless succeeded in educating themselves. They enrolled in night schools, university extension courses and Workers Educational Association (WEA) lessons. They gobbled up popular editions of classic texts produced by Dent and Co., with working-class readers sticking to the classics, particularly Shakespeare, Milton, Macaulay and Carlyle ... A 1906 list of the favourite authors of Labour MPs recalls a lost world of popular learning: Ruskin is number one, followed by Dickens, the Bible and Carlyle, but the list also includes John Stuart Mill, Thomas Macaulay and Adam Smith ...
>
> (Wooldridge 2021: 172)

Again, Sandel's and Wooldridge's points about the compatibility of civic learning and work applies to the compatibility of higher-level intellectual activity pursued for pleasure and work. However, state and private organizations which do or would draw upon individuals who derive pleasure from involvement in higher education understandably have an interest in some form of testing and certification for proficiency and expertise in higher-level intellectual subject matters for the sake of quality control. The awarding of degrees by institutions of higher learning and standardized testing play a pivotal, if not essential, role here. So while testing and certification are in principle peripheral to higher education as advanced intellectual activity for the purpose of enjoyment, various state and private groups have an interest in using them for the purpose of ascertaining which individuals are most qualified for which jobs. After all, what organization would not wish to have the most qualified persons who enjoy the requisite advanced intellectual activity working for it?

Christians and Higher-Level Intellectual Activity

So far in this chapter, I have focused on various issues in higher education generally. What about Christian higher education in particular? As a Christian, I am interested in what does and does not transpire within Christian colleges. What follows consists of some thoughts about various topics relevant to higher-level intellectual activity in a Christian context.

What about the issue of viewpoint diversity? For example, can professors in Christian institutions of higher learning find pleasure in intellectual activity that concerns itself with non-Christian views? I do not see why not. While a Christian university might require that its professors affirm a statement of faith that is more general in nature like the Apostles' Creed or more specific in content like the Catechism of the Catholic Church or the Westminster Catechism, this requirement would in no way prevent those faculty members from seeing the world through the eyes of others with differing beliefs. Thinking about something is not the same as, and does not require, believing it. While seeing might be believing, thinking is not. Indeed, in my own case, a side effect of my thinking about things that I believe are false is that I better understand, and thereby derive more pleasure from, thinking about the things that I believe are true.

But might a Christian university make clear to its faculty members that they can only engage in intellectual activity concerned with Christian views? I do not see why not. Higher-level intellectual activity with this constraint would be a limited source of pleasure for me, so I have never been interested in being a member of such an intellectual community. But I have never considered my lack of interest in advanced intellectual activity with this constraint a good reason for maintaining that others should not be allowed to be members of communities formed around higher-level intellectual activity directed at contents which are exclusively Christian in nature. Once again, as with non-Christian/secular and naturalist institutions of higher education, what is needed is truth-in-advertising. No Christian institution should advertise that it provides a well-rounded, higher-level education if the intellectual activity that takes place therein is only concerned with Christian subjects and ideas.

About forty years ago, the philosopher Alvin Plantinga issued his advice to Christian philosophers. Plantinga maintained that "the Christian philosopher has his own topics and projects to think about" (Plantinga 1984: 256) in distinction from those topics and projects thought about by non-Christians: "[M]y plea is for the Christian philosopher, the Christian philosophical community, to display ... more independence and autonomy: we needn't take as our research projects just those projects that currently enjoy widespread popularity; we have our own questions to think about" (Plantinga 1984: 268). Indeed, according to Plantinga, the Christian philosopher has a "duty" to "work at his own projects—projects set by the beliefs of the Christian community of which he is a part" (Plantinga 1984: 263), which he should serve (Plantinga 1984: 255), and to which he has a "fundamental responsibility" (Plantinga 1984: 262). "Philosophy is a communal enterprise" (Plantinga 1984: 264), and the Christian philosopher's primary community is that comprised of his fellow Christians.

Let us, as does not seem unreasonable for the purposes of this chapter, generalize for the moment Plantinga's comments, so that they apply not only to Christian philosophers but to Christian academicians as a whole, and ask how plausible they are. One feature that is notable about them is the conspicuous absence of any mention of pleasure. Does Plantinga believe the Christian academician in higher education has no desire for experiences of pleasure from higher-level intellectual activity that informs his selection of topics and projects? Like Lewis, I find it hard to believe that the desire for pleasure plays no explanatory role in a Christian academician's intellectual life. According to Plantinga, the Christian academician has a duty to work on his own projects out of his membership in and duty to the Christian community. But might not the Christian academician work on projects that interest him not because it is his duty vis-à-vis the Christian community to do so but because engagement with those projects provides him with experiences of pleasure? Plantinga maintains that the beliefs of the Christian community set projects for Christian academicians. Let us concede that at least in some cases this is so. Would it not be far better if those who derived pleasure from the higher-level intellectual activity concerned with the relevant projects were the people who worked on them? They would likely do a better job at those projects given the pleasure they experienced from the intellectual activity involved, as opposed to those who derived no pleasure from the intellectual activity but were required to take them on anyway because it was their duty to do so.

What about Plantinga's regard for the broader fundamental responsibility of the Christian academician to the Christian community? In the case of Christian philosophers, Plantinga does not spell out in any detail what it looks like for them to serve the Christian community, beyond saying that they should carry out the task of addressing philosophical questions of importance to the Christian community and developing the implications of Christian theism for the whole range of questions philosophers ask and answer (Plantinga 1984: 264). Plantinga would presumably approvingly cite Lewis's work as an apologist (e.g., Lewis's writing of books, his radio broadcasts during the Second World War), as a form of service to the Christian community. And Lewis would surely have insisted that it was because he derived pleasure from higher-level intellectual activity that he was able to carry out his apologetical work. And had Lewis been alive to read Plantinga's written philosophical work, he (Lewis) would probably have believed that Plantinga has had such a significant impact on the contemporary world of Christian and non-Christian thought in higher education because he has enjoyed the work that he has done. As a reader of both Lewis's and Plantinga's work, I believe it is not unreasonable to conclude that both of them pursued higher intellectual activity for the pleasure they derived from it. I suspect it was only because they first pursued the advanced intellectual activity they enjoyed that they were able to be of service to the Christian community.

Some Christians will likely regard the claim that it is permissible for Christians to be concerned with advanced intellectual activity for the sake of pleasure as problematic for, or in direct opposition to, the responsibility to share the Gospel. The Christians I have in mind believe that any and every Christian should be concerned primarily, if not exclusively, with evangelizing the non-Christian world. Everything else, even pleasurable intellectual activity that focuses on Christian content alone, is superfluous.

As I pointed out in Chapter 3, Lewis initially wrestled with whether he as a Christian could justify his life of intellectual activity in academia which he enjoyed. He concluded that his need for money to support himself was innocent and that his advanced intellectual work was an honorable and acceptable way of satisfying his monetary need. Lewis cited as support for his view (Lewis [1940] in 1967: 20) St. Paul's admonition to the Thessalonian Christians that they not be idle busybodies but stick to their work so that they would not be unnecessarily dependent on others (I Thessalonians 4: 11; 2 Thessalonians 3: 11). And Lewis also noted that St. Paul instructed the Ephesians to do honest work so that they might be able to help those in need (Eph. 4:28). Lewis wrote:

> Provided, then, that there was a demand for culture, and that culture was not actually deleterious, I concluded I was justified in making my living by supplying that demand—and that all others in my position

(dons, schoolmasters, professional authors, critics, reviewers) were similarly justified; especially if, like me, they had few or no talents for any other career—if their "vocation" to a cultural profession consisted in the brute fact of not being fit for anything else.

(Lewis [1940] in 1967: 20)

It seems to me that Lewis's thought about this matter was sound: a life of enjoyed work in higher education is respectable. And it also seems to me that Lewis was right to think that those who enjoy higher-level intellectual activity glorify God because pleasure is a beam from its divine source and the smell of deity, as Lewis wrote, hangs about it (Lewis 1992a [1963]: 89, 90). But if the aroma of deity surrounds experiences of pleasure, why do so many Christian people seemingly not detect it?

I am not sure about the answer to this question, but I believe it is not unlikely that it is related to what I will term, for the lack of a better word, the "bibliolatry" of certain Christians. "Where," they want to know, "does the Bible teach that pleasure is intrinsically good?" The correct response is that the Bible does not teach that pleasure is intrinsically good, just as it does not teach that it is *not* intrinsically good or is intrinsically evil. It teaches neither view because it is not a philosophy text which is written to address such a topic. Hence, this question about where the Bible teaches that pleasure is intrinsically good presupposes what is false, namely, that the Bible is a philosophical treatise written for the purpose of answering philosophical questions.[4]

"But if the Bible does not teach anything about the intrinsic goodness of pleasure and, it is appropriate to add, the intrinsic evilness of pain, how do we know that the former is intrinsically good and the latter is intrinsically evil?" Here again I agree with Lewis. We know this from our awareness of our experiences of pleasure and pain. True, we typically do not explicitly talk about pleasure's intrinsic goodness and pain's intrinsic badness because the terminology of intrinsic goodness and intrinsic badness is not in our everyday vocabulary. But what is not explicit in this case is implicit. Lewis claimed the entire Christian tradition, which he was convinced is rooted in common sense, presupposes (hangs upon) the nature of pleasure and pain as intrinsically good and evil respectively: "I have no doubt at all that pleasure in itself is a good and pain in itself an evil; if not, then the whole Christian tradition about heaven and hell and the passion of our Lord seems to have no meaning" (Lewis [1940] in 1967: 21).

"But," someone will retort, "these distinctions about value that Lewis and you make are mistaken. Surely the Bible teaches that pleasure is bad." No. The Bible simply assumes that certain *ways* of pursuing pleasure, but not pleasure itself, are bad (in theological terms, sinful). Lewis understood that some Christians wrongly suppose pleasure is evil in itself. He regarded such individuals as confused: "I know some muddle-headed Christians have talked as if Christianity thought that sex, or the body, or pleasure, were bad in themselves. But they were wrong" (Lewis 2001b [1952]: 98). As Lewis rightly reminded us, certain actions are wicked, and "we must practise in abstaining from [the performance of wicked actions in pursuit of] pleasures which are not in themselves wicked" (Lewis [1944a] in 1970: 54).

In the end, like Lewis, I believe Christians who are suspicious about the intrinsic goodness of pleasure wrongly ascribe the badness or evilness of certain immoral actions performed in pursuit of pleasure to the pleasure itself. These Christians fail to understand that, in Lewis's words, "[i]t is the stealing of the apple that is bad, not the sweetness" (Lewis 1992a [1963]: 89). Because I agree with Lewis's view, which I discussed at length in Chapter 1, I will say no more about the issue here.

Need all higher-level intellectual activity within a Christian context take place in a Christian university? I do not see why it cannot go on outside the university. For example, I do not see why it cannot take place in day and evening informal gatherings or formal classes in local churches. Certain subject matters are obviously more suitable than others for advanced intellectual consideration in local churches. Subjects like biology, chemistry, and physics, when they require laboratories and hands-on experimental work, will have to be situated in physical spaces that are conducive to them. But subjects such as history, language, literature, philosophy, and theology can easily find a home in the local church.

"But c'mon, Goetz, how many Christians do you know who are or would be interested in higher-level intellectual activity in the way that you are describing?" I know. I hear you. Alan Jacobs, an English literature professor who formerly taught at Wheaton College and is currently at Baylor University, both Christian institutions, writes that when he hears from nostalgic former students of his:

> [W]hat they tend to miss most about their college literature classes is the regular opportunity to talk about books, books that a group of people are all reading at the same time. When I quiz them about this nostalgia, they articulate a rather complex position. They do not say they miss reading highly literary texts; after all, they can do that on their own, and usually do ... Rather, they miss the conversation that such books generate.
>
> When I ask whether a book group might not be an adequate substitute for the classroom, or even a superior alternative ... they often disagree ... [T]hose who are not satisfied by book groups tend to give two reasons. The minor one is that the books chosen are rarely challenging enough to provide first-rate conversation. The major one is that too few participants in book groups are interested in really exploring the books: rather, for them, books seem to be an excuse for talking about other matters that they're more deeply interested in, often their own emotional lives.
>
> (Jacobs 2011: 136–7)

My wife's and my experiences with church home groups that supposedly focus on books are like those of Jacobs's former students. There is little substantive talk about the books and much discussion of children, grandchildren, jobs, sports, and whatever. But perhaps, contrary to the experience of Jacobs's former students and my wife and me, there are more Christians who actually do or would enjoy intellectual activity of a more advanced nature but who, for one reason or another, do not find a way to connect with other individuals who also do or would enjoy the same intellectual activity. If these persons do exist, then it seems reasonable to conclude that they need to make their interests more widely known. They will likely encounter opposition from those who do not get pleasure from higher-level intellectual activity and who are deeply suspicious of those who do. In my experience, the opposition, perhaps surprisingly, often comes from members of the clergy who are seemingly afraid that they might lose control of their flocks if members of the latter are allowed to think for themselves.

However, fear is not domiciled among the clergy. In recent years, I have had conversations with several people who, unlike me, either attended and/or teach at protestant evangelical Christian colleges. To a person, they all agree that many parents who send their children to these colleges do so out of fear; fear that their children will not be able to get a job without going to college; fear that their children will be exposed to ideas in a non-Christian/secular university that will lead to their children losing their faith; and fear of feeling inadequately prepared to talk with their children about the advanced intellectual activity they (the children) would encounter in a non-Christian college were they to go there. As a counter to the fears of these parents, Lewis's words merit re-quoting here: "[R]emember how much religious education has exactly the opposite effect to that [which] was intended, how many hard atheists come from pious homes" (Lewis 2007: 507).[5]

I am confident that Lewis would have regarded fear as a bad reason for attending college and perhaps a particular kind of college. Of course, he also disagreed with the parents I have described about the purpose for attending university. He assumed that the primary reason you would attend university is that you derive pleasure from higher-level intellectual activity. And if you go to university for this reason, you will enjoy the intellectual conflicts that arise from the consideration of different ideas and allow those ideas to sort themselves out in your mind over time. I would add that fear of intellectual activity prevents a person from enjoying intellectual activity. Yet, I also believe that a lack of fear of intellectual activity is not sufficient for enjoyment of that activity. People enjoy different things, and those who enjoy intellectual activity are no better as human beings than those who do not enjoy it.

Affordability

Lewis pointed out, as I quoted in Chapter 2, that civil societies have often concluded that people who desire to know should be given the opportunity to associate more formally with others who share the same desire. He was also aware that when the government supports this opportunity with the provision of taxpayer money, then it acquires and exercises control over the intellectual activity of those who desire to know and often insists that certain ideas be considered and taught. In the following comment Lewis was talking about the state's influence over pre-university education, but his point applies equally to the polis's control over higher education: "The State may take education more and more firmly under its wing. I do not doubt that by so doing it can foster uniformity, perhaps even servility, up to a point; the power of the State to de-liberalize a profession is undoubtedly very great" (Lewis [1946c] in 1970: 117).[6] And again,

> I believe a man is happier, and happy in a richer way, if he has "the freeborn mind." But I doubt whether he can have this without economic independence, which the new society is abolishing. For economic independence allows an education not controlled by Government; and in adult life it is the man who needs, and asks, nothing of Government who can criticise its acts, and snap his fingers at its ideology. Read Montaigne; that's the voice of a man with his legs under his own table, eating the mutton and turnips raised on his own land. Who will talk like that when the State is everyone's schoolmaster and employer?
> (Lewis [1958a] in 1970: 314)

Thus, those who believe the purpose of higher education is the experience of pleasure and wish to retain control over the level of intellectual activity that is the source of that pleasure would do well not to accept government money.

How then is higher education pursued for the experience of pleasure to be funded? This a difficult question to answer. The requisite money will have to come from sources other than the government. But who in the private sector will be interested in funding higher education so that certain individuals can experience pleasure? The individuals who derive pleasure from intellectual activity are one obvious source of capital. But if they are unable to pay much or anything at all, various philanthropic organizations might step forward, as well as churches which are committed to bettering the quality of life of people with intellectual needs. Businesses which are interested in finding and/or developing people who derive pleasure from intellectual activity that furthers their (the businesses') interests might also fund higher education.

Those who laugh at not only the idea that the purpose of higher education is the experience of pleasure but also the suggestion that there might be ways of financing higher education for that purpose would do well to remember that those who maintain higher education exists for the purpose of providing jobs, achieving social justice, developing people to run the government, etc., have made a mess of the financing of higher-level intellectual activity. For them to dismiss with a wave of the hand the idea put forth by Lewis and defended in this book about the purpose of higher education might itself be an instance of elitist snobbery. Perhaps these individuals might find that what they care about is not at odds with what Lewis maintained is the aim of higher education. Perhaps the achievement of their goals would be made more realistic by financially supporting those individuals who enjoy higher-level intellectual activity.

Asking the Right Questions

Lewis wrote that the "[h]uman intellect is incurably abstract. Pure mathematics is the type of successful thought. Yet the only realities we experience are concrete—this pain, this pleasure, this dog, this man. While we are loving the man, bearing the pain, enjoying the pleasure, we are not intellectually apprehending Pleasure, Pain or Personality" (Lewis [1944a] in 1970: 65). If Lewis is right about the purpose of higher education, then we would not engage in abstract thought if it were not itself a source of a concrete experience of pleasure. In higher-level intellectual activity, the abstract and the concrete meet and embrace.

I began this book with an anecdote about my answer to a question from a prospective student's father about why he should send his daughter to the college where I teach as opposed to another institution of higher education. I answered him that if his daughter were to take a course from me I would try to teach her how to think, where learning how to think is learning how to ask the right questions. The father told me that I had given the correct answer. Since giving the answer that I did, I have come to believe that what I said was incomplete. I now believe that asking the right questions is important because thinking about and answering them correctly is a source of pleasure. Were he to have sent his daughter to the college where I teach (for the record, I do not know if he did or did not), she would ideally have shared in the experience of pleasure that comes with higher-level intellectual activity.

Notes

Introduction

1. I understand "higher education," strictly speaking, to mean "intellectual activity that occurs at a higher-level." Of course, we regularly use "higher education" (and its synonyms) loosely to refer to the physical spaces within which the higher-level intellectual activity takes place. To avoid unnecessary wordiness, I will often speak loosely and use "higher education" to refer to the physical spaces within which intellectual activity occurs. The context should make clear when I am using "higher education" loosely and when I am using it strictly.
2. I will use "college" and "university" interchangeably. Some, not unreasonably, distinguish between the two. For example, Andrew Delbanco maintains a college "is about transmitting knowledge of and from the past to undergraduate students so they may draw upon it as a living resource in the future. [A university] is mainly an array of research activities conducted by faculty and graduate students with the aim of creating new knowledge in order to supersede the past" (Delbanco 2102: 2). Given I have defined "higher education" as higher-level intellectual activity and this kind of intellectual activity takes place in both colleges and universities as understood by Delbanco, I see no point in firmly delineating between them.
3. By "utilitarian" I mean no more than "useful as a means to an end" or "instrumental." In philosophical circles, "utilitarian" is conceptually more fine-grained and, strictly speaking, implies, as a form of hedonism, that there is one and only one intrinsic good, and one and only one intrinsic evil (for more about hedonism, see Chapter 1). The reader should not import that strict meaning into my use of "utilitarian" in this book.
4. The English public school is roughly equivalent to a particularly prestigious subset of the American private school.
5. *Carpe Diem* was a poem written by C. S. Lewis in 1913, when he was fourteen years of age, and for which he received special recognition by Malvern College, a public school in Great Malvern, England.

6   In the rest of this book, I will use the terms "elitist" and "elitism" to refer to the snobbish, distasteful, morally repugnant attitude which is, unfortunately, too often displayed by those within higher education toward those without.

7   Vedder (Vedder 2019: 17) thinks of "for the purpose of experiencing pleasure" as "the consumption goal" for attending university. To his credit, he acknowledges it as a legitimate reason for going to college. But, someone might be thinking, surely a person can pursue a vocation for the purpose of experiencing pleasure. If so, what is the difference between that person and someone who is involved in higher education for the purpose of experiencing pleasure? Is not the structure of explanation the same in both cases?

Yes, the explanatory structure is the same. However, in terms of the topic of this book, what is principally at issue is whether higher education is pursued for the sake of a vocation, which is in turn pursued for the sake of experiencing pleasure, or whether higher education is pursued directly for the sake of experiencing pleasure. What makes Lewis's view distinctive is that it is an affirmation of the latter alternative, whereas everyone else affirms the former.

8   In his essay "On Stories," Lewis was concerned with the different kinds of sources of pleasure in reading stories, and he settled on the belief that there are different qualities in stories that provide readers with pleasure. As one example, he mentions children who want to hear the same story over and over again (who are like the minority of readers who read the same story over and over again): "The children … ask for the same story over and over again, and in the same words. They want to have again the 'surprise' of discovering that what seemed Little Red Riding Hood's grandmother is really the wolf. It is better when you know it is coming [there is no surprise]: free from the shock of actual surprise you can attend better to the intrinsic surprisingness of the *peripeteia* [the sudden change of circumstances]" (Lewis [1947] in 1994 [1966]: 18).

9   Lewis warned minority readers against harking back to the experience they had on the first occasion of reading a book, setting it up as a norm, and depreciating all subsequent experiences by comparison with it. "You can't, at the twentieth reading, get again the experience of reading *Lycidas* [a poem of Milton's in which he bewails the death by drowning of a learned friend] for the first time. But what you do get can be in its

own way as good" (Lewis 1992a [1963]: 26). He also made clear that readers who are members of the literary minority must not be confused with members of other minorities who either read out of social necessity or are like members of families and circles who must show an interest in hunting or county cricket (Lewis 1961a: 7–8).

10 Mark A. McCarthy writes, "I taught at a major Midwestern university for 40 years ... Throughout my career, but especially in the past few years, I encountered many students who clearly were uninterested in the subject matter, even when it was part of their major. They seemed to believe all that was necessary was to get that pigskin, not necessarily to master the subject matter. As a society, we must stop telling young people that college is the only path to happiness" (McCarthy 2022).

While Lewis would have wholeheartedly agreed with McCarthy that we must stop telling young people that college is the only path to happiness, he would have added that we must also start telling them that higher education is itself a source of and exists for the purpose of providing happiness for those who enjoy higher-level intellectual activity.

11 Michael Oakeshott not only fails to see that the experience of pleasure is the purpose of the university, but he also strikingly claims that the existence of the university, which he says "is a number of people engaged in ... 'the pursuit of learning'" (Oakeshott 1989: 96), has no purpose. When Oakeshott rejects the idea of a purpose for the university, he means the university does not exist for achieving what is useful, where a job, social change, etc. are examples of what is useful. Yet, toward the end of his essay he writes that "[t]he enjoyment of [the pursuit of learning]" is the one thing that every university in Europe provides in some degree for its undergraduates (Oakeshott 1989: 102). What Oakeshott never explains is why enjoyment is not itself a purpose for which the pursuit of learning is useful.

12 For example, Jonathan Marks (Marks 2021a) points out that over fifty years ago, the authors of the Port Huron Statement, a founding document of American student activism, called for "an alliance of students and faculty" to galvanize a new left, taking in "allies in labor, civil rights, and other liberal forces outside the campus." Within the universities, this alliance would "consciously build a base for [its] assault upon the loci of power." From "its schools and colleges across the nations," a "militant left

might awaken its allies." On this view, politics is not an extracurricular activity but the very stuff of higher education. Marks is quoting from Students for a Democratic Society, "The Port Huron Statement," in Flacks and Lichtenstein (2015: 282–3).

Lewis would have said none of us should be surprised by the existence of people who seek to take over higher education for a political purpose. He described "the man whose soul is filled with some great Cause, to which he will subordinate his appetites, his fortune, and even his safety ... [I]t is out of [this] man that something really fiendish can be made; an Inquisitor, a Member of the Committee of Public Safety. It is great men, potential saints, not little men, who become merciless fanatics. Those who are readiest to die for a cause may easily become those who are readiest to kill for it ... The higher the stakes, the greater the temptation to lose your temper over the game" (Lewis 1986b [1958]: 28–9). Lest a reader assume that Lewis, because he was a Christian, thought that those whose souls are captured by a "Cause" are always secularists or atheists, it is important to point out that he believed the worst "Cause" is theocracy:

> Theocracy is the worst of all governments. If we must have a tyrant a robber baron is far better than an inquisitor. The baron's cruelty may sometimes sleep, his cupidity at some point be sated; and since he dimly knows he is doing wrong he may possibly repent. But the inquisitor who mistakes his own cruelty and lust of power and fear for the voice of Heaven will torment us infinitely because he torments us with the approval of his own conscience ... A metaphysic, held by the rulers with the force of a religion, is a bad sign. It forbids them, like the inquisitor, to admit any grain of truth or good in their opponents, it abrogates the ordinary rules of morality, and it gives a seemingly high, super-personal sanction to all the very ordinary human passions by which, like other men, the rulers will frequently be actuated. In a word, it forbids wholesome doubt. A political programme can never in reality be more than probably right ... To attach to a party programme ... the sort of assent which we should reserve for demonstrable theorems, is a kind of intoxication. (Lewis [1946] in 1994 [1966]: 81–2)

It is for reasons like these which Lewis had in mind (concerning theocrats and rulers who hold a metaphysic with the force of a religion) that John McWhorter admonishes his readers to be wary of people like Ibram X. Kendi, whom he likens to members of a priesthood in the new religion which he calls "Woke Racism" (McWhorter 2021).

13 Anscombe's statement is a reminder that while higher education is concerned with more complex conceptual relationships, this does not mean that it is always concerned with assembling simples into complexes. Sometimes it is concerned with disassembling complexes into simples. And this, as Anscombe understood, is hard work.

14 People who seemingly misunderstand Lewis's view of higher education are Melinda and Philip Nielsen in their paper "Education's Discarded Image: C. S. Lewis and the Theological Tradition of the Liberal Arts" (2015). They point out that Lewis's "philosophy of education ... has been so little noticed by critics," which might in part be explained by the fact that Lewis "does not set out to treat a liberal education explicitly and comprehensively ... [but instead] embeds his views in theological or literary arguments" (Nielsen and Nielsen 2015: 272). The Nielsens go on to ask if there are some subjects worth studying not because they lead to a vocation but simply because we are humans. They maintain that Lewis's writings implicitly suggest that the medieval trivium—grammar, rhetoric, and dialectic—and quadrivium—arithmetic, geometry, music, and astronomy—are such subjects, and they believe Lewis thought the trivium and quadrivium could provide the framework for a sound university education (Nielsen and Nielsen 2015: 277) in which students develop an appreciation of the true, the beautiful, and the good, all of which brings glory to God (Nielsen and Nielsen 2015: 281). Nielsen and Nielsen never mention the word "pleasure" and seem completely unaware that the Lewis corpus is metaphorically overflowing with discussions of experiences of pleasure as what provides the purpose for intellectual activity in the university.

15 Higher education in Lewis's day was largely for men. Not so, today:

> Men [in the United States] are abandoning higher education in such numbers that they now trail female college students by record levels.

> At the close of the 2020–21 academic year, women made up 59.5% of college students … The gender enrollment disparity among nonprofit colleges is widest at private four-year schools, where the proportion of women during the 2020–21 school year grew to an average of 61%, a record high …. (Belkin 2021)

The percentages would in many cases become even more unbalanced than they already are were it not for the fact that many men go to college to play a sport. For example, a former president of my college wanted to get rid of the men's football team but concluded he could not because the percentages of men and women students would become even more lopsided than they already were.

Chapter 1

1. In his book *The Pleasures of Reading in an Age of Distraction*, Alan Jacobs asks "*Why* should [books] be read? The first reason … the first in order of importance—is that reading books can be intensely pleasurable" (Jacobs 2011: 10). Thus, he declares that "I am firmly on the side of Lewis … Read what gives you delight" (Jacobs 2011: 23). Jacobs does not explain why Lewis maintained pleasure is the first reason for reading books, which is that pleasure is intrinsically good. That is, it is the intrinsic goodness of pleasure that explains why it is first and foremost reasonable to read for pleasure.
2. Lewis's view of God's relationship to questions about value is found in his answer to what in philosophy is known as Euthyphro's Dilemma, which is named after Socrates's interlocutor, Euthyphro, in Plato's dialogue *Euthyphro*. Therein, a major point of contention is the following dilemma: Do the gods say a certain action is pious because it is pious? Or is the action pious because the gods say that it is pious? Over the course of more than two millennia, piety for the most part has disappeared from the formulation of Euthyphro's Dilemma and has been replaced with the concept of the good, so that today we find the Dilemma most often expressed in something like the following form: Does God say something is good because it is good? Or is something good because God says it is

good? Lewis made it very clear in more than one place that he sided with the former choice:

> With Hooker, and against Dr Johnson, I emphatically embrace the first alternative. The second might lead to the abominable conclusion ... that charity is good only because God arbitrarily commanded it—that He might equally well have commanded us to hate Him and one another and that hatred would then have been right ... God's will is determined by His wisdom which always perceives, and His goodness which always embraces, the intrinsically good. (Lewis 2001f [1940]: 99)
>
> If I had any hesitation in saying that God "made" the *Tao* [the moral law] it [would] only be because that might suggest that it was an arbitrary creation ... : whereas I believe it to be the necessary expression, in terms of temporal existence, of what God by His own righteous nature necessarily is. One [could] indeed say of it *genitum, non factum* [begotten, not made]: for is not the *Tao* the Word Himself, considered from a particular point of view? (Lewis 2007: 1226–7)

As applied to morality and happiness, Lewis's position on Euthyphro's Dilemma amounts to the following: Given that moral principles like "Do not murder," "Do not steal," "Do not lie," and "Do not covet" are fundamentally about the happiness of others, moral principles cannot be a matter of what any being, including God, says or commands because the value of happiness itself is not a matter of what any being says or commands. Lewis believed matters of value are in the nature of things. God created human nature out of which morality flows, but God created human nature in light of His own nature, which, Lewis believed, is the basis of all reality (see Dyer and Watson 2016: 90, 103, 107 for a good treatment of Lewis's view). Because pleasure is intrinsically good and pain is intrinsically evil, they have their value independent of what God says or commands, but not independent of God's nature. Lewis was convinced God could no more make pleasure not intrinsically good and pain not intrinsically evil than He could make Himself exist and not exist at the same time. And because something like hatred is productive of actions that aim to decrease pleasure and/or increase pain in the lives of others, God cannot decree that hatred is good. Were issues of value a function of what God (or anyone else) chooses, then they would ultimately be arbitrary. And Lewis believed this is contrary to the nature of things.

3   Poe's apparent failure to understand the distinction between intrinsic evil and instrumental good illustrates how easy it is to confuse the distinction between intrinsic and extrinsic/instrumental good (evil). For example, Zena Hitz writes the following in her recent book *Lost in Thought: The Hidden Pleasures of an Intellectual Life*: "What does learning look like, stripped of its trappings of fame, prestige, fortune, and social use? In other words, how is it good for its own sake, because of its effect on the learner rather than because of its outward results? ... What sort of effect [on the learner] are we looking for?" (Hitz 2020: 26).

   If learning is intrinsically good, then we are not looking for any effect of it to account for its intrinsic goodness. According to Hitz, learning is intrinsically good because it contributes to a person being more fully human (Hitz 2020: 187); it contributes to a person's dignity (Hitz 2020: 203). But if these contributions make learning good, then learning is extrinsically and instrumentally good.

   Lewis understood how easy it is to confuse means with ends. He complained that John Henry Newman, in one of his *Parochial and Plain Sermons*, "has substituted *religion* for God—as if navigation were substituted for arrival, or battle for victory, or wooing for marriage, or in general the means for the end" (Lewis 1992a [1963]: 30).

4   Julie A. Reuben, in her book *The Making of the Modern University: Intellectual Transformation and the Marginalization of Morality*, discusses at length the possibility of value-free scholarship which is "a persistent and problematic aspect of modern intellectual life" (Reuben 1996: 10). For Lewis, higher education and the scholarly work therein is value-laden in the sense that it exists for the purpose of experiencing the intrinsic goodness of pleasure. However, Lewis believed higher education is value-neutral in the sense that a human mind is able to and does directly apprehend objective reality without any prior epistemological assumptions or presuppositions. For example, Lewis believed a person does not have to assume that God exists or that God does not exist in order to apprehend/know certain things about the world. One of the

things he thought a human mind directly apprehends is the experience of pleasure and its intrinsic goodness.

Some readers might be puzzled: Are there really people who maintain we cannot directly apprehend/have an awareness of anything about the world without assuming, say, that God exists? Yes. Indeed, I suspect that some of the people who read this book might believe this. I have in mind here what are known in certain Christian religious circles as presuppositionalists or, in the words of one former presuppositionalist, "presuppers." Presuppositionalists claim that we cannot know anything, even that we are experiencing pleasure and pain, without assuming that the God of the Bible exists. Examples of presuppositionalists are Cornelius Van Til (Van Til 1969, 1975), Rousas John Rushdoony (Rushdoony 1971), and Gordon H. Clark (Clark 1989).

5   A reviewer of this book in its consideration for publication (a different reviewer than the one mentioned in the Addendum to this chapter) wrote the following: "As the author notes, hedonists claim not only that pleasure is an intrinsic good, but that it is the ONLY intrinsic good. Did Lewis believe that? The author provides no textual support that he did." The reason I provide no textual support for the claim that Lewis believed pleasure is the only intrinsic good is because Lewis believed pleasure is *not* the only intrinsic good, and I have *explicitly* stated he believed it is not. Lewis was a hedonist *about happiness* in the sense that he agreed with hedonists that happiness consists of nothing but experiences of pleasure. However, he disagreed with hedonists that pleasure is the only intrinsic good and, hence, was not, strictly speaking, a hedonist.

6   Lewis provides his own example of an intrinsic evil other than pain. In a letter to his hypothetical interlocutor, Malcolm, in *Letters to Malcolm*, Lewis considered the following objection to his claim that pleasure is intrinsically good: "When I was writing about pleasures last week I had quite forgotten about the *mala mentis gaudia*—the pleasures of the mind which are intrinsically evil. The pleasure, say, of having a grievance. What a disappointment it is—for one self-revealing moment—to discover that the other party was not really to blame?" (Lewis 1992a [1963]: 94). Lewis responded, "But I don't think this leaves my theory (and experience) of ordinary pleasures in ruins" (Lewis 1992a [1963]: 94). Why not in ruins? Because what is intrinsically evil is not the simple pleasure but

the complex whole that consists of pleasure-cum-grievance at someone whom you believe is innocent. That is, given your belief that the person is innocent, you understand that continuing to derive pleasure from a complaint against him is *unjust*. It is the combination of pleasure with an attitude that does not fit, is a mismatch for, the belief that is intrinsically evil. Things are, wrote Lewis, "as Plato said, 'mixed'" (Lewis 1992a [1963]: 94), but they are mixed in the wrong way, in a way which makes the mixture intrinsically evil.

7 For example, when Lewis wrote about the idea of hell, he pointed out that "[o]ur Lord's words usually stress the negative side of it, not what the lost souls get but what they miss. Perhaps we had best leave it at that" (Lewis 2007: 1149).

8 Lewis believed that "modern politics would be impossible without the Myth" (Lewis [1967] in 1967: 92). Those who ascribed to the "Myth" believe that "*everything* is moving 'upwards and onwards' ... [N]othing seems more normal, more natural, more plausible, than that chaos should turn into order, death into life, ignorance into knowledge" (Lewis [1967] in 1967: 86). Lewis maintained the Myth is a philosophical doctrine (as opposed to a scientific hypothesis) and that those who assent to it are motivationally driven to see its realization in this world. If one combines a belief in eudaimonism with a commitment to the Myth, then one ends up with, in contemporary terms, a progressive view that the polis should provide, and its citizens complete, a college education which is necessary for happiness. Lewis said he found the Myth imaginatively attractive. Indeed, he wrote it "appeals to every part of me except my reason" (Lewis [1967] in 1967: 93). And in his own play on the idea of being "woke," Lewis claimed it was the "painful duty" of those who understood the falsity of the Myth "to wake the world" from an enchantment (Lewis [1967] in 1967: 93).

9 In maintaining that there will be no need for acting morally in heaven, Lewis was not claiming that moral principles will not exist in heaven. Given that pleasure is intrinsically good, it is good in every possible world (heaven is a possible world that Christians and others believe will be actual). Therefore, the moral principles arising out of pleasure's intrinsic goodness exist in every possible world where there are or could be experiences of pleasure. Lewis believed that persons in heaven will desire

to act in ways that are moral and, with no opposing desires, will not need to choose to act morally.

10. Lewis made clear in his book *An Experiment in Criticism* that he believed the ultimate purpose of literature is for the reader to experience pleasure. However, he believed

> [t]he real objection to a merely hedonistic theory of literature, or of the arts in general, is that "pleasure" is a very high, and therefore very empty, abstraction ... If you tell me that something is a [source of] pleasure, I do not know whether [the pleasure] is more like [that which comes from] revenge, or buttered toast, or success, or adoration, or relief from danger, or a good scratch. You will have to say that literature gives, not just pleasure, but the particular pleasure proper to it; and it is in defining this "proper pleasure" that all your real work will have to be done. (Lewis 1961a: 133)

Lewis proposed specifying the pleasure that literature provides in terms of the distinction between a good book and a bad book, where this distinction is made in terms of the further distinction between a good reader and a bad reader. A good reader is a person who is open or receptive to what he is reading in the sense that he is open to having his mind enlarged through seeing the world "with other eyes," in imagining "with other imaginations," in feeling "with other hearts" (Lewis 1961a, 137), where this enlargement of mind is a source of pleasure. Thus, a good book is one that is capable of actualizing the stated receptiveness in good readers and providing them with accompanying literary pleasure. And a bad book? Lewis wrote that "[i]n calling [a] book bad we are claiming not that it can elicit bad reading, but that it can't elicit good" (Lewis 1961a: 117).

Chapter 2

1. Lewis linked satisfaction of our basic human needs for food, health, and sex with enjoyable activity in some thoughts about poetry. He regarded poetry as literature which uses language to say something (make utterances) that is detachable from its original context. He claimed the first demand of any utterance is that it should be interesting, that is,

"entertaining, charming, or exciting for the moment [but which also] should have a desirable permanent effect on us if possible—should make us happier, or wiser, or better … It is all of a piece with what we want in other departments of life: a man wants his food to be nourishing as well as palatable, his games to be healthy as well as enjoyable, his wife to be a good companion and housekeeper as well as a pleasing sexual mate" (Lewis 1939b: 119).

2   Lewis made mention of his father's love and purchase of books. It should not be overlooked that his mother, Florence, was quite accomplished academically. She earned first- and second-class honors respectively in logic and mathematics at what is now Queen's University in Belfast, Northern Ireland, and she tutored Lewis in Latin and French when he was a boy. However, she tragically died of abdominal cancer when Lewis was nine years of age. Her death left a huge void in his life. He wrote that "[w]ith my mother's death all settled happiness, all that was tranquil and reliable, disappeared from my life. There was to be much fun, many pleasures … but no more of the old security. It was sea and islands now; the great continent had sunk like Atlantis" (Lewis 1955: 21).

3   A reviewer of this manuscript pointed out that "there is a relatively simple analogue [here] when it comes to other activities like sports or music. In both of these arenas, participants do, in fact, separate themselves into various groups based on degrees of excellence. And they do so precisely for the purpose of maximizing enjoyment. When you're really good at playing the trumpet or playing basketball, it simply isn't as pleasurable to play with others who aren't."

4   At this point, one might ask "Was Lewis opposed to democracy?" In education, Yes. But as a form of government for the polis, No. Concerning the latter, he wrote the following:

> I believe in political equality. But there are two opposite reasons for being a democrat. You may think all men so good that they deserve a share in the government of the commonwealth, and so wise that the commonwealth needs their advice. That is, in my opinion, the false, romantic doctrine of democracy. On the other hand, you may believe fallen men to be so wicked that not one of them can be trusted with any irresponsible power over his fellows.
>
> That I believe to be the true ground of democracy. (Lewis [1945c] in 2001g: 168)

Lewis believed the democratization of education, which he opposed, was a threat to the existence of the democratic polis, which he supported:

> Of course, this [democratization of education] would not follow unless all education became state education. But it will. That is part of the same movement. Penal taxes, designed for that purpose, are liquidating the Middle Class, the class who were prepared to save and spend and make sacrifices in order to have their children privately educated. The removal of this class, besides linking up with the abolishment of education, is ... an inevitable effect of the spirit that says *I'm as good as you*. This was, after all, the social group which gave ... humans ... the over-whelming majority of their scientists, physicians, philosophers, theologians, poets, artists, composers, architects, jurists, and administrators. (Lewis 1961b: 168)

Lewis could at times be blunt:

> An education on [democratic] lines will be pleasing to democratic feelings. It will have repaired the inequalities of nature. But it is quite another question whether it will breed a democratic nation which can survive, or even one whose survival is desirable ... A nation of dunces can be safe only in a world of dunces. (Lewis [1944c] in 1986a: 33)

> [A democratic education is] that nationally suicidal type of education which keeps back the promising child because the idlers and dunces might be "hurt" if it [the child] were undemocratically moved into a higher class than themselves. (Lewis 1988 [1960]: 48)

5   Lewis's belief that higher education does not exist for the purpose of making a student a good man can be contrasted with the following assertion of Nicholas Murray Butler, the President of Columbia University in 1921: "[T]here is one aim which all faculties and schools, all teachers and scholars, have in common—the building of character" (quoted in Reuben 1996: 75). Reuben adds (Reuben 1996: 75) that Charles W. Eliot, the President of Harvard in the late nineteenth and early twentieth centuries, agreed with Butler that "a sense of duty to students

in respect to the formation of character" was "characteristic of all the American faculties." Eliot's claim was made in 1905.

6   The reason the university student is in theory, if not in reality, human (a good man) is because, in Lewis's Platonic conception, his emotions have been trained (beginning before he is able to reason) to support his reason in terms of how he should behave against his desire to pursue pleasure in ways that he believes are immoral. In Lewis's terms, the university student is ideally already a man with a chest which mediates between his belly (desires) and his head (his intellect). Lewis set forth his beliefs about pre-university education in his book *The Abolition of Man* (Lewis 2001d [1944]: Chapter 1). Michael Ward, in his book *After Humanity: A Guide to C. S. Lewis's The Abolition of Man*, writes that Lewis "tackles 'education' in the widest possible sense and takes it to mean something like moral inheritance, the legacy of humane wisdom that the older generation imparts to the younger and which the younger have a duty to hand on in due course. The subject [is] not so much schoolroom pedagogy as moral philosophy …" (Ward 2021: 11).

7   Alan Jacobs rightly reminds us of the difference between the ideal and the reality, and that Lewis's tutees were not always students who arrived in Oxford as individuals who derived pleasure from intellectual activity: "[Lewis's] Oxford students were by and large people who either liked sports and games and social activities naturally or had learned to do so through their school years. Trying to teach his twenty-year old pupils that Spenser or Milton or Chaucer could give *delight*—well, that was a nearly superhuman task. It would have been far better if someone had captured their imaginations a decade earlier, as some of his teachers had captured his …" (Jacobs 2005: 178). Jacobs is one of the few authors writing about Lewis who understands the central role of pleasure in Lewis's belief about the purpose of higher education (and the importance of good pre-university teachers as cultivators of experiences of pleasure in their students).

8   Lewis's conception of pre-university and university education and the relationship between them is reflected in a recent interview with Ian Rowe and Joyanet Mangual, who are opening a charter high school, Vertex Partnership Academies, in the impoverished Bronx neighborhood

of Soundview in New York City. Vertex is an International Baccalaureate (IB) school:

> "The IB program ... stresses critical thinking, the Socratic method, and writing, writing, writing," Ms. Mangual says, stressing that this should help prepare students for higher education. "What students struggle with most in college is not being able to do independent research. We're going to make each student complete a research paper by the end of the 12th grade."
>
> Mr. Rowe, for his part, emphasizes that the school will inculcate what he calls "cardinal virtues": "courage, justice, wisdom and temperance." (Varadarajan 2022)

Like Lewis, Rowe and Mangual believe the virtues should be inculcated before entering university and confirm Lewis's claim that those in university should be able to do independent research, which puts them on a level with their professors/mentors.

9 Lewis wrote that games are played for pleasure. Interestingly, Kathleen Raine, a colleague at Cambridge, recounted that learning for Lewis was a game of play: "I knew C. S. Lewis only during his last years when he was Professor of English at Cambridge ... He seemed to possess a kind of boyish greatness ... He was not, certainly, intellectually boyish ... [except] in the freshness and joyousness with which he carried his learning ... [F]or him learning was a joyful and inexhaustible game ... The element of play was never far away." (Raine 1965: 102–3)

10 Louis Markos, in a section of his book *C. S. Lewis: An Apologist for Education* entitled "C. S. Lewis University," states that "professors would seek to instill a love of and a desire for virtue in their students and strive to help restore in them the traditional stock responses to good and evil" (Markos 2015: 48). However, Lewis believed students at university, if properly educated in primary and secondary schools, should already be morally formed. He did not believe it is the job of a professor to instill a desire and love for virtue and restore stock responses to good and evil.

11 Joel D. Heck, in his book *Irrigating Deserts: C. S. Lewis on Education*, writes that "Lewis agreed with John Henry Newman, who said that the purpose of the university was to train good members of society" (Heck 2005: 30). But Lewis explicitly wrote that he was not able to

make Newman's conclusion about the purpose of higher education his own. Lewis did not believe the purpose of a university education was to train good members of society. That might be a side effect of university learning, but it is not its purpose. Lewis thought education for training good members of society occurs, if things are well ordered, *prior* to entering university.

Heck writes that "we will glean from Lewis's writings the philosophy behind his educational practice" (Heck 2005: 23). Yet, like almost everyone else who writes about Lewis on philosophical topics (which is a small group of individuals), Heck fails to pick up on Lewis's explicit comments about pleasure and its intrinsic goodness. Heck repeatedly reminds his readers that Lewis believed "[t]he task of reading should cause us to lay aside our preconceived ideas so the message of the text comes through to us and has the opportunity to change us" (Heck 2005: 61). But when it comes to Lewis's beliefs about pleasure, Heck, like so many others, cannot lay aside his own preconceived ideas. Two others who find it difficult to disassociate Lewis from Newman are Melinda and Philip Nielsen. They write that "Lewis agrees with Newman that liberal arts education is [in Newman's words] 'not merely a means to something beyond it ... but an end sufficient to rest in and to pursue for its own sake'" (Nielsen and Nielsen 2015: 274). They go on to add that "for Lewis liberal education concerns itself with improving men" (Nielsen and Nielsen 2015: 274). However, Lewis was clear that liberal arts (higher) education is for the purpose of experiencing pleasure, where pleasure is experienced for its own sake, and that someone in higher education should in theory already be a good human being, where being a good human being is the objective of pre-university education.

12 "[T]he whole modern world" had at one point included Lewis himself:

> At an early age I came to believe that the life of culture (that is, of intellectual and aesthetic activity) was very good for its own sake, or even that it was the good for man ... I was awakened from this confused state of mind by finding that the friends of culture seemed to me to be exaggerating. In my reaction against what seemed exaggerated I was driven to the other extreme, and began, in my own mind, to belittle the claims of culture. As soon as I did this I was faced with the question, "If it is a thing of so little

value, how are you justified in spending so much of your life on it?" (Lewis [1940] in 1967: 12)

As we know by now, Lewis answered this question in terms of the value of experiences of pleasure that culture provided him.

13 Lewis mentioned Francis Bacon's belief that knowledge in the form of applied science and magic is rightly used to control nature, which Lewis characterized as knowledge as "a spouse for fruit [what is useful]." He contrasted Bacon's belief about knowledge with the view that knowledge is an end in itself, which Lewis regarded as knowledge as "a mistress for pleasure" (Lewis 2001d [1944]: 78).

14 While Lewis believed the medieval Model of the universe is false, even though it provided him with much pleasure, he was also convinced that the relationship between cosmological models and facts of science is complicated. In terms of the old medieval Model, "[t]here is no question [of its] being shattered by the inrush of new phenomena. The truth would seem to be the reverse; that when changes in the human mind produce a sufficient disrelish of the old Model and a sufficient hankering for some new one, phenomena to support that new one will obediently turn up. I do not at all mean that these new phenomena are illusory. Nature has all sorts of phenomena in stock and can suit many different tastes ... [But nature] gives most of her evidence in answer to the questions we ask her. Here, as in the courts, the character of the evidence depends on the shape of the examination" (Lewis 1964: 221, 223). One feature of the human mind is its preference for simple explanations. Thus, the old Model

> "with Centric and Eccentric scribl'd o're", had been tinkered a good deal to keep up with observations. How far, by endless tinkerings, it could have kept up with them till even now, I do not know. But the human mind will not long endure such ever-increasing complications if once it has seen that some simpler conception can "save the appearances" ... The new astronomy triumphed not because the case for the old became desperate, but because the new was a better tool; once this was grasped, our ingrained conviction that Nature herself is thrifty did the rest. (Lewis 1964: 219–20)

Lewis's thoughts about the relationship between scientific models and facts of nature are similar to those found in Thomas Kuhn's *The Structure of Scientific Revolutions* (Kuhn 1962). However, I am not aware of any reference that Lewis makes to Kuhn's work. Perhaps they were contemporaneously yet independently thinking along the same lines about how science works.

15 In a recent essay in *The Wall Street Journal* about the purpose of art museums, Eric Gibson, the *Journal*'s Arts in Review editor, asserts that

> art museums have played a role in the intellectual and cultural life of the nation on par with that of colleges and universities.
>
> Like higher education, art museums face a crisis of purpose. They are now widely seen as shameful relics of the era of Western colonialism, whose proper social role is to advance a progressive agenda. The doctrine of art for art's sake, the idea that aesthetic values alone should guide their operations, is increasingly taking a back seat to political ideology. (Gibson 2022)

As an example of the politicization of museums, Gibson cites the 150th anniversary of The Metropolitan Museum of Art in New York City in which there was

> an exhibition celebrating its many treasures and the donors who'd helped the museum acquire them … After outlining [two of the biggest donors'] contributions to the museum, the wall texts informed visitors that the fortunes that had made these generous acts possible had been built on, respectively, "intolerable" and "harsh" labor conditions. (Gibson 2022)

Not surprisingly, Gibson's article has given rise to a string of letters to the editor of the *Journal*, one of which is from Kenneth Weine, Chief Communications Officer for The Metropolitan Museum of Art, in which he justifies "[a] modest wall label [which] explained that the collector who donated these pieces benefitted from the sugar industry and slavery" (Weine 2022). Peggy Fogelman, Director of the Isabella Stewart Gardner Museum, Boston, writes "[w]e can both honor the aesthetic and excavate other truths" (Fogelman 2022). In the last of the letters, Charlotte O'Beirne, a sixteen-year-old private citizen, writes that "my generation has inherited a chaotic intellectual landscape. Between arguments about ideology and indoctrination, we have forgotten that, above all, art is made to be enjoyed" (O'Beirne 2022).

Lewis would have commended O'Beirne. Like her, he believed art museums, as a species of culture, exist for the purpose of providing their viewers with experiences of aesthetic pleasure. Lewis would likely have regarded Weine's and Fogelman's efforts at, respectively, explaining the sources of the donor's beneficence and excavating other truths as blinding and paralyzing distractions. Most certainly, he would have considered Gibson's claim about art for art's sake as one more instance of the gross exaggeration of the importance of culture.

Chapter 3

1. Anthony Kronman writes of his mother that her hatred of religion "was the source of energy with which she defended everything that in her mind stood in opposition to religion—science, tolerance, the pleasure of reading ..." (Kronman 2022: 7). Lewis concluded that religion in the form of Christianity was not in the least opposed to science, tolerance, or, most importantly in terms of our present concern, the pleasure of higher-level intellectual activity.

2. Engaging in intellectual activity for pleasure and for the glory of God presupposes that we can perform one and the same action for two (or more) purposes. Lewis seemingly believed that because God created us for the purpose of experiencing pleasure with its intrinsic goodness, an experience which has the aroma of our Creator about it, it makes perfect sense that we would act for both the purpose of enjoying the goodness of what we were created to experience and the purpose of calling attention to (glorifying) our Creator. For further development of Lewis's thoughts about pleasure in relationship to glorifying God, see Chapter 5.

3. Letters concerning these activities are found in Lewis 2004b: the Home Guard (425–6, 432–3), talks to members of the Royal Air Force (471–3), and broadcasts on the BBC (469–71).

4. The difference between a reason to and not to do something is important at this point. In his recent book *The Medieval Mind of C. S. Lewis*, Jason M. Baxter discusses Lewis's concern in "Learning in Wartime" about whether Christians can continue in higher education during a great war like the Second World War. Baxter writes that "[t]he answer, from Lewis ... was

yes, we should" (Baxter 2022: 17). But we must carefully note the way in which the normative notion "should" is introduced here. The problem Lewis addressed about Christians remaining at university in the Second World War arose because they desired, and thereby had a reason, to engage in higher-level intellectual activity for pleasure. Lewis answered that "given our country allows us to remain [in university], this is *prima facie* evidence that the life which we, at any rate, can best lead to the glory of God at present is the learned life" (Lewis [1939a] in 2001g: 56). Lewis's point was not, as Baxter suggests, that Christians had a reason why they *should* remain in higher education during the war, but that there was no outweighing reason why they *should not* remain at university and fulfill their desire for the pleasure of higher-level intellectual activity (their remaining, for which they had a reason, was morally permissible).

Chapter 4

1   Lewis's high estimation of reason is apparent in what was originally an untitled poem (but later entitled "Reason" by Walter Hooper, who edited the book *Poems* (see Lewis 1992b) in which it appears).
    In personal correspondence, Michael Ward informs me that no one really knows when Lewis wrote the poem. His best guess is it was written in the early 1930s around the time of Lewis's conversion to Christianity in 1931, or perhaps slightly later.
2   Lewis believed that the frequent appeal to *ad hominem* attacks, what he called "Bulverism," was in part a reflection of the naturalist's conviction that "reason can play no effective part in human affairs" (Lewis [1944b] in 1970: 274). See Goetz (2018a: 44–5).
3   Some persons might also be wondering *why* people like Rosenberg espouse naturalism. What is the *reasoning* behind an espousal of it? If you are one of these persons, see Goetz (2018a: Chapter 5) for the reasoning and Lewis's response to it.
4   One of the most famous exchanges at meetings of the Socratic Club occurred in 1948 when the philosopher G. E. M. (Elizabeth) Anscombe presented a paper criticizing Lewis's argument from reason against naturalism in his book *Miracles*. In light of her criticisms, Lewis revised

his argument in a second edition of *Miracles*. Some think that Lewis ceased to believe in his argument after the exchange with Anscombe, but it is difficult to explain his revising of the argument in the second edition of *Miracles* had he ceased to believe in the soundness of the argument. In a letter to Professor Thomas Van Osdall dated June 1, 1963, Lewis wrote that "I made a mess of one argument" in the first edition of *Miracles*, and he encouraged Van Osdall to use the second edition of *Miracles* as "the first text" (Peterson 2020: 185). It is plausible to think the argument of which Lewis believed he had made a mess was his argument from reason (the central chapter about the argument from reason (Chapter 3) is the only chapter he rewrote for the second edition). But to admit making a mess of an argument and encouraging someone to use a revised version of it suggests continued belief in the soundness of the argument.

Chapter 5

1. For more on this issue, see Goetz (2018a: 48–54), and Goetz and Taliaferro (2011).
2. Someone might respond, "Does not a person involved in Christian ministry by definition enjoy his or her vocational work, so that there is no need for a purpose statement about enjoyment?" Those who think Christian ministry is always enjoyed by those involved in it should read the private writings of Mother Teresa which describe her decades-long dark night of the soul. See Kolodiejchuk (2007).
3. Lewis provided vocational advice, apparently upon request, to Anglican priests in Wales in 1945 (Lewis [1945a] in 1970: 89–103). Some of what he said is perhaps relevant to what he considered a good theological education. For example, Lewis believed there should be a compulsory paper in every ordination exam on translation of a theological work into vernacular language to facilitate clergy-laity communication, because the language of the priest or pastor is different from that of the parishioner. In terms of theological ideas, Lewis thought the clergy, while defending permanent Christian truths and avoiding "winds of doctrine" (to avoid moving with the times, Lewis urged clergymen to read old books as opposed to new, if they do not have time to read both), should stay

abreast of developments in science, while not relying on them as solid confirmation of Christianity because the deliverances of science are never more than provisional.

4   Lewis understood that for people who are members of a university and enjoy seeing the world through the eyes of others, even the eyes of others with whom they disagree, there is always the danger, which must be resisted, of what is called, in today's terms, a "silo mentality":

> In any fairly large and talkative community such as a university there is always the danger that those who think alike should gravitate together into *coteries* where they will henceforth encounter opposition only in the emasculated form of rumour that the outsiders say thus and thus. The absent are easily refuted, complacent dogmatism thrives, and differences of opinion are embittered by group hostility. Each group hears not the best, but the worst, that the other group can say. (Lewis [1942–3] in 1970: 127)

5   If one thinks of a core curriculum as identical with or similar in relevant respects to a liberal arts education, then Lewis believed higher education is *not* the place for a liberal arts education. Nevertheless, many maintain Lewis believed not only that the university is the proper place for a liberal arts education but also that he spent his life in higher education providing such an education. For example, Louis Markos writes of Lewis that "he devoted his life to providing students with a classical, liberal arts education" (Markos 2015: 32). Derek Keefe writes in personal correspondence, "I ... find it somewhat strange that Lewis is so widely trumpeted as a champion of the liberal arts or general education at the tertiary level [the university level], as his position in such essays as 'Our English Syllabus' [in Lewis 1939a] couldn't be clearer: by the time one reaches university, the days of formalised comprehensive education *should* be over." Keefe goes on to point out that "[i]t may be strange to think of Christian liberal arts colleges as remedial institutions, but for many students ... this is indeed the role they serve."

6   The following quote from the Lewis scholar, Michael Ward, which concerns his illumination of the background for Lewis's writing of the Narnia stories, expresses the idea of licit knowledge that both subtracts from and adds to the pleasures that come from reading the stories:

> Knowledge, except where it is illicit, is always a kind of pleasure, and it is hard to see how our responses to Leonardo and to the Mona Lisa would not be enriched if we could read the silent message in her lips. To prefer our former ignorance would be to adopt a Luddite or obscurantist stance. So with the Narniad: its problems of occasion, composition, and reception are, in varying degrees, "solved" by the arguments mounted in this book [*Planet Narnia*], and to that extent the septet no longer yields the pleasure that it used to, the pleasure we derive from thinking, "There's more going on here than meets the eye." But at the same time these explanations offer up new pleasures, first at the literary-historical level and second at the theological level. (Ward 2008: 233–4)

I believe Lewis, while affirming Ward's point about licit knowledge, would have wondered why illicit knowledge cannot also provide pleasure. What would be the reason for pursuing it, Lewis would have asked, if it were believed that it would not, at any point in time or in any way, be a source of pleasure?

7   Some, perhaps many, people will be bothered by a position like that which I ascribe to Lewis. "How selfish of Lewis," they might respond, "that he would include or exclude topics of intellectual activity on the basis of whether they are a source of pleasure." But why think this is selfish? It surely is possible for individuals, whether inside or outside higher education, to pursue morally permissible pleasures without being selfish. Unless every reason for satisfying one's own interest is selfish, Lewis would have been thoroughly reasonable in including or excluding a topic of intellectual activity for the reason that it did or did not provide him with pleasure.

8   In an article about the religious rights of individuals in pre-university schooling, William Galston writes that "the government has fundamental interests that can override individual claims in some circumstances" (Galston 2022). If we apply Galston's point to higher education, I think Lewis, while conceding it, would have stressed that the fundamental interests of government are best served by people who enjoy the work which the furtherance of its interests requires. Hence, as far as is possible, the government should exercise restraint and not dictate what higher-level intellectual activity must occur in higher education.

Chapter 6

1. Someone might ask, "Where's the evidence in support of the assertion that some people in higher education think about and inculcate only their own points of view?" Here is one example. I and a colleague recently co-authored a textbook in which we present substantive naturalistic and theistic points of view on various topics. We extensively quote naturalists and theists so that readers can see for themselves what each claims about the topics we discuss. One of the reviewers of the manuscript wrote the following: "I'll be upfront here and out myself as a naturalist … I'm willing to entertain the hypothesis that my resistance to the heavy focus on theism in this book springs from the fact that I'm not a theist, so feel free to take my comments above … with a grain of salt. I care about acceptance of doctrinal diversity in the philosophy profession, and am not a Richard Dawkins- / Christopher Hitchens-style militant atheist. I strongly believe there should be room for theistic views in this debate, and I am interested to read them. But I feel duty-bound as a manuscript reviewer for a publishing house to mention that the large majority of professional philosophers are naturalists, many of them ardently so, and it's those philosophers who will decide whether or not to assign this text in their classes." The implied message here is that naturalists will not use the textbook because it provides a substantive presentation of an opposing, in this case theistic, point of view.

2. Zena Hitz writes that "[a]fter graduation, many of my classmates took their supposedly useless liberal arts education out of the ivory tower and into the realms of politics, law, business, journalism, and nonprofit initiatives. They founded schools and peopled law firms, corporate boards, *The New York Times*, international nongovernmental organizations, and high reaches of the US government. They found, in other words, that study for its own sake—that is, study without visible results or high-prestige credentials—was enormously useful for other ends" (Hitz 2020: 6). The only quibble I have with Hitz is one that Lewis had, which is that, strictly speaking, study is not for its own sake. It is for pleasure. Hitz asks, "What does learning look like, stripped of its trappings of fame, prestige, fortune and social use? In other words, how is it good for its own sake, because of its effect on the learner rather than

because of its outward results" (Hitz 2020: 26). As I explained in endnote 3 of Chapter 1, if study/learning is good for its own sake, it is not good because of its results, whether inward or outward. Interestingly, when Hitz looks for and dismisses an inward effect of study on the learner, the first alternative she discusses is pleasure (Hitz 2020: 26).

3   Albert Lewis kept his son, Jack, financially afloat while the latter was a student at Oxford. Albert wrote in his diary on October 11, 1923, that "[w]hile Jack was at home I repeated my promise to provide for him at Oxford if I possibly could, for a maximum of three years this summer. I again pointed out to him the difficulty of getting anything to do at [age] 28 if he had ultimately to leave Oxford" (W. H. Lewis n. d.: 148). It is doubtful Albert believed Jack literally could not have found something else to do other than being an academician in Oxford. What Albert likely meant was that Jack could not have found something else to do that he would have enjoyed as much as being an academician in Oxford. Most of Lewis's friends while studying at Oxford went on to do other things. Surely, Lewis could have done so too, even though he would have been, at least initially, deeply disappointed and unhappy.

4   Given I have maintained that the Bible is not a philosophy text that addresses topics like the values of pleasure and pain, someone will understandably ask, "What is the Bible about, if it is not a philosophy text?" The short answer, and it must be short for the purposes of this book, is that the Bible is about the history of Israel and Israel's place in God's redemptive plan for human beings. Given this purpose, the Bible, as I have already suggested, assumes certain beliefs such as that we experience pleasure and pain and that these are respectively intrinsically good and evil. "What are a couple of other examples of things the Bible assumes we believe without reading it?" Lewis believed that "[w]hen the apostles preached, they could assume even in their Pagan hearers a real consciousness of deserving the Divine anger. The Pagan mysteries existed to allay this consciousness, and the Epicurean philosophy claimed to deliver men from the fear of eternal punishment. It was against this background that the Gospel appeared as good news" (Lewis 2001f [1940]: 48). I am confident Lewis would also have insisted that another belief people have without reading the Bible is that we are souls that have

bodies. And I agree with Lewis. People often ask me where the Bible teaches that we are souls. I respond that the Bible does not teach that we are (or are not) souls because it is not a philosophy text. It simply takes for granted what ordinary people believe about the existence of the soul, which is that it exists and is separable from its physical body (see Goetz 2012a, 2015b, 2018b).

5   While many Christian parents send their children to Christian colleges in an effort to shield them from higher-level intellectual activity that they fear will lead to their offspring questioning and, perhaps, renouncing their Christian faith, Lewis believed this intellectual activity can be helpful for Christian belief. For example, Lewis had the senior devil, Screwtape, instruct the younger devil, Wormwood, not to let the patient under his care engage in reasoning because it might very well lead him to Christianity:

> The trouble about argument is that it moves the whole struggle onto the Enemy's [God's] ground. He can argue too … By the very act of arguing, you awake the patient's reason; and once it is awake, who can foresee the result? Even if a particular train of thought can be twisted so as to end in our favour, you will find that you have been strengthening in your patient the fatal habit of attending to universal issues and withdrawing his attention from the stream of immediate sense experiences. Your business is to fix his attention on the stream. Teach him to call it "real life" and don't let him ask what he means by "real." … Above all, do not attempt to use science (I mean, the real sciences) as a defence against Christianity. They will positively encourage him to think about realities he can't touch or see. There have been sad cases among the modern physicists. If he must dabble in science, keep him on economics and sociology; don't let him get away from that invaluable "real life." But the best of all is to let him read no science but to give him a grand general idea that he knows it all and that everything he happens to have picked up in casual talk and reading is "the results of modern investigation." Do remember you are there to fuddle him. From the way some of you young fiends talk, anyone would suppose it was our job to *teach*! (Lewis 1961b: 8, 10)

6   It is interesting to note that Lewis believed that a polis which seeks to gain more control over education will not

> encourage or even tolerate any radically Christian elements in its State system of education. Where the tide flows toward increasing State control, Christianity, with its claims in one way personal and in the other way ecumenical and both ways antithetical to omnicompetent government, must always in fact ... be treated as an enemy. Like learning, like the family, like any ancient and liberal profession, like the common law, it gives the individual a standing ground against the State. (Lewis [1946c] in 1970: 118)

Bibliography

Annas, Julia. 1993. *The Morality of Happiness*. Oxford: Oxford University Press.

Ansberry, Clare. 2021. "Rethinking Happiness," *The Wall Street Journal*, March 12.

Aristotle. 1962. *Nicomachean Ethics*, translated by Martin Ostwald. Indianapolis, IN: The Bobbs-Merrill Company.

Armstrong, David. 1978. "Naturalism, Materialism and First Philosophy." *Philosophia* 8: 261–76.

Arnold, Matthew. 2006. *Culture and Anarchy*. Oxford: Oxford University Press.

Baggini, Julian. 2004. *What's It All about: Philosophy and the Meaning of Life*. Oxford: Oxford University Press.

Balint, Benjamin. 2021. "A Literary Impressario." *The Wall Street Journal*, February 20–1.

Baxter, Jason M. 2022. *The Medieval Mind of C. S. Lewis: How Great Books Shaped a Great Mind*. Downers Grove, IL: IVP Academic.

Belkin, Douglas. 2021. "'I Just Feel Lost.' Young Men Abandon College." *The Wall Street Journal*, September 7.

Bloom, Paul. 2007. "Religion Is Natural." *Developmental Science* 10: 147–51.

Bloomberg, Michael R. 2022. "Republican Censors Go for Woke." *The Wall Street Journal*, August 22.

Bobrow, Emily. 2022. "Joseph McShane." *The Wall Street Journal*, July 16–17.

Boswell, James. 2008. *The Life of Samuel Johnson*, edited by David Womersley. London: Penguin Classics.

Brewer, Derek. 2005. "The Tutor: A Portrait." In Como, 115–51.

Carpenter, Humphrey. 1997. *The Inklings: C. S. Lewis, J. R. R. Tolkien, Charles Williams, and Their Friends*. London: HarperCollins.

Clark, Gordon H. 1989. *Three Types of Religious Philosophy*. Jefferson, MD: The Trinity Foundation.

Coghill, Nevill. 1965. "The Approach to English." In Gibb, 51–66.

Cohen, Ben. 2022. "America's Greatest Math Team Shares Its Secrets." *The Wall Street Journal*, July 16–17.

Como, James T., ed. 2005 [1979]. *Remembering C. S. Lewis: Recollections of Those Who Knew Him*. San Francisco, CA: Ignatius.

Cumhaill, Clare Mac and Rachael Wiseman. 2022. *Metaphysical Animals: How Four Women Brought Philosophy Back to Life*. London: Chatto & Windus.

Dawkins, Richard. 2012. *The Magic of Reality: How We Know What's Really True*. Great Britain: Transworld Publishers.

De Caro, Mario and David Macarthur, eds. 2004. *Naturalism in Question*. Cambridge, MA: Harvard University Press.

Delbanco, Andrew. 2012. *College: What It Was, Is, and Should Be*. Princeton, NJ: Princeton University Press.

Dyer, Justin Buckley and Micah J. Watson. 2016. *C. S. Lewis on Politics and the Natural Law*. Cambridge: Cambridge University Press.

"Fermat's Last Theorem." 1996. *BBC Horizon*, January 15. https://www.bbc.co.uk/player/episode/b0074rxx/horizon-19951996-fermat's-last-theorem

Finley, Allysia. 2021. "Rebellion in the Faculty Lounge." *The Wall Street Journal*, May 21. https://www.wsj.com/articles/rebellion-in-the-faculty-lounge-11621619432

Flacks, Richard and Nelson Lichtenstein, eds. 2015. *Sources and Legacies of the New Left's Founding Manifesto*. Philadelphia, PA: University of Pennsylvania Press.

Fogelman, Peggy. 2022. "Museums, Politics and the Experience of Art." *The Wall Street Journal*, September 12.

Galston, William A. 2022. "What Rights Do Hasidic Schools Have?" *The Wall Street Journal*, September 14, A17.

Gibb, Jocelyn, ed. 1965. *Light on C. S. Lewis*. New York: Harcourt, Brace, and World.

Gibson, Eric. 2022. "When Connoisseurs Yield to Commissars." *The Wall Street Journal*, September 3–4.

Goetz, Stewart. 2012a. "Is N. T. Wright Right about Substance Dualism?" *Philosophia Christi* 14: 183–91.

Goetz, Stewart. 2012b. *The Purpose of Life*. New York: Continuum.

Goetz, Stewart. 2015a. *A Philosophical Walking Tour with C. S. Lewis: Why It Did Not Include Rome*. New York: Bloomsbury.

Goetz, Stewart. 2015b. "Substance Dualism." In *The Ashgate Research Companion to Theological Anthropology*, edited by Joshua Farris and Charles Taliaferro, 125–37. Burlington, VT: Ashgate.

Goetz, Stewart. 2018a. *C. S. Lewis*. Oxford: Wiley Blackwell.

Goetz, Stewart. 2018b. "On the Nature of Human Persons and the Resurrection of the Body." *Journal of Analytic Theology* 6: 300–12.

Goetz, Stewart and Charles Taliaferro. 2011. *A Brief History of the Soul*. Chichester, UK: Wiley-Blackwell.

Harrington, Mary. 2022. "Should Conservatives Abolish Higher Education?" *The Post*, June 28. https://unherd.com/thepost/should-conservatives-abolish-higher-education/

Heck, Joel D. 2005. *Irrigating Deserts: C. S. Lewis on Education*. Saint Louis, MO: Concordia Publishing House.

Heil, John. 2020. *Philosophy of Mind: A Contemporary Introduction*, 4th edition. New York: Routledge.

Hill, Catherine B. 2021. "Letter to the Editor." *The Wall Street Journal*, January 29.

Hitz, Zena. 2020. *Lost in Thought: The Hidden Pleasures of an Intellectual Life*. Princeton, NJ: Princeton University Press.

Hooper, Walter. 1979. "Oxford's Bonny Fighter." In Como 2005, 241–308.

Hooper, Walter. 1996. *C. S. Lewis: Companion and Guide*. New York: HarperCollins.

Jacobs, Alan. 2005. *The Narnian: The Life and Imagination of C. S. Lewis*. New York: HarperCollins.

Jacobs, Alan. 2011. *The Pleasures of Reading in an Age of Distraction*. Oxford: Oxford University Press.

Jacobs, Alan. 2013. *The Book of Common Prayer: A Biography*. Princeton, NJ: Princeton University Press.

Johnson, Samuel. 1807. *Prayers and Meditations*, 4th edition, edited by George Strahan. London: T. Cadell and W. Davies.

Kant, Immanuel. 1956. *Groundwork of the Metaphysic of Morals*, translated by H. J. Paton. New York: Harper and Row.

Kendi, Ibram X. 2019. *How to Be an Antiracist*. London: The Bodley Head.

Kim, Jaegwon. 2005. *Physicalism, or Something Near Enough*. Princeton, NJ: Princeton University Press.

Kolodiejchuk Brian, M. C. 2007. *Mother Teresa: Come Be My Light; The Private Writings of the "Saint of Calcutta."* New York: Doubleday.

Kronman, Anthony. 2019. *The Assault on American Excellence*. New York: Free Press.

Kronman, Anthony. 2022. *After Disbelief: On Disenchantment, Eternity, and Joy*. New Haven, CT: Yale University Press.

Kuhn, Thomas S. 1962. *The Structure of Scientific Revolutions*. Chicago, IL: The University of Chicago Press.

Lawlor, John. 1965. "The Tutor and the Scholar." In Gibb, 67–85.
Lewis, C. S. 1930. *De Bono et Malo*, CSL/MS-34/X, The Marion E. Wade Center, Wheaton College, Wheaton, IL.
Lewis, C. S. 1936. *The Allegory of Love*. Oxford: Oxford University Press.
Lewis, C. S. 1939a. *Rehabilitations and Other Essays*. Oxford: Oxford University Press.
Lewis, C. S. 1939b. *The Personal Heresy: A Controversy*. London: Oxford University Press.
Lewis, C. S. [1939a]. "Learning in Wartime." In Lewis 2001g, 47–63.
Lewis, C. S. [1939b]. "The Fifteenth-Century Heroic Line." In Lewis 1969, 45–57.
Lewis, C. S. [1939–1945?]. "De Futilitate." In Lewis 1967, 57–71.
Lewis, C. S. [1940]. "Christianity and Culture." In Lewis 1967, 12–36.
Lewis, C. S. [1941]. "The Weight of Glory." In Lewis 2001g, 25–46.
Lewis, C. S. 1942. *A Preface to Paradise Lost*. New York: Oxford University Press.
Lewis, C. S. [1942–43]. "The Founding of the Oxford Socratic Club." In Lewis 1970, 126–8.
Lewis, C. S. [1943]. "My First School." In Lewis 1986a, 23–6.
Lewis, C. S. [1944a]. "Answers to Questions on Christianity." In Lewis 1970, 48–62.
Lewis, C. S. [1944b]. "Bulverism." In Lewis 1970, 271–7.
Lewis, C. S. [1944c]. "Democratic Education." In Lewis 1986a, 32–6.
Lewis, C. S. [1944d]. "Myth Became Fact." In Lewis 1970, 63–7.
Lewis, C. S. [1944e]. "On the Reading of Old Books." In Lewis 1970, 200–7.
Lewis, C. S. [1944f]. "The Inner Ring." In Lewis 2001g, 141–57.
Lewis, C. S. [1945a]. "Christian Apologetics." In Lewis 1970, 89–103.
Lewis, C. S. [1945b]. "Meditation in a Toolshed." In Lewis 1970, 212–15.
Lewis, C. S. [1945c]. "Membership." In Lewis 2001g, 158–76.
Lewis, C. S. [1946a]. "A Reply to Professor Haldane." In Lewis 1994, 74–85.
Lewis, C. S. [1946b]. "Modern Man and His Categories of Thought." In Lewis 1986a, 61–6.
Lewis, C. S. [1946c]. "On the Transmission of Christianity." In Lewis 1970, 114–19.
Lewis, C. S. [1946d]. "Period Criticism." In Lewis 1982, 113–17.
Lewis, C. S. [1946?] "Man or Rabbit?" In Lewis 1970, 108–13.
Lewis, C. S. [1947]. "On Stories." In Lewis 1994, 3–21.

Lewis, C. S. [1948a]. "Kipling's World." In Lewis 1969, 232–50.
Lewis, C. S. [1948b]. "The Trouble with 'X.'" Lewis 1970, 151–5.
Lewis, C. S. [1950]. "The Literary Impact of the Authorised Version." In Lewis 1969, 126–45.
Lewis, C. S. [1952]. "On Three Ways of Writing for Children." In Lewis 1982, 31–43.
Lewis, C. S. [1953]. "Review of Alan M. F. Gunn, *The Mirror of Love: A Reinterpretation of* The Romance of the Rose." In Lewis 2013, 240–7.
Lewis, C. S. [1954]. "A Note on Jane Austen." In Lewis 1969, 175–86.
Lewis, C. S. 1954. *Poetry and Prose in the Sixteenth Century*. Oxford: Oxford University Press.
Lewis, C. S. 1955. *Surprised by Joy*. New York: Harcourt.
Lewis, C. S. [1955]. "Lilies That Fester." In Lewis 1987, 31–49.
Lewis, C. S. [1956]. "Imagination and Thought in the Middle Ages." In Lewis 2005, 41–63.
Lewis, C. S. [1957]. "Is History Bunk?" In Lewis 1986a, 100–4.
Lewis, C. S. [1958a]. "Is Progress Possible?: Willing Slaves of the Welfare State." In Lewis 1970, 311–16.
Lewis, C. S. [1958b]. "Religion and Rocketry." In Lewis 1987, 83–92.
Lewis, C. S. 1961a. *An Experiment in Criticism*. Cambridge: Cambridge University Press.
Lewis, C. S. 1961b. *The Screwtape Letters and Screwtape Proposes a Toast*. New York: Macmillan.
Lewis, C. S. 1962. "*Ex Libris*." *The Christian Century*, 79, June 6, 719.
Lewis, C. S. [1963a]. "Cross-Examination." In Lewis 1970, 258–67.
Lewis, C. S. [1963b]. "The Seeing Eye." In Lewis 1967, 167–76.
Lewis, C. S. [1963c]. "We Have No 'Right to Happiness.'" In Lewis 1970, 317–22
Lewis, C. S. 1964. *The Discarded Image: An Introduction to Medieval and Renaissance Literature*. Cambridge: Cambridge University Press.
Lewis, C. S. 1967. *Christian Reflections*. Grand Rapids, MI: Eerdmans.
Lewis, C. S. [1967]. "The Funeral of a Great Myth." In Lewis 1967, 82–93.
Lewis, C. S. 1969. *Selected Literary Essays*, edited by Walter Hooper. Cambridge: Cambridge University Press.
Lewis, C. S. 1970. *God in the Dock*. Grand Rapids, MI: Eerdmans.
Lewis, C. S. 1982. *On Stories: And Other Essays on Literature*. New York: Harcourt Brace.

Lewis, C. S. 1986a. *Present Concerns*. New York: Harcourt.
Lewis, C. S. 1986b [1958]. *Reflections on the Psalms*. New York: Harcourt.
Lewis, C. S. 1987. *The World's Last Night and Other Essays*. New York: Harcourt.
Lewis, C. S. 1988 [1960]. *The Four Loves*. New York: Harcourt.
Lewis, C. S. 1991 [1922–27]. *All My Road Before Me: The Diary of C. S. Lewis*. New York: Harcourt.
Lewis, C. S. 1992a [1963]. *Letters to Malcolm: Chiefly on Prayer*. New York: Harcourt.
Lewis, C. S. 1992b. *Poems*. New York: Harcourt, Inc.
Lewis, C. S. 1992c [1933]. *The Pilgrim's Regress*. Grand Rapids, MI: Eerdmans.
Lewis, C. S. 1994 [1966]. *Of Other Worlds: Essays and Stories*. New York: Harcourt, Inc.
Lewis, C. S. 2001a [1961]. *A Grief Observed*. New York: HarperSanFrancisco.
Lewis, C. S. 2001b [1952]. *Mere Christianity*. New York: HarperSanFrancisco.
Lewis, C. S. 2001c [1960 rev. ed.]. *Miracles*. New York: HarperCollins.
Lewis, C. S. 2001d [1944]. *The Abolition of Man*. New York: HarperSanFrancisco.
Lewis, C. S. 2001e [1946]. *The Great Divorce*. New York: HarperSanFrancisco.
Lewis, C. S. 2001f [1940]. *The Problem of Pain*. New York: HarperSanFrancisco.
Lewis, C. S. 2001g. *The Weight of Glory and Other Essays*. New York: HarperCollins.
Lewis, C. S. 2003a [1938]. *Out of the Silent Planet*. New York: Scribner.
Lewis, C. S. 2003b [1945]. *That Hideous Strength*. New York: Scribner.
Lewis, C. S. 2004a. *The Collected Letters of C. S. Lewis: Volume I; Family Letters 1905–1931*, edited by Walter Hooper. New York: HarperSanFrancisco.
Lewis, C. S. 2004b. *The Collected Letters of C. S. Lewis: Volume II; Books, Broadcasts, and The War 1931–1949*, edited by Walter Hooper. New York: HarperSanFrancisco.
Lewis, C. S. 2005. *Studies in Medieval and Renaissance Literature*. Cambridge: Cambridge University Press.
Lewis, C. S. 2007. *The Collected Letters of C. S. Lewis: Vol. III; Narnia, Cambridge, and Joy, 1950–1963*, edited by Walter Hooper. New York: HarperSanFrancisco.
Lewis, C. S. 2013. *Image and Imagination*, edited by Walter Hooper. Cambridge: Cambridge University Press.
Lewis, C. S. [n.d.] "De Audiendis Poetis." In Lewis 2005, 1–17.

Lewis, Warren Hamilton. n.d. *C. S. Lewis: A Biography*. Unpublished typescript in the Marion E. Wade Center, Wheaton College, Wheaton, IL.

Lewis, Warren Hamilton. 1934. *Memoirs of the Lewis Family: 1850–1930, Volume V*. Leeborough Press.

Lindop, Grevel. 2015. *Charles Williams: The Third Inkling*. Oxford: Oxford University Press.

Loomis, Steven R. and Jacob P. Rodriguez. 2009. *C. S. Lewis: A Philosophy of Education*. Basingstoke, UK: Palgrave Macmillan.

McCarthy, Mark. A. 2022. "The Misguided Push toward 'College for All,'" *The Wall Street Journal*, September 13.

McWhorter, John. 2021. *Woke Racism: How a New Religion Has Betrayed Black America*. Great Britain: Forum.

Maher, Bill. 2021. Bill Maher: "Higher Education" Is a Racket That Sells You a Very Expensive Ticket to the Upper Middle Class | Video | RealClearPolitics, June 10.

Markos, Louis. 2015. *C. S. Lewis: An Apologist for Education*. Camp Hill, PA: Classical Academic Press.

Marks, Jonathan. 2021a. *Let's Be Reasonable: A Conservative Case for Liberal Education*. Princeton, NJ: Princeton University Press.

Marks, Jonathan. 2021b. "What Universities Owe." *The Constitutionalist*, June 23. https://theconstitutionalist.org/2021/06/23/what-universities-owe/

Marks, Jonathan. 2022. "Do We Really Need to Rethink Academic Freedom?" *The Bulwark*, May 13.

Marsden, George M. 2014. *The Twilight of the American Enlightenment*. New York: Basic Books.

Mill, John Stuart. 1964. *The Autobiography of John Stuart Mill*. New York: Signet Classics.

Milton, John. 1957. "Of Education." In *John Milton: Complete Poems and Major Prose*, edited by Merritt Y. Hughes, 630–9. New York: The Odyssey Press.

Mitchell, Josh. 2020. "Apprenticeships Offer Path into Middle Class." *The Wall Street Journal*, October 20.

Montás, Roosevelt. 2021. *Rescuing Socrates: How the Great Books Changed My Life and Why They Matter for a New Generation*. Princeton, NJ: Princeton University Press.

Newman, John Henry. 1996. *The Idea of a University*. New Haven, CT: Yale University Press.

Nielsen, Melinda and Philip Nielsen. 2015. "Education's Discarded Image: C. S. Lewis and the Theological Tradition of the Liberal Arts." *Pro Ecclesia* 24 (3): 271–88.

Oakeshott, Michael. 1989. "The Idea of a University." In *The Voice of Liberal Learning: Michael Oakeshott on Education*, 95–104. New Haven, CN: Yale University Press.

O'Beirne, Charlotte. 2022. "Art Is More Than an Ideological Battleground." *The Wall Street Journal*, September 21.

Oderberg, David S. 2020. *The Metaphysics of Good and Evil*. New York: Routledge.

Olgers, Greg. 2021. "Hope Forward to Travel South by Southwest." *News from Hope College*, 9.

Oppenheimer, Mark. 2021. "The Power of Purpose-Driven Schools." *The Wall Street Journal*, July 31–August 1.

Papineau, David. 1993. *Philosophical Naturalism*. Oxford: Blackwell.

Papineau, David. 2002. *Thinking about Consciousness*. Oxford: Clarendon Press.

Peterson, Michael L. 2020. *C. S. Lewis and the Christian World View*. Oxford: Oxford University Press.

Pieper, Josef. 1964. *Leisure the Basis of Culture*. New York: Pantheon Books.

Plantinga, Alvin. 1984. "Advice to Christian Philosophers." *Faith and Philosophy* 1: 253–71.

Poe, Harry Lee. 2021. *The Making of C. S. Lewis: From Atheist to Apologist*. Wheaton, IL: Crossways.

Raine, Kathleen. 1965. "From a Poet." In Gibb, 102–5.

Reuben, Julie A. 1996. *The Making of the Modern University: Intellectual Transformation and The Marginalization of Morality*. Chicago, IL: The University of Chicago Press.

Rorty, Richard. 1998. *Achieving Our Country*. Cambridge, MA: Harvard University Press.

Rose, John. 2021. "How I Liberated My College Classroom." *The Wall Street Journal*, June 24.

Rosenberg, Alex. 2011. *The Atheist's Guide to Reality: Enjoying Life without Illusions*. New York: W. W. Norton & Company.

Rosenberg, Alex. 2018. *How History Gets Things Wrong: The Neuroscience of Our Addiction to Stories*. Cambridge, MA: MIT Press.

Rushdoony, Rousas J. 1971. *The One and the Many*. Nutley, NJ: Craig Press. N.p.

Sandel, Michael. 2020. *The Tyranny of Merit: What's Become of the Common Good?* New York: Farrar, Straus, and Giroux.
Sayer, George. 2015. "Recollections of C. S. Lewis." In White, Wolfe, and Wolfe, 175–8.
Sen, Amartya. 2021. *Home in the World: A Memoir*. New York: Liveright Publishing Company.
Sidgwick, Henry. 1966. *The Methods of Ethics*, 7th edition. New York: Dover Publications.
Silverstein, Matthew. 2000. "In Defense of Happiness: A Response to the Experience Machine." *Social Theory and Practice* 26: 279–300.
Simon-Thomas, Emiliana. 2021. Quoted in Clare Ansberry's "Rethinking Happiness," *The Wall Street Journal*, March 12.
Storey, Benjamin and Jenna Silber Storey. 2021. *Why We Are Restless: On the Modern Quest for Contentment*. Princeton, NJ: Princeton University Press.
Stroud, Barry. 2004. "The Charm of Naturalism." In De Caro and Macarthur, 21–35.
Van Inwagen, Peter. 2011. "C. S. Lewis' Argument against Naturalism." *Journal of Inklings Studies* 1: 25–40.
Van Riel, Gerd. 1999. "Does Perfect Activity Necessarily Yield Pleasure? An Evaluation of the Relation between Pleasure and Activity in Aristotle, *Nicomachean Ethics* VII and X." *International Journal of Philosophical Studies* 7: 211–41.
Van Til, Cornelius. 1969. *Defense of the Faith, vol. II: A Survey of Christian Epistemology*. USA: den Dulk Christian Foundation.
Van Til, Cornelius. 1975. *A Christian Theory of Knowledge*. Nutley, NJ: Presbyterian and Reformed Publishing Co.
Vanauken, Sheldon. 1987. *A Severe Mercy*. New York: HarperSanFrancisco.
Varadarajan, Tunku. 2022. "The Weekend Interview with Ian Rowe and Joyanet Mangual: Build a School, Get Sued by the Union." *The Wall Street Journal*, July 9–10.
Vedder, Rickard K. 2019. *Restoring the Promise: Higher Education in America*. Oakland, CA: The Independent Institute.
Wain, John. 1954. *The Spectator* 193: 405. In Lewis 2007, xiii.
Ward, Michael. 2008. *Planet Narnia*. New York: Oxford University Press.
Ward, Michael. 2021. *After Humanity: A Guide to C. S. Lewis's* The Abolition of Man. Park Ridge, IL: Word on Fire Academic.
Weine, Kenneth. 2022. "The Met Replies on the Politics of Art Museums." *The Wall Street Journal*, September 10–11.

White, Nicholas. 2006. *A Brief History of Happiness*. Oxford: Blackwell.

White, Roger, Judith Wolfe, and Brendan Wolfe, eds. 2015. *C. S. Lewis and His Circle: Essays and Memoirs from the Oxford C. S. Lewis Society*. New York: Oxford University Press.

Williamson, Timothy. 2011. "What Is Naturalism," *The New York Times*, September 4. http://opinionator.blogs.nytimes.com/category/the-stone/

Wiltsey, Kathy. 2021. "Obituary." *Wall Street Journal*, February 27–8.

Wolff, Alexander. 2021. *Endpapers: A Family Story of Books, War, Escape, and Home*. New York: Atlantic Monthly Press.

Wolterstorff, Nicholas. 2008. *Justice: Rights and Wrongs*. Princeton, NJ: Princeton University Press.

Wood, Will C. 2020. "College Degrees, Race and Better-Paid Jobs." *The Wall Street Journal*, July 2.

Wooldridge, Adrian. 2021. *The Aristocracy of Talent: How Meritocracy Made the Modern World*. New York: Skyhorse Publishing.

Zaleski, Philip and Carol Zaleski. 2015. *The Fellowship: The Literary Lives of the Inklings: J. R. R. Tolkien, C. S. Lewis, Own Barfield, Charles Williams*. New York: Farrar, Strauss, and Giroux.

Index

Angell, Robert C. 164
Annas, Julia 37–8
Anscombe, Elizabeth 21, 184, 199–200
Aquinas, St Thomas 53, 159
Argument from Reason 102–5
Aristotle 37, 47, 158, 159
Armstrong, David 102
Arnold, Matthew 41, 69, 70, 136
Atman, Non-Atman 90–1
   See also Soul
Augustine, St 13, 161
Aurelius, Marcus 41
Austen, Jane 34

Bacon, Francis 196
Baggini, Julian 88, 89
Baker, Leo 90
Balint, Benjamin 96
Barbour, John 72
Barfield, Owen 74, 162
Baxter, Jason M. 198–9
Belkin, Douglas 185
Bennett, Arnold 15
Bloom, Paul 130–1
Bloomberg, Michael R. 156, 157
Bodle, Rhona 98
Boethius 53
Boswell, James 49, 50
Brewer, Derek 63–4
Buddhism 90–1
Butler, Nicholas Murray 192
Byron, Lord 34

Camus, Albert 88
Carpenter, Humphrey 63
Chaucer, Geoffrey 24, 45, 193
Clark, Gordon H. 188
Coghill, Neville 62–3

Cohen, Ben 14
Conway, John 12
Culture 45, 67, 69, 70, 78, 83, 90, 92, 95, 97, 158, 172–3, 195–6, 198
Curricula 133–40, 161–2

Dante 13, 60, 145
Davis, Miles K. 120–1, 122, 123
Dawkins, Richard 107–8, 110, 112, 203
Delbanco, Andrew 19, 70, 180
Dewey, John 7
Diversity, Equity, and Inclusion 7–8, 101, 156, 184
Dobb, Maurice 137
Dyer, Justin Buckley 81, 186
Dyson, Hugo 63

Eliot, Charles W. 192–3
Elitism/Elitist 9, 58, 81, 121–3, 147–9, 181
Equality 57–60, 63, 119, 191
Eudaimonism/Eudaimonist 36–9, 189
Euthyphro 185, 186
Evans, I. O. 24
Every, Brother George 40
Evil
   Extrinsic 32, 97, 187
   Intrinsic 30–1, 33, 35–6, 40, 78, 173–4, 180, 186, 188–9, 204
   Moral 41
   Non-moral 39–40
Explanation
   Causal vs. Purposeful 105–10

Fermat's Last Theorem 12
Finley, Allysia 120–1
Flacks, Richard 183

Fogelman, Peggy 197, 198
Frazer, Will 13, 14
Functionalism 114

Galston, William A. 202
Gibson, Eric 197, 198
Good
  Extrinsic 21, 31–2, 55, 71–5, 79–80, 97, 151, 187
  Intrinsic 21, 30–1, 33, 34, 35–6, 40, 46, 47, 53, 54, 66–7, 71, 74, 78, 79–80, 85, 88–9, 114–15, 142, 146, 159, 173–4, 180, 185–6, 187–8, 189, 195, 198, 204
  Moral 40, 148
  Non-Moral 39–40, 46, 68, 136
Greeves, Arthur 14, 26, 35, 44, 62, 162
Gunn, Alan 23

Happiness
  Hedonist View of 29–36
Harrington, Mary 11
Heck, Joel D. 194, 195
Hedonism 29–30, 180
  Paradox of 49–52
Heil, John 114
Herbert, George 13
Hill, Catherine B. 5
Hitz, Zena 39, 187, 203–4
Hooker, Richard 13, 71, 186
Hugo of St. Victor 40

Inner Ring 151–5
Instrumentalism 4–19, 21–2, 31–2, 55–6, 65–6, 71–5, 79–80, 97, 119, 150–1, 180, 187

Jacobs, Alan 50, 175, 185, 193
Johnson, Samuel 49–50, 186

Kant, Immanuel 49, 50
Keefe, Derek 201

Kendi, Ibram X. 7–8, 184
Kim, Jaegwon 113–14
Kronman, Anthony 8–9, 198
Kuhn, Thomas S. 196–7

Lawlor, John 98
Leavis, F. R. 70
Lewis, Albert 204
Lewis, Florence 191
Lewis, Warren Hamilton 6–7, 51, 141, 204
Liberal Education 123–6, 184, 195, 201, 203–4
  and Core Curricula 135–7
Loomis, Steven R. 141, 142

Maher, Bill 119, 120
Mangual, Joyanet 193–4
Mann, Heinrich 96
Markos, Louis 194, 201
Marks, Jonathan 11, 124, 125, 182–3
Marsden, George M. 126
McCarthy, Mark 182
McCaslin, James 11
McShane, Father Joseph M. 5
McWhorter, John 166–7, 184
Mental, nature of 44, 102–3
Mill, John Stuart 41, 50, 81, 168
Milton, John 6, 13, 168, 181, 193
Mitchell, Josh 10–11
Model, The Medieval 75–7, 196
Montás, Roosevelt 135, 136, 161
Morris, William 34
Mother Teresa 200
Murdoch, Iris 21
Myth 26, 35, 189

Naturalism
  and Explanation 105–10
  and Pleasure 112–16
  versus Secularism 126
Newman, John Henry 67–8, 187, 194–5
Neylen, Mary 23

Index

Nielsen, Melinda 184, 195
Nielsen, Philip 184, 195

Oakeshott, Michael 182
O'Beirne, Charlotte 197, 198
Oderberg, David S. 31, 40
Olgers, Greg 7
Oppenheimer, Mark 117

Papineau, David 102
Patmore, Coventry 13
Pieper, Josef 158, 159
Plantinga, Alvin 170-2
Plato 112, 113, 185, 189, 193
Poe, Harry Lee 32, 187
Pope, Alexander 159

Qualia 112-16
Quick, Canon Oliver Chase 29, 30

Raine, Kathleen 194
Reasoning 102-5
Reuben, Julie A. 164-5, 187, 192
Robinson, Joan 137
Rodriguez, Jacob P. 141, 142
Rorty, Richard 7, 18
Rose, John 11
Rosenberg, Alex 106-7, 108, 112, 199
Rowe, Ian 193-4
Rushdoony, Rousas John 188

Sandel, Michael 8, 9, 10, 11, 81, 167-8
Sarnak, Peter 12
Sayer, George 98
Sayers, Dorothy L. 145
School
    Primary and Secondary 57-60
Sen, Amarta 137
Sidgwick, Henry 50
Silverstein, Matthew 73

Simon-Thomas, Emiliana 36
Socrates 185
Soul 130-1, 204-5
    See also Atman, Non-Atman
Spenser, Edmund 13, 193
Storey, Benjamin 5
Storey, Jenna Silber 5
Stroud, Barry 101

Tillich, Paul 97
Tolkien, J.R.R. 63, 75

Utilitarianism 4, 180

Van Deusen, Mary 14, 30, 97
Van Inwagen, Peter 101
Van Osdall, Thomas 200
Van Riel, Gerd 48
Van Til, Cornelius 188
Vanauken, Sheldon 17
Varadarajan, Tunku 194
Vedder, Rickard K. 4-5, 181

Wain, John 13, 14
Ward, Michael 193, 199, 201-2
Watson, Micah J. 81, 186
Weber, Max 158
Weine, Kenneth 197, 198
White, Nicholas 29
Wiles, Andrew 12, 13
Williams, Charles 149, 150
Williamson, Timothy 101
Wiltsey, Kathy 13, 14
Wolff, Alexander 96
Wolff, Kurt 96
Wolterstorff, Nicholas 37
Wood, Will C. 5-6
Wooldridge, Adrian 81, 168

Zaleski, Carol 63
Zaleski, Philip 63